# Basic Training
## FOR
# DUMMIES®

**by Rod Powers**
Recognized expert in all U.S. Military matters

WILEY

John Wiley & Sons, Inc.

**Basic Training For Dummies®**

Published by
**John Wiley & Sons, Inc.**
111 River St.
Hoboken, NJ 07030-5774
www.wiley.com

For general information on our other products and services, please contact our Customer Care Department within the U.S. at 877-762-2974, outside the U.S. at 317-572-3993, or fax 317-572-4002.

For technical support, please visit www.wiley.com/techsupport.

Wiley also publishes its books in a variety of electronic formats and by print-on-demand. Some content that appears in standard print versions of this book may not be available in other formats. For more information about Wiley products, visit us at www.wiley.com.

Library of Congress Control Number: 2011930311

ISBN 978-0-470-88123-1 (pbk); ISBN 978-1-118-08896-8 (ebk); ISBN 978-1-118-08897-5 (ebk); ISBN 978-1-118-08898-2 (ebk)

Manufactured in the United States of America

10  9  8  7  6  5  4  3  2

WILEY

# About the Author

**Rod Powers** joined the United States Air Force in 1975 intending to become a spy. He was devastated to learn that he should've joined the CIA instead because the military doesn't have that particular enlisted job. Regardless, he fell in love with the military and made it both a passion and a career, retiring with 23 years of service. Rod spent 11 of those years as a First Sergeant, helping to solve the problems of the enlisted corps.

Since his retirement from the military in 1998, Rod has become a world-renowned military careers expert. Through his highly popular U.S. Military Information website on About.com (http://usmilitary.about.com), Rod has advised thousands of troops about all aspects of the U.S. Armed Forces career information.

Rod is the proud father of twin girls, both of whom enjoy successful careers in the United States Air Force. Rod currently resides in Daytona Beach, Florida, with his pet tomato plant, Oscar. Even today, Powers tries to run his life according to long-lived military ideals and standards, but he gets a bit confused about why nobody will obey his orders anymore . . . not even Oscar.

# Dedication

To all the women in my life: Jeanie, Chrissy, Milani, Autumn, Charissa, Joy, Shilynn, Katie, Sue, Barb, Patty, Crystal, Amber, Linda, Camryn, Cindy, Denise, Dana, Hope, Robin, and Sheri. This book *is not* dedicated to Jackie — she had her chance.

# Author's Acknowledgments

The author wants to thank Autumn McLeod for reading my drafts and making sure my ramblings made some kind of sense. Also, her husband, Jake, for educating me about Coast Guard basic training and for looking over the Coast Guard portions of this book. Many thanks to my outstanding literary agent, Barb Doyen, for putting this project together and helping convince the publisher that there was a valid need for this book. Special thanks to the Army, Navy, and Air Force recruiting services, as well as Thomas J. Cutler of the Air Force, for making sure I covered all the basics of basic training.

Many thanks to Tracy Boggier, my Acquisitions Editor and Kelly Ewing, my sensational Project Editor.

Finally, I send more special thanks to the recruiting commands of the United States Army, Air Force, Navy, Marine Corps, and Coast Guard, especially the recruiters assigned to the Volusia County Mall, for providing invaluable resource information.

## Publisher's Acknowledgments

We're proud of this book; please send us your comments at http://dummies.custhelp.com. For other comments, please contact our Customer Care Department within the U.S. at 877-762-2974, outside the U.S. at 317-572-3993, or fax 317-572-4002.

Some of the people who helped bring this book to market include the following:

*Acquisitions, Editorial, and Media Development*

**Project Editor:** Kelly Ewing

**Acquisitions Editor:** Tracy Boggier

**Assistant Editor:** David Lutton

**Editorial Program Coordinator:** Joe Niesen

**General Reviewers:** Jake McLeod, Thomas J. Cutler, Grant Kellow

**Editorial Supervisor and Reprint Editor:** Carmen Krikorian

**Editorial Assistant:** Rachelle S. Amick

**Art Coordinator:** Alicia B. South

**Cover Photos:** © iStockphoto.com/ Konstantin Tavrov

**Cartoons:** Rich Tennant (www.the5thwave.com)

*Composition Services*

**Project Coordinator:** Patrick Redmond

**Layout and Graphics:** Lavonne Roberts, Corrie Socolovitch

**Proofreaders:** Cynthia Fields, Lauren Mandelbaum

**Indexer:** BIM Indexing & Proofreading Services

---

**Publishing and Editorial for Consumer Dummies**

    **Kathleen Nebenhaus,** Vice President and Executive Publisher

    **Kristin Ferguson-Wagstaffe,** Product Development Director

    **Ensley Eikenburg,** Associate Publisher, Travel

    **Kelly Regan,** Editorial Director, Travel

**Publishing for Technology Dummies**

    **Andy Cummings,** Vice President and Publisher

**Composition Services**

    **Debbie Stailey,** Director of Composition Services

# Table of Contents

# Introduction

●  ●  ●  ●  ●  ●  ●  ●  ●  ●  ●  ●  ●  ●  ●  ●  ●  ●  ●  ●  ●  ●  ●  ●  ●  ●  ●  ●  ●  ●  ●  ●  ●  ●  ●  ●

*I*f you're reading this book, there's a very good chance that you've joined the military and are just waiting for your date to roll around to ship out for military basic training. Maybe you're wondering what you're in for, or maybe you plan to be an honor graduate and want to study up on some of the things you'll need to know to impress your instructors. Perhaps you have a close family member or friend attending military basic training and want to know what they're going through. In any case, buying this book was a good decision. In *Basic Training For Dummies,* you can find out exactly what goes on in military basic training, as well as a few tips of what you can do to prepare in advance.

## About This Book

Depending on your branch of choice, military basic training is between 6 weeks and 13 weeks long. Although a lot of new information is packed into this short amount of time, you can get a head start on required military knowledge, as well as a heads-up about what to expect during basic training, by reading through the chapters of this book.

*Basic Training For Dummies* gives you a blow-by-blow look at all five branches of the U.S. Military and their basic training courses, as well as tips and techniques that can help make your basic training experience more rewarding.

My entire purpose in writing this book is to help you get the most out of your initial military training experience. There's so much to learn in such a short period of time, and a little advanced knowledge will certainly enhance your basic training adventure. As the old axiom says, "Preparation is half the battle."

## Conventions Used in This Book

The following conventions are used throughout the text to help point out important concepts and make the text easier to understand:

  ✔ All Web addresses appear in `monofont`. ***Note:*** Some Web addresses may extend to two lines of text. If you use one of these addresses, just type the address exactly as you see it, pretending that the line break doesn't exist.

✔ New terms appear in italic and are closely followed by an easy-to-understand definition.

✔ **Bold** text highlights important points and the action parts of numbered steps or processes.

In addition, each branch of the military uses terminology specific to it. For example, the Army calls its drill instructors drill sergeants and basic training basic combat training. Throughout this book, I use general terms, rather than the specific ones, whenever I'm talking about multiple branches.

# What You're Not to Read

This book contains a number of sidebars (the shaded gray boxes). These sidebars are full of interesting information about basic training, but you don't have to read them if you don't want to — they don't contain anything you simply *must* know in order to do your best at military basic training.

You also run across special icons, titled *Technical Stuff,* from time to time. These sections include concise, detailed information (interesting but nonessential) about the topic at hand, but the info probably can't help you pass military basic training. You can safely skip these tidbits, if you want.

If you already know which branch of the military's basic training programs you're going to attend, you can skip over information about the other services. For example, if you're going to attend Army basic training, you can safely skip over the section about Navy aircraft and ships. However, military basic training for all branches are very similar, so information about one branch's system very well could help you with a different branch's basic training.

# Foolish Assumptions

While writing this book, I made a few assumptions about you — namely, who you are and why you picked up this book. I've assumed the following:

✔ You may be nervous about attending military basic training and need some information so that you know what you're getting yourself into.

✔ You're curious about what goes on in military basic training on a day-to-day basis.

✔ You want to know what you can study in advance to help make your military basic training experience as rewarding as possible.

# How This Book Is Organized

There is a method to the madness . . . a reason why this book is organized the way you see it today. I organized this book according to subject matter. Material having to do with preparing for basic training is organized together, what to expect for each branch is grouped in succession, and information about graduating from basic training is in one area.

This book isn't organized to reflect how various events will occur during basic training, but rather by the significance of the events. You can read about more important events before you read about requirements that are of lesser priority.

I also include two appendixes — one on military justice and one on military history — to help you prepare for basic training.

## Part I: The Basics about Basic

If you have no clue about what to expect during military basic training, then this part is for you. I talk about what you can expect in a day at basic training, no matter which branch you're in. You also get a peek at what happens on the firing range and tips on which basic training jobs you may want to volunteer for (and which ones to avoid at all costs).

## Part II: Getting Ready for Basic

Believe it or not, you can do some things in advance to make your basic training experience a little bit easier. In this part, you find out what you need to know about military ranks, military life, and the military law and justice (and hopefully you'll never have to apply the latter knowledge!). You also find out what you need to do to get in shape for basic training.

## Part III: Heading to Basic Training

You can't just jump on a plane or bus and show up at basic training. If it were that easy, it wouldn't be the U.S. Military. In this part, you find out what you should bring with you to basic training and what to avoid packing at all costs. You can also read about final in-processing at MEPS and what to expect when you get to your basic training location to begin your new life.

# Part IV: Basic Training Life, Branch by Branch

Part IV includes the meat of this book. Here, you discover exactly what to expect in each of the services' basic training programs, including daily a ctivities, equipment, and how to interact with your classmates and instructors. I dedicate a chapter to each military branch so that I can point out each area's special nuances.

# Part V: Wrapping Up Basic Training

All good things must come to an end, and so it is with military basic training. Turn to this part if you're interested in graduation events and basic training awards.

# Part VI: The Part of Tens

This book is a *For Dummies* book, so it's not complete without a Part of Tens. If you want to get right down to it and find out some of the most important information for doing well in military basic training and you like your info presented in easily digestible lists, turn to Part V. This part gives you basic training tips and advice on how to keep that mean instructor off your back.

# Icons Used in This Book

Throughout this book, you find icons that help you use the material in this book. Here's a rundown on what they mean to you:

This icon alerts you to helpful hints regarding basic training. Tips can help you save time and avoid frustration.

This icon reminds you of important information you should memorize (or at least read carefully).

This icon flags information that may prove hazardous to your plans of conquering military basic training. Often, this icon accompanies common mistakes or misconceptions people have or questions about basic training.

This icon points out information that is interesting, enlightening, or in-depth but info that isn't necessary for you to read. You may or may not find these concepts helpful to you during basic training, but knowing the info may make basic training a little more rewarding.

# Where to Go from Here

You don't have to read this book from cover to cover in order to do well during military basic training. People have different strengths and weaknesses, and the format of this book is designed to be read in the manner that best suits you. You may be a whiz in physical training and choose to skip the fitness sections entirely and use your time in areas you feel you need more information.

If you do choose to skip chapters, I highly recommend you skim through those chapters anyway, taking note of Tip, Warning, and Remember icons, because these morsels of info include important factors about your basic training experience.

I suggest that you begin with Chapters 1 and 2, however. That way you can get a feel for what goes on during military basic training and what you'll need to know. This plan of attack helps you set up logical and effective goals to maximize your military basic training adventure.

No matter where you start, I wish you luck on your upcoming military journey. I hope you find your time at military basic training as rewarding as I did!

# Part I
# The Basics about Basic

The 5th Wave      By Rich Tennant

"It's an Armed Services aptitude test taken on a computer, and you're telling me my hours of experience playing World of Warcraft count for <u>nothing</u>?!"

# In this part . . .

In this part, you discover what to expect during an average basic training day, what basic training jobs you should volunteer for (and which ones you should avoid like the plague), as well as the proper way to handle a military weapon without accidentally shooting yourself or others.

# Chapter 1

# Forewarned Is Forearmed

**In This Chapter**

▶ Taking a look at the military basic training method

▶ Preparing is half the battle

▶ Detailing basic training

**M**ilitary basic training is all about being prepared for any situation. That preparation includes gathering intelligence about situations you're likely to face in the future. I merely provide a means for smart young folks to gather a little intelligence about what's in store for them. I predict that those who are smart enough to read through this book before attending military basic training will have a higher chance of graduation and success, thereby allowing them to contribute to the most powerful military in the world, and that can't be a bad thing.

## Brushing Up on Military Missions

The United States Military branches exist to defend the United States against all enemies and to provide combat capabilities anywhere in the world in support of United States security objectives.

While it's sometimes hard to tell (the Army has aircraft and ships, and the Navy, Air Force, Marine Corps, and Coast Guard have ground forces), each branch has specific missions.

### Army mission

The Army exists to serve the American people, defend the Nation, protect vital national interests, and fulfill national military responsibilities. The Army makes up the nation's largest and most extensive military ground capabilities. Currently, approximately 499,000 active duty Army troops are backed up by 700,000 National Guard and Army reservists. The Army is responsible to provide necessary forces and capabilities in support of the National Security and Defense Strategies of the United States.

The Army's mission is codified by federal law:

- ✔ Preserve the peace and security and provide for the defense of the United States, the Commonwealths and possessions, and any areas occupied by the United States
- ✔ Support the national policies
- ✔ Implement the national objectives
- ✔ Overcome any nations responsible for aggressive acts that imperil the peace and security of the United States

## Air Force mission

The mission statement of the United States Air Force is *"fly, fight, and win in air, space, and cyberspace."*

Like the other branches, the official mission of the USAF has been established by federal law.

Title 10, Section 8062 of the U.S. Code defines the mission of the USAF as follows:

- ✔ To preserve the peace and security and provide for the defense of the United States, the Territories, Commonwealths, and possessions, and any areas occupied by the United States
- ✔ To support national policy
- ✔ To implement national objectives
- ✔ To overcome any nations responsible for aggressive acts that imperil the peace and security of the United States

## Navy mission

The mission of the United States Navy is to protect and defend the right of the United States and its allies to move freely on the oceans and to protect the country against her enemies.

Federal law defines the mission of the United States Navy as follows:

- ✔ To prepare the naval forces necessary for the effective prosecution of war

- ✔ To maintain naval aviation, including land-based naval aviation, air transport essential for naval operations, and all air weapons and air techniques involved in the operations and activities of the Navy.

- ✔ To develop aircraft, weapons, tactics, technique, organization, and equipment of naval combat and service elements

## Marine Corps mission

The United States Marine Corps serves as the amphibious forces of the United States. Its mission is detailed in Title 10, Section 5063 of the United States Code (USC):

- ✔ The seizure or defense of advanced naval bases and other land operations to support naval campaigns

- ✔ The development of tactics, technique, and equipment used by amphibious landing forces

- ✔ Such other duties as the President may direct

## Coast Guard mission

The Coast Guard is the only U.S. military service not organized under the Department of Defense. Instead, the Coast Guard falls under the Department of Homeland Security.

Even so, the Coast Guard is one of the official branches of the U.S. Military. Title 10, section 101(a)(4) of the U.S.C. says, "The term 'armed forces' means the Army, Navy, Air Force, Marine Corps, and Coast Guard." Additionally, Title 14, Section 1 states, "The Coast Guard as established 28 January 1915, shall be a military service and a branch of the armed forces of the United States at all times."

In time of war, the President can direct all, or part of, the Coast Guard under the service of the Navy.

## Military history

Sir Francis Bacon once said, "History makes men wise." The Uniform Services certainly subscribe to this idea. In basic training, you study the history of your branch and take a written test about famous military events and famous military people who have come before you. In order to graduate from basic training, you need to pass this test, and if you want a shot at honor graduate or distinguished graduate, you need to score very well on this test.

The U.S. Coast Guard is the only U.S. Military branch that routinely engages in civilian law enforcement during peacetime. Section 2 of 14 U.S.C authorizes the Coast Guard to enforce federal law.

The Coast Guard statutory missions as defined by law are divided into homeland security missions and nonhomeland security missions. Nonhomeland security missions are

- ✔ Marine safety
- ✔ Search and rescue
- ✔ Aids to navigation
- ✔ Living marine resources (fisheries law enforcement)
- ✔ Marine environmental protection
- ✔ Ice operations

Homeland security missions are

- ✔ Ports, waterways, and coastal security (PWCS)
- ✔ Drug interdiction
- ✔ Migrant interdiction
- ✔ Defense readiness
- ✔ Other law enforcement

# Building a G.I. from Scratch

When I went to Air Force basic training as a young 18-year-old kid, there was no Internet, and there were no books about military basic training. The only sources of information about what to expect during basic training were your recruiter and family members who probably went through basic about

100 years before you. Your recruiter would simply say, "It's easy. Don't worry about it," and leave it at that. (After all, his job was to get you on a plane, not to scare you to death.)

When I got off the plane in San Antonio, Texas, and that guy in the Smokey-the-Bear hat immediately started yelling at me for (what seemed to me) no reason, I remember thinking, "Oh, my. I signed up for four years to this??!"

I had no way of knowing that basic training and military training instructors were only a very small part of military life, and those MTIs at the airport certainly weren't about to tell me. I didn't know that they weren't allowed to hit me. I thought anyone of them could pick me up and throw me across the airport. I wondered if I had time to write out a quick last will and testament before one of them got their mitts on me.

When I first started writing about military basic training on my website (`http://usmilitary.about.com`), I got a lot of hate e-mail from military basic training instructors. According to many of them, by letting the cat out of the bag and letting out all of their secrets, I was diluting the basic training experience, taking away their ability to "shock and awe," and therefore making their jobs harder. I disagree.

I can describe the military basic training experience in one sentence. It's all about breaking a person down and rebuilding him from the bottom up. The breaking down process begins immediately upon arrival. Basic training instructors don't want you to think things through — they want you to automatically react, but react in the right way. That's why there's so much repetition in basic training. You don't think; you just do" But, you have to *do* it the military way.

In basic training, there's an old saying: "There's the right way to do something, the wrong way to do something, and the military way." It really should read, "The right way, the wrong way, and *the basic training way*," because innovation and better ways to do something are encouraged in the military — just not while you're in basic training. Save your "better ideas" for after you graduate and join the "real" military.

The first few weeks of military basic training is dedicated to breaking you down. During this period, you'll find that you can't do anything right. Even if you do it right, it'll be wrong. Nobody's perfect, and military drill instructors are trained to ferret out those imperfections and make sure that you know about them.

After you've been completely ripped apart, the real training begins — teaching you to do things the "basic training way," without even having to think about it — you just react. If a military basic training instructor can make this reaction happen, then he has done his job.

# Making the Basic Training Experience a Little Bit Easier

A lot of memorization goes on during basic training. Maybe you're the type of person who can easily concentrate while some mean, large person is screaming in your face 24 hours per day, or maybe you're more like me — you'd rather do your learning in a nice, quiet, relaxing environment. Unfortunately, you're not going to find any nice, quiet, relaxing areas during basic training, so your only other option is to try to memorize this required knowledge before you depart. Part II should be able to help you with your memorization work.

One of the first things you'll be required to know is the military rank/insignia system, especially for the branch you've decided to join. In addition, if you're in the Marines, you will be required to have a basic understanding of the Navy rank structure because the Marine Corps was derived from and falls under the Department of the Navy.

Everyone in the military wears insignia, which are often called *stripes* for enlisted folks, and you should know what those stripes mean. If you call a sergeant major a private, I can guarantee you won't like the results. Chapter 5 can help you out with military ranks.

Along those lines, you should commit to memory the proper way to address drill instructors in your particular branch. Just to add to the confusion, each branch does it differently. Don't worry; I give you the straight dope in Part IV.

If you're joining the Army, Navy, Marine Corps, or Coast Guard, it's important that you memorize the rules for a sentry. Instructors in these branches like to keep you on your toes by popping out of nowhere, and asking you something like, "What's the third rule of a sentry?" Responding with the correct answer is *always* preferable to not knowing. If the Air Force is your choice of service, you don't have to worry about this memorization. As an Air Force basic training sentry, you'll carry a book with you at all times during sentry (dorm guard) duty, and you can quickly look up the information, if needed.

Many new basic training recruits make the mistake of thinking, "I don't need to get in shape in advance. Basic training will get me into shape." Big mistake. By far the biggest reason for getting "set back" in military basic training and not graduating on time is failing to meet the physical fitness graduation standards. You have only a few short weeks in basic to meet very high physical fitness standards for graduation, and — if you show up out of shape — you can't do it. You won't fail military basic training for being out of shape (the instructors won't let you), but they'll keep you in basic training as long as it takes for you to pass the standards. You can read more about required fitness standards in Chapter 8.

If you have a little extra time, make sure that you look over Chapter 7 on military law and what constitutes a crime in the military in Appendix A. You don't have to memorize this information, but you should know basic facts, such as if you disobey an order, you can go to military prison for more than five years.

You'll do a lot of marching during military basic training. While I explain the basics of marching and the standard drill commands in Chapter 9, it certainly wouldn't hurt to practice them or even join your school's marching band or Junior ROTC program for a little advance practice.

# Getting There Is Half the Fun

Going to military basic training isn't like leaving home to go to college. You can't just pack whatever you want to bring — there are rules about what you must have, and more rules about what you can't have. Fortunately, if your recruiter forgets to give you the official list of bring and don't-bring items, I give you a little advice in Chapter 10.

Traveling to your basic training location usually involves a plane ride, but you can't simply buy a plane ticket and show up. You have to process first through your local Military Entrance Processing Station (MEPS), which will arrange (and pay for) your travel. You can find out details about this process in Chapter 11.

Basic training doesn't officially begin until several days after you arrive (although from your point of view, it may seem to begin earlier!). The first few days are spent *in-processing* — that is, doing all the paperwork to tell the massive government information system that you're now part of the U.S. Military. The term in-processing means more than just giving you a uniform and issuing you a military ID card, though. Part III gives you an idea of what to expect during your first few days of basic.

# Getting Specific about Each Branch's Training

Several years ago, there was talk of creating a purple basic training — one basic training program for all of the branches, kind of like what the Naval Academy does with Navy and Marine Corps officers. This idea never got past the "what if" stage. While similar processes are involved in turning young men and women into disciplined military members, the specific subject areas, disciplines, rules, and processes vary too widely among the military branches to ever create a viable joint basic training program. The meat of military basic training is in the details, and Part IV of this book is where I take you through the day-to-day activities of each branch in separate chapters.

This is the only book I know of that details the basic training programs of all the branches, under one cover, and I think it can help with your basic training experience to find out what the new members of the other branches go through in order to go from recruit to trained military member.

However, while many aspects of military basic training are different, many are similar, or even exactly the same. I devote Chapter 2 to those similarities, explaining those aspects of military basic training that are the same (or nearly the same) for all of the branches.

# Juggling Basic Training Jobs

You may think that military basic training is run by the drill instructors, and, in some ways, that's correct. Instructors are the gods of military basic training and are there to ensure that everything goes according to their divine plan. However, almost everything else that goes on during basic training is accomplished, planned, and supervised by the basic training recruits themselves.

As with life itself, there are good jobs in basic training and jobs that suck. The trick is getting chosen for one of the good jobs while leaving the sucky jobs for others. The problem is, it's usually not a matter of volunteering for any specific basic training duties. The drill instructors hand out the jobs, and there are few (if any) rules. The drill instructors pretty much get to assign the jobs as they see fit.

However, you can do a few things to increase your chances of getting one of the good basic training jobs. Chapter 3 includes all you need to know.

# Taking a Shot at Weapons Training

It wouldn't be a book about military basic training if I didn't talk a bit about firing guns. Excuse me, I mean "weapons."

In the military, especially during basic training, never, ever refer to your rifle or pistol as a gun. *Guns* are those very big shooting things used on combat ships. Guns you carry in the military are called rifles or pistols or sometimes your "weapon."

Most drill instructors believe they can teach a monkey to shoot. But they'd much rather teach a monkey than try to teach a farm boy who's grown up with weapons his entire life. Teaching someone the correct (military) way from scratch is much easier than trying to eliminate bad habits that have likely arisen from several years of doing it wrong.

The U.S. Military has more than 200 years of experience in firing weapons and hitting what is aimed at. It's best to remember this history, even if you were the original Wyatt Earp prior to basic training. If you know nothing more about shooting than what I explain in Chapter 4 when you first arrive at basic training, you'll probably do much better on the firing line than if you've spent your entire life on a farm shooting pistols and rifles.

If you have significant experience with weapons, I know you won't believe me. For some unknown reason, nobody ever does on this particular point. However, it's been proven time and time again. You're much more likely to earn a qualification or even win a weapons award (see Chapter 4) in basic training if you've never seen a gun than if you grew up your entire life hunting.

# Gearing Up for Graduation

No matter which of the services you decide to join, your ultimate goal is to graduate from military basic training and begin your new life as a valued member of America's armed forces.

Military basic training graduation is no small thing. The event rivals anything you may have gone through during your high school, or even college, graduation ceremony. As a very minimum, the event will include a formal military parade, where your family and loved ones can gape at you in your new military dress uniform as you march by in all your military splendor.

In some branches, you get a day or two on the town, while in other branches, you go immediately on leave (vacation time). For those who get leave immediately following basic training, you're usually allowed only a week or two before you have to proceed to your first duty assignment. In any event, graduation day is a day you'll remember and cherish for the rest of your life.

# Basic Training Does Not a Career Make

Assuming that you graduate, basic training is just the beginning of your military experience. Many recruits will leave basic training and proceed immediately to their military job school. A few may get a little time off after basic to go home and visit family and friends. Some may proceed directly from basic training to their first military duty station, getting their job training on the job, or delaying specific military job training for a future date.

Each military branch has different policies, and within those policies, there is room for specific individual career paths. Chapter 3 gives you an idea of what you can expect after you complete military basic training.

# Basic Training Can Be a Rewarding Experience

I get e-mail all the time from readers of my military information website (http://usmilitary.about.com) who want to know what they can do to win an award in basic training. I usually respond by telling them that those who try for an award rarely win one. Usually, those who win the awards are those who do their very best without even thinking about it.

However, depending on the branch, you can earn several awards during your basic training experience. Did you know that you can earn a military medal just for graduating from basic training? It's true. It's called the National Defense Service Medal, and it's awarded to those who volunteer to serve in the military during times of conflict. I explain all about this medal in Chapter 20.

Other basic training awards are based on doing specific things better than anyone else. All the branches have an honor graduate or distinguished graduate program, which recognizes the recruits who had the best overall performance during basic training. Some branches even make a competition out of almost every single aspect of basic training. The Army rewards the top soldier during each training cycle with the Soldier of the Cycle award for each basic training company. Others offer only a few rewards and reserve those for the basic training graduation ceremony.

# Chapter 2

# A Day in the Life of Basic Training

**R**egardless of branch, many aspects of military basic training are the same. You have to march, you wake up extremely early, and you have drill instructors screaming at you like crazy persons.

It's all a part of the process of taking a spoiled civilian kid and turning him into a confident, professional member of the U.S. armed forces.

## Getting That Morning Wake-Up Call

In military basic training, there's no such thing as sleeping in. You'll get up at 5 a.m., every single day.

Waking up in the morning is an adjustment process that's the same for every single basic training class. When you first arrive, the drill instructors require a lot of noise, yelling, and jostling to get everyone out of the rack. Then, sometime around week 4, all it takes is for the drill instructor to enter the room in the early morning and quietly say, "Get up," and everyone pops out of their bunks immediately and begins their morning routine. It's an amazing adjustment.

## Calling Home

You'll have several chances during basic training to call home, but making a phone call is not a right; it's a privilege that has to be earned.

Because calling home is an earned privilege (for your group) and is different for everyone depending on how your basic training unit performs, you may get only one phone call during your entire time at basic, or you may get as many as eight or ten chances to call home. There's just no way to tell.

Generally, your first phone call lasts a few minutes, giving you just enough time to say, "I love you, and here's my mailing address." The instructor will give you a time limit on your phone calls. Your group travels to the pay phone area where you must wait in line for your turn.

How many calls you're allowed to make, how much time you get, and where the phone area is (indoors or outdoors) depends on which branch you're in.

# Just a Little Off the Sides: Haircuts

Haircuts are a rite of passage during military basic training. Almost immediately after arrival, your hair will be cut so short that it almost feels like you were shaved bald (guys, only).

After the initial haircut, you'll get a trim at least once per week during basic training. However, during the weekly trim, depending on which branch you're in, your hair may not be entirely cut off again, and the sides and the back may just be evened up.

You can actually estimate how long someone has been in basic training, depending on which branch you're in, by the length of their hair. Brand new male recruits have virtually no hair at all, those who have been there a week or two have a little bit of stubble, and those who are getting ready to graduate have an inch or so of hair showing.

Except for the Navy, women do not have to get their hair cut. However, when in uniform (which is all the time in basic training), women must wear their hair in such a way that the hair does not protrude past the bottom of the collar, and is not below the eyebrows. If your bangs are grown out, they must be long enough to be tied into a bun.

Navy gals, you will get your hair cut so that it meets the preceding standards at all times. You can let your hair grow back after basic training, as long as you continue to wear it in such a way that you meet the standards while in uniform.

# Cleaning Up: Showers

In basic training, you take group showers. There's no way out of communal showers. They're required. Everyone in your barracks will enter the shower room assigned to your barracks when commanded. The shower area is one large tiled room with multiple shower heads along the walls. Your instructor will give you a time limit for your shower and tell you when you may take your shower during the day or night.

In Marine Corps boot camp, the first couple of weeks will be spent doing things "by the numbers." This is true for hygiene time as well. When everyone is packed into their showering area, a drill instructor will give you an allotted time (by counting down from a certain number) to clean individual parts of your body and then rinse. Being able to take a full shower without a DI giving commands is also a rite of passage.

Over the years, I've received more e-mail concerns about this aspect of military basic training than any other factor. It seems recruits are scared or self-conscious to be naked in front of other recruits during shower time. When I went to basic training, group showers weren't a big deal because daily group showers were required after high school physical education.

Don't waste energy worrying about this aspect of basic training. I can guarantee that when it happens, you'll be so nervous or scared of your drill instructor that you won't worry about the shower.

When my twin daughters attended Air Force basic training a few years ago, they were so nervous about this aspect of training that they almost decided to change their mind and not ship out. I almost had to drag them to MEPS when the final day came. They were scared silly about having to shower in front of other people.

During their basic training graduation, I asked them how they got through having to take group showers. They looked at me like I was crazy. They didn't even remember being nervous about it! Go figure.

# Hearing from Home: Mail Call

In basic training, mail call is everyone's favorite time of day, except for the days when they don't get mail.

## Letters from home

When I was in Air Force basic training (about 100 years ago), I didn't receive any mail for the first four weeks. I was in a low, low place and ready to give it up or, worse, hurt myself.

Then one afternoon the TI performed mail call and called my name 18 times! It seems that for some reason, my mail had gotten lost in the system and apparently spent a significant amount of time sitting on someone's desk before he finally determined who I was and where I was and got my mail to me.

Unfortunately, I was performing dorm guard duty at the time, and you're not allowed to read mail during mail call. When I got off dorm guard duty, it would be time for lights out, and you can't read mail after lights out, either. My first chance to read mail wouldn't be until the next evening's mail call period.

However, my TI noticed that this was the first mail I'd received in basic training, and because more than four weeks had passed, he took pity on me. Right after mail call, he took me to the side and said, "Powers, I'm taking the flight outside for a little drill practice. We'll be gone about 45 minutes. Remember, you're not allowed to read any of that mail while we're gone, okay?" Then, he winked at me. That was the first time I realized that my TI was really an okay guy and not the ogre I thought him to be.

Mail call is usually every evening, Monday through Saturday. At the end of the duty day, the drill instructor will enter the barracks, call out names, and pass out mail. You're then usually granted about one hour of free time to read your mail. If you read fast, you may even have a few extra minutes to write a quick letter back.

Ask your family, friends, and loved ones to send you lots of mail during your time in basic training. I can't emphasis enough how much hearing from home helps, even if you don't have much free time available to answer. Also, be sure to ask for written mail only. Do not ask for items such as food, money, and prohibited items (which will be addressed when you arrive at basic training).

# Hitting the Sack: Lights Out

In all the branches' basic training programs, bedtime is usually 2100, or 9 p.m., except during times of special events, such as night exercises.

In basic training, *lights out* means go to sleep. It does not mean talk to your buddies, study, or write a letter home. However, these kinds of distractions generally aren't a problem. In basic training, you'll be so tired all the time that falling asleep at night shouldn't be an issue. What is more difficult is trying to keep from falling asleep during class time.

At the very beginning of basic training, the chief drill instructor will spend the night with you in the barracks. As you progress in training, the drill instructor will likely go home each night. However, basic training staff is constantly monitoring the barracks using closed circuit cameras. If you're not quietly in your bunks, you can expect a surprise night-time visit from your drill instructor.

Depending on which branch you're in, you may even have three or four DIs assigned to your platoon, and each a night a certain DI will stay in the barracks with the platoon. You are never without supervision.

# Gathering for Instructor Time

Every night (usually right after mail call) is instructor time. During this time, the drill instructor gathers everybody into the day room to go over information you need to learn and usually give you an overview of the next day's events.

During the first couple of weeks of basic training, communication during instructor time is one-way — in other words, the instructor talks, and the recruits listen. Gradually, this meeting changes to a session where questions and comments are permitted from the students.

At the very beginning of basic training, you'll learn to hate instructor time, because it seems to be set up so that the drill instructor is doing nothing except keeping you from much needed sleep. However, as weeks go on and you're allowed to make comments and ask questions, you'll start to look forward to instructor time, and it will become a period where you can pick up information that is beneficial to your basic training experience.

Listen closely during instructor time, because the instructor will often drop hints about important information you should know concerning the next day's events. For example, if the instructor says, "I want everyone to get a very good night's sleep tonight," that's not just your instructor being polite. (Basic training instructors are never polite when talking to recruits.) What the instructor's comments really mean is that tomorrow will be a very rough day.

# Surviving Inspections

Basic training inspections are a way of life. Some inspections will be formal and graded, usually conducted by a commissioned officer or someone else high in the chain of command. These inspections are generally pass/fail, and failing them is a good way to get sent back in basic training time.

Inspections by your drill instructor will be less formal, but will happen almost daily, and consequences of messing up are usually immediate (a chewing out or intense physical training, such as doing push-ups until you can't feel your arms anymore!).

There will come a time when you and your teammates begin to think that you are smarter than your instructor, and you've discovered an easier way to do things. Don't count on it.

# Meeting Your Battle Buddies

In basic training, you will be put under more stress and for a longer period of time than you have experienced during your entire life. Unfortunately, this type of stress provides fertile grounds for improper (even dangerous) behavior, such as suicide attempts or running away (AWOL).

To combat this problem, the services make sure that you're never, ever alone during basic training. One of your classmates will be assigned to be your battle buddy. Your battle buddy will be your best friend from the very first day of basic training to the very last day.

# Going on a Sick Call

In the military, *sick call* simply means going to see the doctor because you don't feel well. Sick call hours are usually first thing in the morning, immediately following the breakfast meal.

You must obtain your instructor's permission before attending sick call.

At sick call, you probably won't see an actual doctor. Instead, you'll likely be attended to by a physician's assistant (PA) or hospital corpsman. If the problem is too tough for the PA to handle or if you need prescription medication, the PA will refer you to an actual physician.

Do not attempt to fake an illness or injury in order to get out of training. If you go to sick call and they find nothing wrong with you, you can be assured that your instructor will hear about it, and the consequences of *malingering* will not be pleasant.

# Getting Shot (the Medical Kind)

During the first two weeks of basic training, you'll receive more immunizations than you knew existed. The good news is that you don't get all of these shots at one time. Your instructor will march your unit to the shot clinic, where you will receive a few of these shots and then take you back a couple days later for more.

Not long ago, the services used to use high compression air guns for basic training vaccinations. (You know, those neat "phfffft" guns you see on _Star Trek?_) However, the problem with these neat devices is that if you move, they'll cut the heck out of your arm. After a few chopped up arms, the services went back to the trusty old needle.

# Payday!

When you report to basic training, you must have a bank account. If you don't, one will be opened for you at the local on-base bank. The military services are not set up to pay you by cash or check. All pay is made by direct deposit to a bank account. If you don't have a bank account, you can't get paid.

You won't have available time to pay personal bills during basic training. It's a good idea to establish a bank account before leaving for basic, and then give a trusted loved one access to the account that can handle those financial matters from home until you return.

In basic training, all recruits are entitled to base pay. In 2010, the base pay rate for an E-1 is $1,447.20 per month. You will receive one half of that amount in each bi-monthly paycheck.

If you have dependents (spouse/children), you will also receive a housing allowance, which is designed to provide a household for your dependents. The housing allowance amount depends on the location where your dependents live, but for an E-1 with dependents, it ranges from $400 per month to $1,100 per month. Base pay is subject to income tax, but the housing allowance is tax-free.

# Chowing Down

In basic training, you receive three meals per day. Most of the time, these are hot meals served in the chow hall (called *dining facility* in the Air Force and Army, and *galley* or mess hall in the Marine Corps, Navy, and Coast Guard).

Chow hall meals in basic training are not slow, leisurely events. You have a limited amount of time (about 15 minutes) to sit down and consume your meal. Even though the chow hall serves it, recruits are not allowed sweets or even sodas in some of the branches.

After basic training, you'll enjoy your meals in the chow hall much, much more. Most military chow halls today include an extensive salad bar, a station for full meals such as fried chicken, seafood, Mexican food, and pastas, along with a snack line that includes hamburgers, hotdogs, chili, fries, and other junk-food items. Plus, you're allowed to consume sodas and dessert!

The chow halls in basic training are limited. You usually have a salad bar, but the snack line is generally off limits to recruits. If you don't like the choices offered in the full meal line, that's just tough. It's that or go hungry. The basic training chow hall food will be reminiscent of the choices offered at a high school cafeteria — not very appetizing.

One thing has changed for the positive in military basic training chow halls from days past. In the old days, the rule in the chow hall was that you had to eat everything on your plate. That rule no longer exists. You no longer have to eat everything you take, if you don't feel like it. Basic training is all about getting into shape, not stuffing your mouth with food you don't really want.

No matter what, time in the chow hall isn't social hour. Do not look around or make any conversation with others.

# Chapter 3

# Training for Military Jobs

*A*lthough you'll remember your basic training for life, it's not the totality of your military training and experience. Before you can be an asset to the military and start to be productive, you have to learn a military job. After all, the military can't afford to continue to pay you just so that you can run around saying, "Yes, sir" and "No, sir" all the time.

After basic training (in most cases), you must attend a school to teach you how to do your specific military job. For example, if you're supposed to be a military cook, someone has to teach you how to cook those eggs over-easy while preparing bacon for hundreds of other people at the same time.

## Leave/Vacation After Basic

Everyone in the military earns 2.5 days of leave (vacation time) for every month of active duty service. That doesn't mean you get to use your vacation any time you want. Leave approval is subject to the "needs of the service." That means if the military or your unit has something important going on (such as your training), you can't take leave at that time. Supervisors and/or commanding officers must approve all leave.

Unless you have a verified family emergency (death or serious injury/illness of an immediate family member), you're not allowed to take leave during basic training.

If you joined the Navy or Air Force, you're not usually allowed to take leave until you finish your military job training. The one exception to this rule is that you're usually allowed to take a week or so of leave if you're attending job training during the Christmas week.

The Marine Corps grants ten days of leave immediately following basic training graduation, prior to reporting to the School of Infantry. The Coast Guard grants one week of leave following Coast Guard basic training, prior to reporting to the first duty assignment.

While on leave, you're responsible for all travel expenses. The military will pick up the tab for transportation directly from your old duty station to your new duty station, but if you have to go out of your way to get to your leave location, you pay the difference.

Most new recruits (except in the Coast Guard) then go directly from basic training to a military job school to discover how to do their new military job.

# Army MOS Training

The Army calls their enlisted jobs *Military Occupation Specialties,* or MOS. If you have a combat arms job, such as infantry, or armor (tank driver), the Army combines basic training and job training into one single course, called OSUT, or One-Station-Unit-Training. In such cases, there is no basic training graduation ceremony. One day, your drill sergeant will wake you up as usual and say something like, "Okay, basic training is over, and now job training starts."

Your graduation ceremony (see Chapter 19) will occur after the job training portion of OSUT.

If you do not have a combat arms MOS, following your basic training graduation ceremony, you'll be bussed or flown to your Army AIT (Advanced Individual Training) base to go through training for your particular Army MOS (job).

Going through Army AIT is much like going to college, with the exception of mandatory PT (exercise sessions) each morning and the fact that you're not allowed to skip any classes. However, at the end of the class day, you're generally on your own until the next morning. Do you want to stop and grab a beer at the end of the day? Feel free (assuming, of course, that you're of legal age). Want to hang out in the post library, each evening? It's allowed! You still have platoon sergeants, who are in charge of you during AIT, but they seem to be of the kinder, gentler sort than what you experienced in basic training.

# Air Force Job Training

Everyone goes directly from Air Force basic training to Air Force job training locations, which the Air Force calls *tech school*. Where you go for Air Force tech school depends on the job you were selected for. Many Air Force job schools are conducted at Lackland AFB in Texas, so your travel to tech school may just mean a short march down the street.

A few years ago, the Air Force discovered that giving new recruits total off-duty freedom immediately after basic training wasn't working so well. Too many new basic training graduates spent too much time drinking and partying and not enough time studying and learning their new Air Force jobs. The Air Force responded by implementing a *phase system* for all of its tech schools, which returns after-basic freedoms to recruits very slowly, during the tech school learning process.

The Air Force Technical School phase program consists of three phases. As airmen advance in each phase, they receive more privileges. The phase program begins on the day you arrive at the technical school and (in most cases) ends when you graduate technical training and proceed to your first permanent duty assignment.

## Phase 1

Phase 1 begins at your very first second of arrival at an Air Force tech school. During your time in phase 1, you

- Will remain on base at all times.

- Will not purchase, possess, or consume alcohol.

- Will wear military uniform on and off duty. However, you may wear civilian attire inside your dormitory.

- Will adhere to a call to quarters (curfew) of 2200 (10 p.m.) to 0400 (4 a.m.) Sunday through Saturday.

- Will eat three meals per day, Monday through Friday, in a base dining facility (chow hall).

- Will not operate, ride in, or utilize a private motor vehicle (PMV). Training/operations group commanders may make exceptions on a case-by-case basis.

- Will have your room inspected a minimum of once per week, but not on the same day every week.

✔ Will make your bed with issue sheets and a bedspread or blanket. Personalized bedspreads or comforters are not authorized.

✔ Will not hang pictures of any kind on the walls or lockers. However, pictures in a frame, no larger than 8 inches by 10 inches, may be displayed on your desktop, but must not be of a sexually explicit or degrading nature.

✔ May have an alarm clock or radio alarm clock on your nightstand or desk.

✔ May not possess or use a television or stereo in your dormitory room. You may, however, use existing televisions or stereos located in dayrooms or common areas.

✔ Will march to and from all locations.

✔ Will participate in a formal open ranks inspection a minimum of once per week.

✔ May use a personal electronic device (cellphone, MP3 player, laptop, and so on) inside your dormitory during nonduty hours only.

You remain in phase 1 until 14 calendar days after arrival. If you fail any of the requirements, you may be extended in phase 1 for even longer.

# Phase 2

In phase 2, you've achieved a higher level of knowledge and proficiency and are expected to be a model Airman. With greater privileges come greater responsibilities. You're expected to follow, promote, and encourage all Airmen to adhere to standards. You're held accountable and supervised commensurate with your time in service.

During this phase, you

✔ Will remain in uniform and on station during duty hours. If you go off station, you must wear the appropriate blue uniform combination and remain in the local area as determined in writing by the training/operations group commander.

✔ May consume alcohol on base only if you're of legal age, but not during the duty week or 12 hours prior to duty.

✔ May ride in and operate a private motor vehicle (PMV) after duty hours.

✔ Will adhere to a call to quarters (curfew) of 2200 (10 p.m.) to 0400 (4 a.m.) on evenings prior to duty days and a curfew of 2400 (midnight) to 0400 on evenings prior to nonduty days.

✔ Will have your room inspected a minimum of one time while in phase 2. You must keep your room according to local guidelines, but may personalize your room.

✔ Will march to and from all locations during duty hours.

✔ Will participate in a formal open ranks inspection a minimum of one time while in phase 2.

✔ May use a personal electronic device (such as cellphones, laptop, and MP3 players) after duty hours only.

✔ Will pass all required open ranks and room evaluations prior to progressing to phase 3.

Phase 2 runs from the 15th calendar day through the 35th calendar day of Air Force tech school.

# Phase 3

During phase 3, you're expected to be a responsible wingman for newer airmen. You require minimal supervision and only random spot-checks for adherence to standards. Your knowledge, proficiency, and conduct should rival that of a permanent party airman, and you're afforded privileges as such.

During this phase, you

✔ Will remain in uniform and on station during duty hours.

✔ Will not consume alcohol 12 hours prior to duty. (You must be of legal age to consume alcohol.)

✔ Will not possess or consume alcohol in the dormitory or immediate surrounding area. Those who choose to drink alcohol will do so responsibly and not bring discredit to the Air Force, in or out of uniform.

✔ Have no restrictions on the use of private motor vehicles (PMVs).

✔ Will adhere to a call to quarters (curfew) of 2200 (10 p.m.) on evenings prior to duty days.

Phase 3 runs from the 36th calendar day through completion of all technical training and departure for permanent duty assignment.

## *Other restrictions*

While in Air Force technical training, some restrictions apply, regardless of what training phase you are in:

- ✔ You can't smoke on base at any time.

- ✔ You can't visit the dormitory rooms of any member of the opposite sex.

- ✔ You can't visit any permanent party dormitory rooms, on-base housing units, or the rooms of anyone assigned TDY (temporary duty) on the base.

- ✔ While in phase 1 or phase 2, you may not rent or visit any off-base hotel rooms.

These restrictions apply until you graduate from Air Force tech school and proceed to your first permanent duty assignment. If your particular Air Force job requires that you attend multiple tech schools, you remain in the phase system while attending such training.

# *Navy Rating Training*

The Navy calls its job training *A school.* All Navy enlisted ratings (jobs) have an A school, which teaches you the fundamentals of your new Navy job.

Unlike the Air Force, you have no special restrictions on your off-duty freedoms during Navy A school (unless you've enlisted in one of a handful of special jobs, such as Navy SEAL).

If you're in a normal rating, attending Navy A school is very much like attending a regular college program, in that after class you can go play, assuming that you haven't been assigned to any extra duties (such as watch).

Of course, like other military branches, you'll also have mandatory PT (exercise) sessions at least three days per week.

After graduation from A school, a few new sailors attend *C school,* while most are assigned to their first ship or permanent duty station. C school is advanced training within your rating (job). For example, if you attended A school for general computer maintenance, it may be followed with C school to teach you how to work on a specific complicated computer system. Being chosen for C school means that you have proven that you're qualified to be trained in an advanced area of the job.

# Marine Corps Training

All Marine basic training graduates get ten days of leave immediately following basic training graduation. Enjoy your ten days off because following your R&R, you have to report to one of the Marine Corps schools of infantry. The Marines have two such schools: one located on the East coast and one on the West coast. If you attended Marine Corps basic training at Parris Island, you'll probably attend the school of infantry at Camp Geiger in North Carolina, while those who attended basic training in San Diego will probably attend the school of infantry at Camp Pendleton in California.

It's often said that all Marines are infantrymen first, and whatever Marine Corps job they happen to hold is a distant second. The Marine Corps certainly believes this philosophy, because all Marines attend one of the schools of infantry, even if their Marine Corps job is not as an infantryman.

Attending a school of infantry doesn't leave much time for grabbing a quick beer after work or spending the evening watching reruns of "I Love Lucy." Think of this training as one long practice war game.

Those who are assigned to Marine Corps infantry job attend a 51-day course after they return from graduation leave, and this course is actually their Marine Corps job training. Upon graduation from the school of infantry, they will proceed to their first permanent duty assignment.

Marines who are not assigned to infantry jobs also attend the Marine Corps school of infantry for 22 days, where they learn basic battle skills. Upon graduation, they proceed to their normal Marine Corps job training. After job training, these Marines proceed to their first permanent duty assignment.

# Coast Guard Training

The Coast Guard is the only service that doesn't send new recruits to job training immediately after basic training. Instead, following basic training leave, new recruits are sent directly to their new permanent duty assignment.

At your first duty assignment, you'll be classified as an *undesignated seaman* (SN), *fireman* (FN), *or airman* (AN), which basically means you don't have a specific rating (job) and are available to do anything at all that the Captain needs to have done on the ship or base. These tasks include general work, such as swabbing the deck or helping load and fire the big guns. Pretty much whatever needs to be done, you do.

After two or three years as an undesignated seaman, you're given the chance to *strike* (apply) for a specific rating (job), meaning you can apply for the job. If you receive the job, you work for a nonrate in that field until you're promoted.

This system has its advantages. In the other branches, you select your job in advance, based on what you've read about it in an official military recruiting job description. These job descriptions are designed to make any job sound interesting and exciting. In the Coast Guard, you get a couple of years to actually scope out the various jobs before making any choices.

After you strike for a job (assuming that job is available), the Coast Guard will send you to the official school for that job, assuming that you agree to re-enlist for an additional four years.

Of all the services, a job in the Coast Guard is the most like having a civilian job. Few Coast Guard ships go on patrols that are longer than a day long. Most of the time, your ship goes out on patrol and then returns to its port at the end of the same day. When off-duty, you're generally allowed to do whatever you want to do (as long as it's legal, of course).

# Chapter 4

# On the Firing Line (Weapons Range)

*I*t wouldn't be the U.S. Military if it didn't involve firing weapons. You get your first crack at firing actual military weapons during your last few weeks of basic training.

Weapons training differs greatly among the different branches' basic training programs. Without doubt, Marine Corps recruits fire the most rounds during basic training programs. They're followed by the Army, the Air Force, the Navy, and finally, the Coast Guard.

Regardless of the branch, you can't graduate from military basic training without proving that you can handle a military weapon without shooting yourself, your classmates, or your instructors.

## Discovering the Weapons Used in Basic

Many types of weapons are used in the United States Military. However, in military basic training, you're required to be familiar with only a few weapons. If your military job requires you to know about additional weapons and how to use them, you'll receive additional training during your military job school.

## M-16A2 assault rifle

The M-16A2 rifle (see Figure 4-1) is the standard military rifle used for combat. It's carried by pretty much every military member in a combat zone. Most people simply call it the M-16.

Some of the military branches have converted to the M-16A4 rifle, which is the upgrade to the M-16A2, so don't be surprised if you receive that rifle instead.

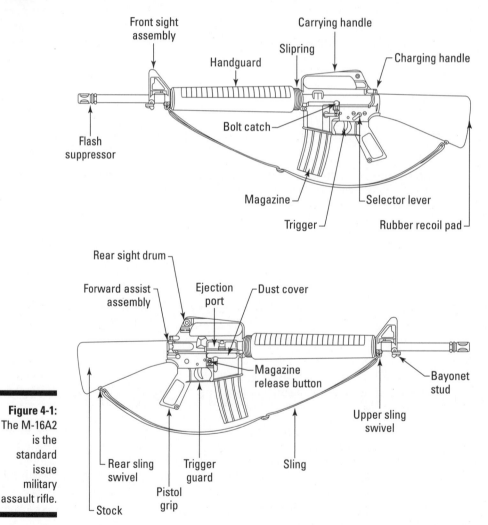

**Figure 4-1:** The M-16A2 is the standard issue military assault rifle.

The M-16 has been around in one version or another since the Vietnam War. (The first version, the M16A1, entered Army service in 1964.) Its longevity is credit to its usefulness as a general assault weapon. The M-16 is quite simply one of the finest military rifles ever made (although advocates of the M-4 Carbine, described in the next section, may argue with me).

The rifle is simple to operate and puts out a lot of lead. The M16A2 5.56mm rifle is a lightweight, air-cooled, gas-operated, magazine-fed, shoulder or hip-fired weapon designed for either automatic fire (3-round bursts) or semiautomatic fire (single shot) through the use of a selector lever. The weapon has a fully adjustable rear sight.

The bottom of the trigger guard opens to provide access to the trigger while wearing winter mittens or chemical protective gear. The upper receiver/ barrel assembly has a fully adjustable rear sight and a compensator that helps keep the muzzle down during firing. The steel bolt group and barrel extension are designed with locking lugs that lock the bolt group to the barrel extension, allowing the rifle to have a lightweight aluminum receiver.

In basic training, recruits of the Army, Air Force, and Marine Corps will fire this weapon. Navy recruits will fire a computerized simulator of the M-16 rifle. This simulator is almost like firing the real thing. (The computerized rifle even kicks and makes a loud noise).

The Coast Guard is the only branch that does not fire the M-16 rifle during basic training. However, Coast Guard recruits receive classroom training, explaining how to fire the weapon, and practical training for disassembly, cleaning, and reassembly. If you later receive a Coast Guard job that requires you to carry an M-16, you'll go through additional training, including actually firing the weapon.

## M-4 Carbine

The M-4 combat assault rifle first entered Army service in 1997. The rifle is the standard weapon used by some Army units, such as the 82nd Airborne Division, and special operations units, such as Army Rangers.

With a shortened barrel and collapsible stock, the M-4 is ideal for close quarter marksmanship where little weight and quick action are required. Firing a standard 5.56 millimeter round (the same as the M-16), the weapon weighs a mere 5.6 pounds (empty). A revised rear sight allows for better control of the weapon out to the maximum range of the ammunition used. With the PAQ-4 (Infrared Sight) mounted on the forward rail system, the M-4 can be fitted for increased firepower.

The M-4 Carbine can also be fitted with the M-203 40mm grenade launcher. The M-203 is a lightweight, compact, breech loading, pump action, single shot launcher. The launcher consists of a hand guard and sight assembly with an adjustable metallic folding, short-range blade sight assembly, and an aluminum receiver assembly, which houses the barrel latch, barrel stop, and firing mechanism. The launcher is capable of firing a variety of low velocity 40mm ammunition. The launcher also has a quadrant sight that may be attached to the M-4 carrying handle and is used when precision is required out to the maximum effective range of the weapon.

Some Army recruits (usually those in infantry training) will get a chance to carry and qualify with the M-4 instead of the M-16. Many infantry Marines will be trained on the M-4 during Marine Corps infantry training, which follows basic training.

## M-9 pistol

Did you know that in combat, mostly officers carry handguns? Most enlisted don't. Notable exceptions are military police and special operations forces.

The M-9 pistol is the primary sidearm for all military services, except the Coast Guard. It entered the services in 1985 (1990 for the Army). The adoption of the M-9 pistol was the result of a congressional mandate to equip all U.S. services with a standard handgun.

The M-9 meets the strict requirements for functional reliability, speed of first shot, rapidity of fire, speed of reloading, range, penetration, and accuracy to 50 yards. Also, the pistol's components are interchangeable, allowing this weapon to be pieced together from the parts of others.

If you attend Army basic training, you'll fire the M-9 pistol before you graduate. The other branches do not fire the M-9 during military basic training.

The Air Force used to fire the M-9 pistol during basic training. However, the Air Force very recently deleted this requirement, as few Air Force enlisted members are required to carry a pistol in combat.

## Sig Sauer P229 DAK pistol

While the other branches use the M-9 as their standard issue pistol, the Coast Guard belongs to the Department of Homeland Security, not the Department of Defense, and therefore it uses the standard weapons used by the Department of Homeland Security.

The P229 DAK .40 S&W pistol (see Figure 4-2) is the standard sidearm for the Department of Homeland Security and therefore the Coast Guard. The P229 DAK is a compact, double-action pistol. The pistol weighs only 6.5 pounds and fires double action only. A key feature of this pistol is quick and easy dis-assembly for cleaning. All you have to do is lock the slide back and remove the magazine. The DAK model also includes a double-strike capability.

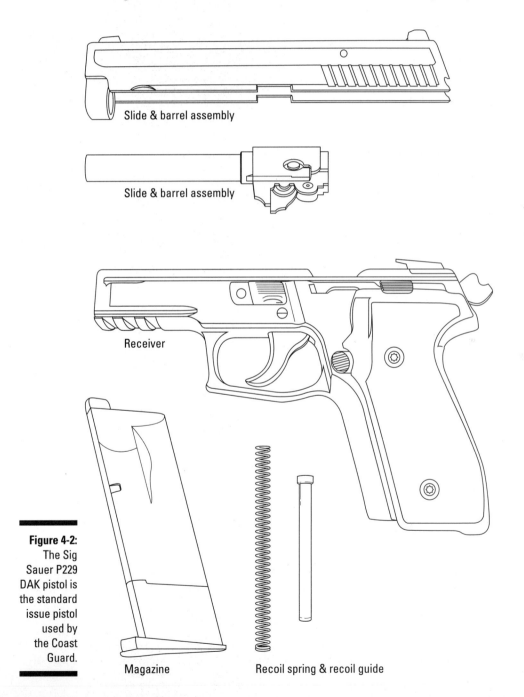

Slide & barrel assembly

Slide & barrel assembly

Receiver

Magazine

Recoil spring & recoil guide

# Thinking about Weapons Safety

You must obey numerous safety rules any time you are around military weapons. Treat all weapons as if they are loaded.

A weapon is never safe to handle until you have cleared it. Ensure that it's unloaded. ***Note:*** You'll receive detailed instructions on how to clear the weapon during your classroom training. Pay attention! Clearing the weapon is one of the most important things you will learn.

Follow these safety rules:

- ✔ Never point a weapon at anyone or anything you do not intend to shoot.

- ✔ Keep your weapon pointed in a safe direction at all times.

- ✔ A weapon is equipped with a mechanical safety. Keep it on Safe when it isn't being fired.

- ✔ Never engage in horseplay when handling (or you're around) weapons.

- ✔ If you have to take medication, inform your instructor so that you can be watched more closely.

- ✔ Do not handle the weapon until you're told to do so.

- ✔ While on the range, keep the weapon pointed toward the target at all times.

- ✔ Immediately obey all commands on the range.

- ✔ Immediately remove finger from the trigger upon hearing "Cease fire," regardless of who gives it.

Safety violations on the range or anywhere else can cause serious or fatal injury to you or others. They can also cause extensive damage to military property. A military weapon is not a toy; it can kill a person with one round. Remember, a weapon is only as safe as the person using it.

# Home, Home on the Range

Weapons qualifications courses differ significantly from one military branch to another. Different branches train on different weapons during basic training and have different requirements to qualify.

During your basic training, you're given the chance to become an expert with your weapon. You receive training by instructors in a school-type setting, as well as hands-on experience out in the field. You're also tested on your accuracy with your weapon and must pass the minimum standards for your services' weapons training before moving on to graduation and job training.

# Army qualification course

Army basic marksmanship training consists of three phases. Training to become a marksmen lasts approximately two to three weeks and ends with qualification testing where you must pass with a minimum score in order to proceed to graduation. Just passing the marksmanship training course will earn you an Army marksmanship badge. You must hit 23 to 29 out of the 40 targets in order to earn the marksmanship qualification. If you do a little better (30 to 35), you qualify for the sharpshooter badge. To get an expert badge, you must hit 36 to 40 of the targets.

## Phase 1

During the first phase, you learn how to disassemble, clean, and reassemble your weapon as well as safe handling procedures. You also find out how to safely load and unload the weapon, but you won't actually be firing during this phase.

Phase 1 of training includes

- Disassembly and assembly of your weapon
- Identification of parts
- Function check
- Magazine loading and unloading
- Ammunition types and care
- Loading/unloading your weapon
- Correcting malfunctions (SPORTS)
- Front and rear sights adjustments
- Peer coaching
- Eight cycles of function and troubleshooting

*SPORTS* is an acronym to remind you of steps to take to clear a weapons malfunction. It stands for Slap, Pull, Observe, Release, Tap, and Shoot.

During phase 1, you'll also learn and practice the four fundamentals of Army marksmanship:

- **Steady position:** The steady position teaches you how to correctly grip and handle your weapon during firing and nonfiring stances. You also learn how to position your elbow, support the weapon, relax your muscles, and feel the natural point of aim.
- **Aiming:** The aiming fundamental includes correct sight alignment and proper eye focus. You also find out how to establish and maintain a viable sight picture.

> ✔ **Breath control:** In order to hit what you're aiming at, you must know and practice proper breath control. When you fire the weapon, you hold your breath. Breathing while firing will cause the bullet to move up or down, missing your intended target.
>
> ✔ **Trigger squeeze:** When you fire a weapon in the Army, you do not pull the trigger. Instead, you gently squeeze it. Pulling the trigger results in the weapon shifting left or right so that the bullet misses the intended target.

## Phase 2

During phase 2, you get to actually fire your weapon. You don't have to wear all your combat gear during this phase. The objective is to just get you used to safely and accurately handling your weapon.

Until recently, you were required to wear all your combat gear (flack vest, canteen web belt, steel helmet, and gas mask carrier) any time you were on the basic training firing range. The Army has eliminated this requirement until after you achieve your basic rifle qualification.

During phase 2, you spend six hours learning how to group your shots and eight hours practicing setting your sights so that you can hit the target. Your instructor then spends six hours giving you feedback about your downrange performance and advice on how to improve your marksmanship ability.

## Phase 3

During phase 3 of training, you actually complete the official Army qualification course. You must pass the minimum standards in order to graduate from Army basic combat training.

During this phase, you shoot targets (single and pop-up) from three firing positions:

> ✔ **Supported prone,** in which you stand and fire with your rifle supported by a barricade
>
> ✔ **Unsupported prone,** where you stand and fire without anything to support your rifle
>
> ✔ **Foxhole** (replaced the kneeling position), where you kneel and shoot from within a simulated foxhole.

The foxhole position allows you to support your weapon on the solid ground. In my experience, foxhole is the most stable firing position.

In order to qualify, you must hit at least 23 out of 40 pop-up targets at ranges varying from 5 meters to 300 meters (approximately 80 to 327 yards).

# Air Force qualification course

In order to graduate from Air Force basic training, you must complete (and qualify on) the Air Force rifle (M-16) qualification course.

The Air Force used to also require qualification on the M-9 pistol during basic training, but this requirement was recently eliminated.

During the actual firing, you'll fire a total of 80 rounds at a man-sized target (upper body only) at ranges from 75 meters to 300 meters (1 meter = 1.094 yards). The range at Lackland is a short range, so you'll actually be firing from only 25 yards away. However, the target sizes are shrunk to represent the proper sizes at the specified distances (75 meters, 175 meters, and 300 meters).

The Air Force conducts its basic training weapons qualification course in three phases.

Airmen who hit the target at least 35 times qualify for the Small Arms Expert Ribbon.

### Phase 1: Battle sight grouping and zero

During this phase, you're sighting in the rifle. After each shot group, you (and the instructor) examine the target. The instructor then gives you advice (such as how to breathe properly or not jerk the trigger) to correct anything that you're doing wrong. Additionally, the instructor tells you how to adjust your sights to correct your grouping.

All the shots in Phase 1 are in the *prone, supported position,* where you're lying on your stomach on the ground, at a slight angle to the target, with your rifle supported on top of a sandbag. The targets for this phase are all man-sized targets at 75 meters.

The following list shows the shot groups for phase 1 training, which includes 16 rounds total. After each group, you're to check your target and make sight adjustments:

- Four rounds (one magazine with 4 rounds loaded) at 75 meters.
- Three rounds (one magazine with 3 rounds loaded) at 75 meters.
- Three rounds (one magazine with 3 rounds loaded) at 75 meters.
- Three rounds (one magazine with 3 rounds loaded) at 75 meters.
- Three rounds (one magazine with 3 rounds loaded) at 75 meters.

### Phase 2: Practice

During the practice phase, you fire a total of 24 rounds from 4 different positions. A couple of twists are thrown in here. First of all, each round is timed, and you'll have to reload a fresh magazine during the round. Keep your head and don't rush, because you have time to make your shots count and still change the magazine and shoot again, within the prescribed time limit. During the practice round, you fire at a man-sized target at 175 meters.

The following describes the three supported positions you'll use during phase 2:

- ✔ **Prone supported:** Six rounds (two magazines with 3 rounds loaded in each), at 175 meters, 50-second time limit.

- ✔ **Kneeling supported:** Six rounds (two magazines with 3 rounds loaded in each), at 175 meters, 50-second time limit.

- ✔ **Over barricade supported**: Six rounds (two magazines with 3 rounds loaded in each), at 175 meters, 50-second time limit.

### Phase 3: Qualification

Phase 3 is the phase that really counts. You fire a total of 40 rounds at a man-sized target at 300 meters. To pass the qualification course, you must hit the target at least 20 times. The following list describes the specific ways you must qualify using supported and unsupported positions:

- ✔ **Prone supported:** Ten rounds (one 4-round magazine, two 3-round magazines), at 300 meters, 90-second time limit.

- ✔ **Prone unsupported:** Ten rounds (one 4-round magazine, two 3-round magazines), at 300 meters, 90-second time limit.

- ✔ **Kneeling supported:** Ten rounds (one 4-round magazine, two 3-round magazines), at 300 meters, 90-second time limit.

- ✔ **Over barricade supported:** Ten rounds (one 4-round magazine, two 3-round magazines), at 300 meters, 90-second time limit.

## Navy qualification course

Discharging a full automatic weapon on a ship is definitely not a good idea. Therefore, during Navy basic training, you won't get to fire the M-16 rifle. Instead, you qualify with the M-9 pistol and the Mossberg 500 shotgun.

The Navy is unique in that before you get to handle an actual weapon, you get a chance to fire the weapon on a computerized simulator. In fact, by the time you actually pick up a real weapon, you'll almost be an expert.

Before you even proceed to the firing range, you'll complete several hours of weapons training in the classroom. These briefings include range safety, drawing and holstering your pistol and shotgun and clearing barrel procedures (loading and unloading the weapon) as well as marksmanship fundamentals, weapons characteristics, the names of parts, and the operation of and assembly/disassembly of your pistol and shotgun.

You also complete at least three hours of *dry firing,* where you practice safely firing the weapon without any ammunition.

### M-9 qualification course

The standard Navy M-9 pistol qualification course has three phases, consisting of a total of 48 live rounds:

- ✔ **From the 3-yard line:** You fire a total of 12 rounds from the 3-yard line. With your strongest hand supported, you fire two rounds with a time limit of four seconds. You then holster your weapon and repeat the first firing sequence. You then repeat this process, except this time, you reload the additional six rounds and switch to your weak hand.

- ✔ **From the 7-yard line:** During this section, you fire a total of 12 rounds from the 7-yard line. The first three times, you fire the weapon two rounds, strong hand supported. Then you have ten seconds to fire two more rounds, reload, switch hands, and fire two more rounds. After holstering your weapon, you have eight seconds to draw and fire your last two rounds.

- ✔ **From the 15-yard line:** In this part, you fire a total of 24 rounds from the 15-yard line. Again, using your strong hand, you fire two rounds in four seconds, repeat, and then fire four rounds before holstering your weapon. You then move to the kneeling position, where you fire 4 rounds, reload 12 rounds, and then fire another 4 rounds before holstering your pistol. Finally, you have eight seconds to draw and fire your remaining eight rounds.

In order to graduate from Navy recruit training, you must achieve a minimum score of 180 points (see the next section). Each area of the human-shaped target is worth a certain number of points. Vital areas (such as chest and head) are worth more than areas such as legs and wrist.

### Shotgun range qualification

The Navy shotgun qualification course consists of four firing stations. Station 1 is 25 yards standing behind a tall barricade. Station 2 is 20 yards in a kneeling position with a low barricade. At station 3, you stand from 15 yards with no barricade. Station 4 is the standing position with no barricade at ten yards.

- ✔ **Station 1:** At station 1, you shoot five rounds from a standing position behind a tall barricade. You then load four rounds before proceeding to station 2.

- ✔ **Station 2:** From the kneeling, aimed fire position behind a low barricade, you fire four rounds, reload an additional four rounds, and proceed to station 3.

- ✔ **Station 3:** Here, you fire four rounds from the shoulder position with no barricade and reload three rounds before proceeding to the last station.

- ✔ **Station 4:** No barricade is at station 4, where you fire with the shotgun supported on your hip. You fire a total of three shots, reloading once, and then clear your weapon. (Make sure that your weapon is unloaded and safe.)

Each shotgun shell consists of nine pellets. In order to qualify, at least 30 of your shotgun pellets must hit each target. Out of a possible score of 162 points, you must score a minimum of 90 points to qualify.

### Navy marksmanship awards

There are no awards for shotgun qualification, although you must successfully qualify to graduate from Navy recruit training. The Navy Pistol Marksmanship Ribbon, Navy Sharpshooter Award, and Navy Expert Pistol Medal may be earned on the Navy Handgun Qualification Course. In order to earn a marksmanship award, you must obtain 180 to 203 points. To qualify as a sharpshooter, you must score between 204 and 227. The highest award, the Expert medal, is awarded to those who score 228 or higher.

## Marine Corps weapons qualification course

Unlike the other branches, Marine recruits qualify with the same M-16 rifle they've been carrying around with them throughout the entire basic training course. Therefore, you should treat your rifle well every day to make sure that it's in good shape for qualification day.

The Marine Corps basic training marksmanship course consists of three distinct phases.

### Phase 1: Weapons introduction

During this phase, you find out all about the M-16A2 rifle. You're even required to memorize your particular rifle's serial number. You spend a considerable amount of time taking your rifle apart, cleaning it, and putting it back together. You're also required to memorize the four rules of Marine Corps rifle safety:

- ✔ Treat every weapon as if it were loaded.
- ✔ Never point your weapon at anything you do not intend to shoot.
- ✔ Keep your finger straight and off the trigger until you intend to fire.
- ✔ Keep your weapon on safe until you intend to fire.

You will also learn another weapons safety rule when you get out of basic training: Be absolutely sure of your target and what is behind it.

During Marine Corps basic training, you must never refer to your M-16 as a gun. Doing so will result in a massive tirade from your drill instructor. Marine Corps M-16s are always called your weapon or your rifle.

During the first phase, you'll also receive several hours of classroom instruction on proper marksmanship techniques so that you'll be able to hit the target when the time comes.

### Phase 2: Snap in/grass week

During snap-in week, you're primarily in a classroom setting where you learn the four standard Marine Corps firing positions (standing, kneeling, sitting, and prone). This phase of your training isn't conducted by a drill instructor, but rather by a Marine who holds the MOS (job) of a Primary Marksmanship Instructor (PMI).

The PMI teaches you how to adjust your sights, how to adjust for weather conditions, and how to successfully hit what you're aiming at. During this phase of training, you actually get to fire a computerized version of your weapon, which will give you a good indication of how you'll do when you actually visit the firing range.

### Phase 3: Firing week

During firing week, you actually get to fire your weapon for the first time. The week begins with practice on the firing range. Half of your platoon will fire the weapon, while the other half sets up targets. Then you swap.

The course of fire includes shooting at targets that are 200, 300, and 500 yards away from the prone, sitting, kneeling, and standing positions. It's interesting to note that the Marine Corps is the only branch that has recruits shooting from distances as far as 500 yards away.

At the end of the week, you get a chance to fire on the actual qualification course. The course is the same as the one you used in practice, but this time, it counts. If you fail to qualify, you won't proceed in basic training with the rest of your platoon. You'll be sent back to complete rifle instruction all over again, thereby delaying your graduation date.

In order to qualify, you fire a total of 50 rounds, worth up to 5 points each (depending on where you hit the target). The maximum possible points you can earn on this course is 250. To pass the course, you must earn at least 190 points, which will qualify you to wear the Marine Corps marksmanship badge. To become a sharpshooter, you must earn at least 210 points. In order to win status as an Expert, you must receive a score of at least 220 points.

## Coast Guard marksmanship qualification course

The Coast Guard is unique in that you don't have to pass the weapons firing course in order to graduate from their basic training program. In order to finish Coast Guard basic, you just have to go through the course, not actually meet any particular qualification score.

If you fail to qualify during basic training and your Coast Guard job requires you to use weapons, you'll need to qualify before you can actually be assigned to those particular Coast Guard duties.

You begin by visiting the firing range, where a Coast Guard gunner's mate teaches you the fundamentals of firing the Sig Sauer P299 .40 Cal. pistol. At the firing range, you discover how to properly handle the weapon. Handling the weapon is followed by some dry firing and some shooting time on the computerized firing program. On the following Monday or Tuesday, you return to the range for the real thing.

Any violation of safety procedures will result in an immediate course failure, and you'll be required to return to the range within seven days to try again. See "Thinking about Weapons Safety," earlier in this chapter.

Like the Navy M-9 pistol range, you fire a total of 48 rounds, at distances ranging from 3 yards to 15 yards. Different areas of the target are worth different numbers of points, ranging from 0 to 5 points each. In order to qualify, you must achieve a score of 114 to 128 points.

To be designated as a Sharpshooter, you must score between 129 and 143 points. Those who achieve more than 143 points are designated an Expert. Those who are certified as a Sharpshooter or an Expert are entitled to wear the Coast Guard pistol ribbon, with the appropriate device to indicate Sharpshooter or Expert status.

# Part II
# Getting Ready for Basic

The 5th Wave                    By Rich Tennant

"It was Lieutenant Hooper's idea. He thought it would be nice to add some rustic charm to the unit by stenciling the tanks. This, for instance, is part of our 'Country Cupboard' attack squad."

# In this part . . .

An old military axiom states "preparation is half the battle." Your experience at military basic training will be much more pleasant if you do a little advance preparation. Fortunately, you were smart enough to buy this book, so you're ahead of the power curve.

In this part, you find out a few simple tidbits that will get you on your way to a successful experience at military basic training. You get the inside scoop on what to pack and what you should leave at home. You also discover the importance of getting in shape before you head out. You also get a sneak preview of what's covered in the classroom: military ranks and chain of command, military law and history, and military drill.

If you like to be prepared, you won't want to miss this part.

# Chapter 5

# Getting a Head Start on Military Ranks

· · · · · · · · · · · · · · · · · · · · · · · · · · · · · · · · · · · · · · · · · · · · · · · · · · · · · · · · · · ·

## In This Chapter

▶ Memorizing military ranks

▶ Becoming clear about the chain of command

· · · · · · · · · · · · · · · · · · · · · · · · · · · · · · · · · · · · · · · · · · · · · · · · · · · · · · · · · · ·

A lot of information is thrown at you during military basic training. You'll be expected to memorize a staggering amount of information. No problem, right? After all, you did this during high school. However, in high school, you had a few hours to hit the books every evening before bedtime. During basic training, you'll be lucky to have a few minutes here and a couple of minutes there to take a look at your notes. The rest of your free time is taken up with getting scolded by your drill instructors, marching somewhere or other, performing guard duty, getting your uniform ready to wear the next day, and preparing your barracks area for inspection. In order to add to the basic training stress factor, you're not given much free time to study.

Your basic training experience will be a whole lot less stressful if you enter into it with some required military knowledge already stamped on your brain. I could probably write an entire book on this topic. However, my evil masters at Wiley Publishing have limited me to one chapter. This is inarguably the most important chapter in this book. Before you leave for basic, take time to study this chapter closely. You'll thank me during your basic training graduation ceremony.

## Becoming Familiar with Military Ranks

Everyone in the military has a rank. Rank defines who you are in the military hierarchy. If you have a higher rank than someone else, you can tell them what to do. If someone else has a higher rank than you, they can tell you what to do.

There are three hierarchies of military rank: enlisted members, warrant officers, and commissioned officers (often referred to as simply *officers*). Warrant officers out-rank all enlisted members, and commissioned officers out-rank all enlisted members and warrant officers.

A military member's rank is denoted by insignia worn on their uniform.

## Enlisted corps

Enlisted members are often called the backbone of the military. While enlisted members hold the lower pay grades, they perform a majority of the actual work. Enlisted members who hold the pay grades of E-1 or E-2 are usually in a training status — in other words, they are learning about the military or learning how to perform their military jobs. Those in the pay grades of E-3 or E-4 are usually trained technicians who do much of the hands-on work. The rank chart in Figure 5-1 shows you what military enlisted insignia actually looks like.

Enlisted personnel with the pay grades of E-5 or E-6 are noncommissioned officers, or working supervisors. The reason they are called noncommissioned officers is that other officers receive their *commission* (authority) by an act of Congress, whereby enlisted members in the higher pay grades derive their authority via military regulations. Therefore, while noncommissioned officers may have similar authority as commissioned officers, that authority comes from a different place. Noncommissioned officers perform their share of the hands-on work while providing direct supervision to lower-ranking enlisted members.

In the Navy and Coast Guard, noncommissioned officers are referred to as petty officers.

## Air Force

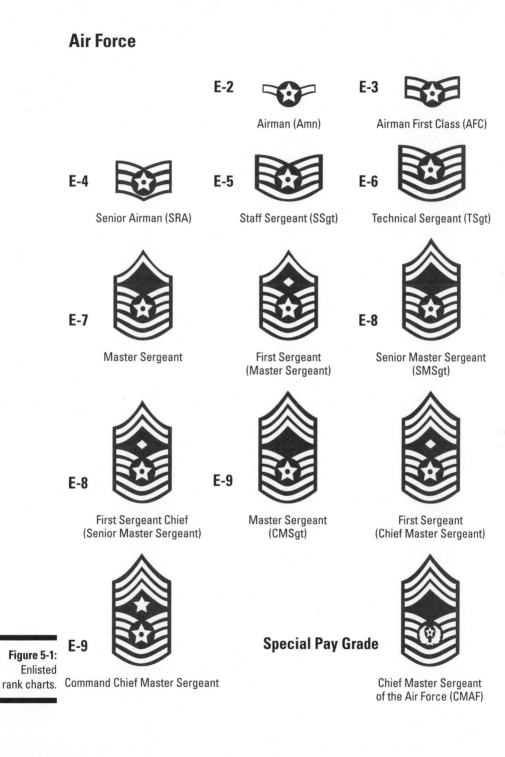

E-2 — Airman (Amn)

E-3 — Airman First Class (AFC)

E-4 — Senior Airman (SRA)

E-5 — Staff Sergeant (SSgt)

E-6 — Technical Sergeant (TSgt)

E-7 — Master Sergeant

First Sergeant (Master Sergeant)

E-8 — Senior Master Sergeant (SMSgt)

E-8 — First Sergeant Chief (Senior Master Sergeant)

E-9 — Master Sergeant (CMSgt)

First Sergeant (Chief Master Sergeant)

E-9 — Command Chief Master Sergeant

**Special Pay Grade**

Chief Master Sergeant of the Air Force (CMAF)

**Figure 5-1:** Enlisted rank charts.

## Army

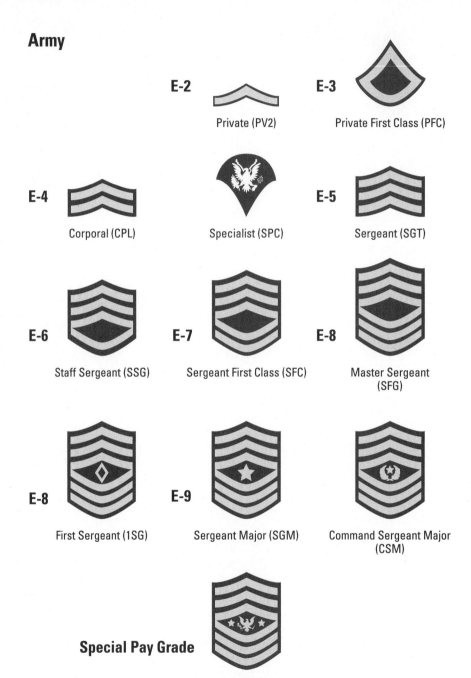

**E-2** Private (PV2)

**E-3** Private First Class (PFC)

**E-4** Corporal (CPL)

Specialist (SPC)

**E-5** Sergeant (SGT)

**E-6** Staff Sergeant (SSG)

**E-7** Sergeant First Class (SFC)

**E-8** Master Sergeant (SFG)

**E-8** First Sergeant (1SG)

**E-9** Sergeant Major (SGM)

Command Sergeant Major (CSM)

**Special Pay Grade**

Sergeant Major of the Army (SMA)

## Marine Corps

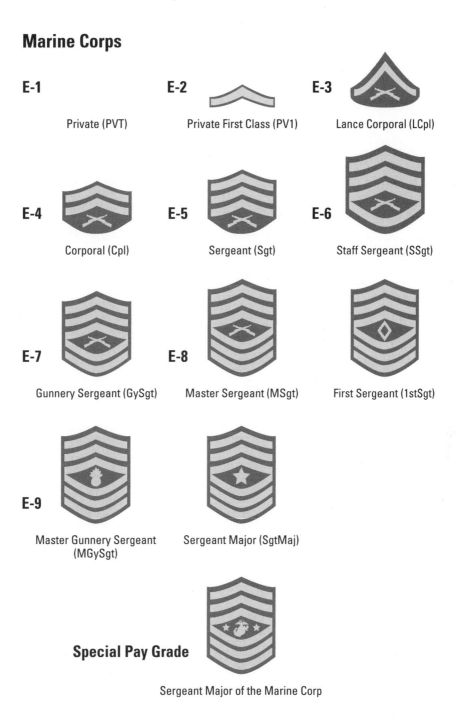

**E-1**

Private (PVT)

**E-2**

Private First Class (PV1)

**E-3**

Lance Corporal (LCpl)

**E-4**

Corporal (Cpl)

**E-5**

Sergeant (Sgt)

**E-6**

Staff Sergeant (SSgt)

**E-7**

Gunnery Sergeant (GySgt)

**E-8**

Master Sergeant (MSgt)

First Sergeant (1stSgt)

**E-9**

Master Gunnery Sergeant
(MGySgt)

Sergeant Major (SgtMaj)

### Special Pay Grade

Sergeant Major of the Marine Corp

## Navy/Coast Guard

E-1

Seaman Recruit (SR)

E-2

Airman (AMN)

E-3

Seaman (SN)

E-4

Petty Officer Third Class (PO3)

E-5

Petty Officer Second Class (PO2)

E-6

Petty Officer First Class (PO1)

E-7

Chief Petty Officer (CPO)

E-8

Senior Chief Petty Officer (SCPO)

E-9

Master Chief Petty Officer (MCPO)

**Special Pay Grade**

Master Chief Petty Officer of the Navy (MCPON)

Senior noncommissioned officers (chief petty officers for the Navy and Coast Guard) are those in the pay grades of E-7 through E-9. These enlisted members are highly proficient in their military jobs, but are primarily supervisors and managers. Think of them as company employees who have worked their way up the ranks to become company managers.

### First Sergeants

First Sergeants exist only in the Army, Marine Corps, and Air Force. The Navy and Coast Guard do not have this unique military position. In the Army and Marine Corps, First Sergeant is a rank in the pay grade of E-8. In the Air Force, a First Sergeant can be in the pay grade of E-7, E-8, or E-9, and the position is a special-duty assignment. The First Sergeant is denoted by the distinctive diamond above their military insignia (refer to Figure 5-1).

First Sergeants are the principle assistant and advisor to the unit commanding officers for all matters affecting enlisted members. The First Sergeant carries the authority of the commanding officer when it involves enlisted members assigned to a unit. For example, an Air Force First Sergeant in the pay grade of E-7 can order a squadron enlisted member in the pay grade of E-9 to get a haircut, and that command would be the same as if the commanding officer issued the order.

While the Navy and Coast Guard do not have First Sergeants, they do have senior enlisted positions that are similar. For example, on Navy and Coast Guard ships, the senior enlisted member is often designated as the Command Master Chief and on submarines is known as the Chief of the Boat, or COB. They perform duties similar to the First Sergeant in the non-seagoing branches. While they don't wear any special rank insignia, they do wear a special pin that identifies their special status.

### Other senior enlisted members

While the First Sergeant takes care of the needs of enlisted members at the unit level, other senior enlisted personnel take care of these needs for the entire military base. These senior NCOs work directly for the installation commander and are in charge of all enlisted matters on the base. These enlisted members are nearly always in the pay grade of E-9. In the Army, these NCOs are called *command sergeant majors*. The Air Force calls them *command chief master sergeants,* and the Marine Corps designates them as *sergeant majors*.

There are also senior enlisted members in charge of all other enlisted members in each branch of service. Only one per service exists, and each works directly for the most senior officer of their service and has a separate pay grade. (In other words, they make more money than any other enlisted person in their service.) In the Army, this person is called the Sergeant Major of the Army (SMA). The Air Force's senior NCO is the Chief Master Sergeant of the Air Force (CMAF). The Marines have the Sergeant Major of the Marine Corps (SgtMajMC). The Navy and Coast Guard's top dog enlisted members are the Master Chief Petty Officer of the Navy and Master Chief Petty Officer of the Coast Guard, (MCPON and MCPCG) respectively. Figure 5-1 can give you an idea of what their special insignia looks like.

## *Warrant officers*

With the exception of Army helicopter pilots, all warrant officers are former enlisted members with 8 to 14 years experience doing a specific military job. I like to think of warrant officers as the scientists of the military — they're highly trained technical specialists, with some supervisory responsibility.

Enlisted members, regardless of pay grade, who apply for Army flight training and become helicopter pilots are promoted to warrant officer immediately upon graduation from Army flight school.

There are only five warrant officer ranks, and they differ somewhat for each service. See Figure 5-2 for an overview.

## Where are the Air Force warrant officers?

The Air Force is the only military service that doesn't have warrant officers. Why?

As the story goes, in the old days, the highest enlisted pay grade was E-7. Many enlisted members were promoted to the highest enlisted rank after only 10 or 12 years of service. What did they have left to look forward to? What would keep them motivated to excel?

The Department of Defense asked Congress to approve the so-called enlisted super-grades, in the pay grades of E-8 and E-9. In exchange, the services would agree to eliminate the warrant officer pay grades. Congress agreed and created the E-8 and E-9 pay grades, but forgot to eliminate the authorization for warrant

officers. The Air Force was the only branch to stick to the deal and eliminate warrant officers. The other branches accepted the new super-grades, but failed to discontinue the warrant officer ranks.

This story has proven not to be true, but Air Force folks like to believe it. What actually happened is that the Air Force conducted a comprehensive review of warrant officer utilization as technicians and midlevel managers in 1959. They determined that structure, training, and retention needs were best served by eliminating their warrant officer program. The last active duty Air Force warrant officer retired in 1980, and the last Air Force Reserve warrant officer retired in 1992.

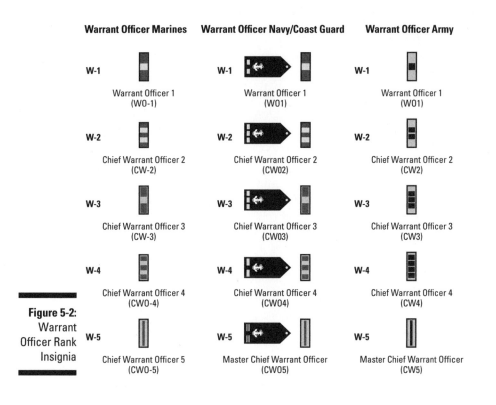

**Figure 5-2:**
Warrant
Officer Rank
Insignia

## Officer ranks

Officers are sometimes referred to as commissioned officers because officers are appointed (commissioned) by the President of the United States, acting as military commander-in-chief. However, the term is misleading because warrant officers in the pay grade of W-2 and above also receive a commission.

Commissioned officers are in charge of the military. Even the lowliest officer (O-1) outranks the highest warrant officer or enlisted member. The chart in Figure 5-3 shows the insignia for different commissioned officer ranks.

Even though the lowest officer technically outranks the highest enlisted member, you won't find any second lieutenant (O-1) giving orders to the Sergeant Major of the Army. Why? Because the SMA works directly for the Army Chief of Staff (COS), the highest ranking officer in the Army. If a sergeant major did give orders to him, that O-1 is liable to find himself reassigned as the officer in charge of plant growth at the North Pole if he sufficiently irritates the Army COS's primary enlisted adviser.

## Army/Air Force/Marines

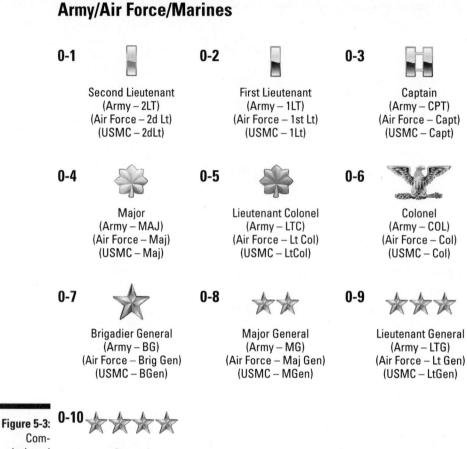

**0-1** Second Lieutenant
(Army – 2LT)
(Air Force – 2d Lt)
(USMC – 2dLt)

**0-2** First Lieutenant
(Army – 1LT)
(Air Force – 1st Lt)
(USMC – 1Lt)

**0-3** Captain
(Army – CPT)
(Air Force – Capt)
(USMC – Capt)

**0-4** Major
(Army – MAJ)
(Air Force – Maj)
(USMC – Maj)

**0-5** Lieutenant Colonel
(Army – LTC)
(Air Force – Lt Col)
(USMC – LtCol)

**0-6** Colonel
(Army – COL)
(Air Force – Col)
(USMC – Col)

**0-7** Brigadier General
(Army – BG)
(Air Force – Brig Gen)
(USMC – BGen)

**0-8** Major General
(Army – MG)
(Air Force – Maj Gen)
(USMC – MGen)

**0-9** Lieutenant General
(Army – LTG)
(Air Force – Lt Gen)
(USMC – LtGen)

**Figure 5-3:**
**Com-**
**missioned**
**officer**
**insignia.**

**0-10** General
(Army – GEN)
(Air Force – Gen)
(USMC – Gen)

## Navy/Coast Guard

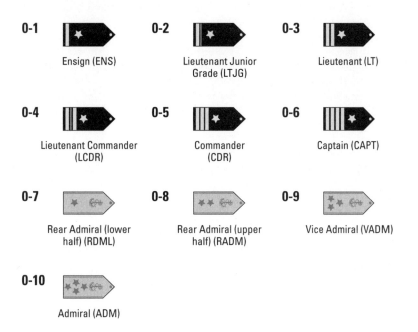

O-1 Ensign (ENS)

O-2 Lieutenant Junior Grade (LTJG)

O-3 Lieutenant (LT)

O-4 Lieutenant Commander (LCDR)

O-5 Commander (CDR)

O-6 Captain (CAPT)

O-7 Rear Admiral (lower half) (RDML)

O-8 Rear Admiral (upper half) (RADM)

O-9 Vice Admiral (VADM)

O-10 Admiral (ADM)

With few exceptions, all commissioned officers must be college graduates. In some branches (such as the Army and Marines), you can become a junior commissioned officer (O-1) with just three or so years of college, but you must complete your degree before you're eligible for promotion.

### Commanding officers

The commanding officer is usually the highest-ranking officer in the unit. He is often referred to as the commander. In the Navy and Coast Guard, the boss is often called the Captain. Commanding officers are given special powers. For example, only a commanding officer can punish someone under the provisions of Article 15 of the Uniform Code of Military Justice (UCMJ). You can find out more about the UCMJ in Chapter 7.

### Special officers

Some military officers receive their commission based on their military job. For example, all military doctors and nurses are commissioned officers. All military lawyers are commissioned officers. Military scientists (those with PhDs and such) are commissioned officers. These officers have limited authority within the scope of their duties. For example, a military scientist in the pay grade of O-6 can order an enlisted lab technician to perform a scientific test, but she's not able to order enlisted members to "take that hill." A military doctor can order an enlisted medical technician to take someone's blood pressure, but he can't order an infantry soldier to engage the enemy.

Officers wear special rank insignia, often called brass, on the collars and headgear (or cover) of their military uniforms. Figure 5-3 shows what these insignia look like.

# Basic Training Chain of Command

Everyone in the military has a chain of command. The chain of command is used to issue orders (downward) and to ask for clarification and resolve problems (upward).

The military chain of command is such an integral part of military life that you'll be required to memorize your basic training chain of command within the first week or two of arrival. In fact, your instructors will often ask you questions about the chain of command, and this topic will probably be your first written test during basic training.

Unfortunately, you can't memorize the entire basic training chain of command in advance because you won't know before your arrival exactly which basic training squadron or unit you'll be assigned to. And even if you did know your assignment, key personnel might change before you get there.

## How the chain of command works

If the President of the United States, as the commander-in-chief, decides that he wants your basic training barracks painted purple, he wouldn't call you directly, even though you're the one who will actually do the work. Instead, he would call the secretary of defense, who would then call the secretary of the Army, who would contact the Army Chief of Staff, and so on until the directive finally reaches your drill instructor, who would then order you to paint the barracks.

Conversely, if the Air Force forgets to pay you this month, you wouldn't walk directly into the Oval Office to complain to the President. Instead, you'd speak to your drill instructor, who would try to resolve the issue. If he couldn't, he'd ask the senior drill instructor for help. If the senior drill instructor had no luck solving your pay problem, she'd speak with the unit First Sergeant. If the First Sergeant couldn't get the problem fixed, he'd ask the commanding officer for help, and onward and onward up the chain, until you finally get paid.

## Army BT chain of command

The chain of command in Army basic training runs from the lowest ranking recruit (you) all the way to the President of the United States. Simply, the Army basic training chain of command is as follows:

- ✔ Recruit (that's you)
- ✔ Drill Sergeant (you'll probably have more than one, and they'll be led by the senior drill sergeant).
- ✔ Executive Officer (in Army basic training, this is usually your senior drill sergeant).
- ✔ Company Commander
- ✔ Battalion Commander
- ✔ Brigade Commander
- ✔ Division Commander
- ✔ Corps Commander
- ✔ Army Chief of Staff
- ✔ Secretary of the Army
- ✔ Secretary of Defense
- ✔ Commander-in-Chief (President of the United States.)

## Air Force BT chain of command

As with all military organizations, Air Force basic training also has a designated chain of command:

- ✔ Recruit (you)
- ✔ Training Instructor
- ✔ Flight Chief (will be a senior training instructor, or T.I.)

- ✔ Squadron commander
- ✔ 373rd Training Group commander
- ✔ 37th Training Wing commander
- ✔ Air Education and Training Command Commander
- ✔ Air Force Chief of Staff
- ✔ Secretary of the Air Force
- ✔ Secretary of Defense
- ✔ Commander-in-Chief (President of the United States)

## Navy BT chain of command

The Navy's basic training chain of command is designed to imitate the same chain of command you will see on many Navy ships:

- ✔ Recruit (guess who?)
- ✔ Company Commander (CC), also known as the Recruit Division Commander (RDC), or your training instructor
- ✔ Division Leading Chief Petty Officer (LCPO)
- ✔ Division Officer (DO)
- ✔ Military Training Assistant (MTA)
- ✔ Military Training Officer (MTO)
- ✔ Executive Officer RTC (XO)
- ✔ Commanding Officer RTC
- ✔ Chief of Naval Education and Training
- ✔ Chief of Naval Operations
- ✔ Secretary of the Navy
- ✔ Secretary of Defense
- ✔ Commander-in-Chief (President of the United States)

# Marine Corps BT chain of command

The Marine Corps basic training chain of command is a bit tricky because there is no Department of the Marine Corps. While technically a separate branch of the U.S. Military, operationally the Marine Corps falls under the command and control of the Department of the Navy. The Marine Corps basic training chain of command is as follows:

- Recruit (that would be you)
- Drill Instructor (DI)
- Company Commander
- Battalion Commander
- Regimental Commander
- Division Commander
- Chief of Naval Education and Training
- Commandant of the Marine Corps
- Secretary of the Navy
- Secretary of Defense
- Commander-in-Chief (President of the United States)

# Coast Guard BT chain of command

While the Coast Guard (like the Navy) is a seagoing service, the Coast Guard basic training chain of command is somewhat different from the Navy basic training chain of command:

- Recruit (you)
- Company Commander (CC)
- Lead Company Commander (LCC)
- Section Commander (SC)
- Battalion Commander (BC)
- Battalion Officer (BO)

- ✔ Regimental Officer (RO)
- ✔ Training Officer (TO)
- ✔ Executive Officer (XO)
- ✔ Commanding Officer (CO)
- ✔ Coast Guard Commandant
- ✔ Secretary of Homeland Security
- ✔ Commander-in-Chief (President of the United States)

# Chapter 6

# Doing Things the Military Way

· · · · · · · · · · · · · · · · · · · · · · · · · · · · · · · · · · · · · · · · · · · · · · · · · · · · · · · · · · · ·

## In This Chapter

▶ Taking guard duty for fun and profit

▶ Becoming accustomed to customs

▶ Speaking to your instructors

▶ Telling time the military way

· · · · · · · · · · · · · · · · · · · · · · · · · · · · · · · · · · · · · · · · · · · · · · · · · · · · · · · · · · · ·

*T*he military does things differently from what you're probably used to, and basic training is designed to teach you how to do common tasks and chores the military way.

Although nobody has ever tried to steal a military base, most of the services want you to learn how to guard the base anyway. The services also have specific ways, called customs and courtesies, of how you're supposed to deal with those of higher rank, Heck, the military even tells time differently than most civilians. Basic training will teach you that it's not really 4 p.m., but rather it's 1600 hours.

## Discovering How Sentries Act

In military basic training, you perform a great deal of guard duty. Such guard duty is called *sentry duty.* I guess that the powers-that-be must feel there are a lot of criminals who are intent on stealing. Recruits guard military barracks rooms most of the day. Only authorized people (your drill instructors and other recruits) are allowed to enter unescorted. In Army, Navy, Marine Corps, and Coast Guard basic training, you'll be assigned to guard other things as well as the barracks, just to give you a little extra practice. Of course, this guard duty practice has a serious purpose; the time may come when you have to guard something vital in the line of duty.

While Air Force basic training recruits pull guard duty (called *dorm guard*), they don't have to memorize any sentry rules. Air Force basic training troops perform dorm guard duties sitting at a desk behind a locked dormitory door with a list of written instructions. If a person isn't on the access list, the dorm guard simply does not open the door. If she is on the access list, the door is opened. What could be simpler?

# Navy, Marine Corps, and Coast Guard

The Army, Navy, Marine Corps, and Coast Guard have a dedicated list of rules that sentries must memorize and be able to recite word for word upon request. These rules are called the *General Orders for Sentries,* or sometimes just *General Orders.*

You're required to memorize the following in order so that you can recite a specific order number, if asked.

1. **To take charge of this post and all government property in view.**

   When you're performing sentry duties, you're in charge of your post. That means that no one except your training instructor, no matter what their rank, can change your orders. Even if a 4-star general approaches and demands that you let him pass, you can't do so if his name isn't on your access list. Only your training instructor can give someone who is not on the list permission to enter the barracks.

   In basic training, other training instructors often try to bluff their way past recruits performing guard duties. If they succeed, that means they get to rub it in to your drill instructor. It also means that your drill instructor will probably have you for lunch.

   When performing guard duty, you're also responsible to protect all government equipment and property that is within site, even though it may be outside of the area of your assigned post.

2. **To walk my post in a military manner, keeping always on the alert and observing everything that takes place within sight or hearing.**

   This means you don't slouch, you don't keep your hands in your pockets, and you don't sit down. Always be vigilant by looking around you at all times. Don't let those tricky training instructors try to pull a fast one on you. If you see or hear anything unusual, don't ignore it — investigate it.

3. **To report all violations of orders I am instructed to enforce.**

   For example, if someone tries to trick his way past you, mark it in your logbook and report it to your training instructor, even if that person wasn't successful.

Use common sense. If it's 2 a.m. and your training instructor is sleeping, it can probably wait until first thing in the morning, unless your training instructor has specifically ordered you to wake him up if anything unusual happens.

4. **To repeat all calls from posts more distant from the guardhouse (or the Quarterdeck) than my own.**

These days, sentries can usually make their reports from modern electronics, such as radios and field telephones. However, if a power outage or other communications problem occurs, the age-old practice of relaying information can be very important. Your training instructor may even order you to simulate a power outage or communications failure to see how you handle it.

5. **To quit my post only when properly relieved.**

This rule may seem evident, but I can guarantee you that at least one person during your time at basic will make the mistake of leaving his watch post and go to bed, if their relief is late. This mistake is very serious in basic training and will almost surely result in severe punishment.

*Marine Corps version:* To receive, obey, and pass on to the sentry who relieves me, all orders from the Commanding Officer, Officer of the Day, Officers, and Non-Commissioned Officers of the guard only.

*Navy version:* To receive, obey, and pass on to the sentry who relieves me, all orders from the Commanding Officer, Command Duty Officer, Officer of the Deck, and Officers and Petty Officers of the Watch only.

*Coast Guard version:* To receive, obey, and pass on to the sentry who relieves me, all orders from the Commanding Officer, Field Officer of the day, Officer of the day, and all Officers and Petty Officers of the Watch.

6. **To obey all special instructions that are given and to relay those instructions on to my relief.**

The Marine Corps, Navy, and Coast Guard all have slightly different versions of order 6, mostly because of different terminology used for those in charge. This order essentially means that you obey all special instructions that are given to you for your watch, and that you pass those instructions on to your relief.

7. **To talk to no one except in the line of duty.**

Guard duty is not the time to chat and gossip with your basic training buddies. You have a job to do, and you're expected to do it. If someone tries to engage you in conversation, politely tell them that you're on duty and can't chat.

8. **To give the alarm in case of fire or disorder.**

While this rule seems pretty straightforward, keep in mind that those tricky training instructors may stage a fire or disturbance to see whether they can sneak someone past you. Stay alert to everything!

- *Marine Corps version:* To call the Corporal of the Guard/Officer of the Deck in any case not covered by instructions.

- *Navy version:* To call the Petty Officer of the Watch in any case not covered by instructions.

- *Coast Guard version:* To call the Petty Officer of the watch in any case not covered by instructions.

Again, the different versions are only a matter of terminology. When in doubt, ask. During military basic training, the only stupid question is the one not asked.

9. **To salute all officers and all colors and standards not cased.**

Even though you're in charge of your post, that doesn't mean you don't engage in normal military customs and courtesies. When outdoors, enlisted members must salute all officers and warrant officers. Additionally, all officers are addressed as sir or ma'am. Warrant officers may be addressed as Mr. or Ms.

*Colors* and *standards* mean the United States flag. Regular flags are called *colors,* while vehicle flags are often called *standards.* The colors are saluted when it's fixed to a staff, mast, or pike (for example, when flown from a flagstaff or carried in a parade). A flag is considered *cased* when it's furled and placed in a protective covering. Flags that are cased aren't saluted. If you're on duty during morning *reveille* (when the flag is raised) or evening *retreat* (when the flag is lowered), you should face and salute the flag only if your duties allow.

10. **To be especially watchful at night and during the time for challenging, to challenge all persons on or near my post, and to allow no one to pass without proper authority.**

You challenge a person by saying, "Halt! Who goes there?" Once a person answers, if she's on your access list, say, "Advance to be recognized." If you're challenging a group, you should allow them to advance only one at a time. If you're not satisfied with a person's identification, you must detain her and call the individual in charge of the watch. When two or more individuals approach from different directions at the same time, challenge each in turn and require each to halt until told to proceed.

# *Army*

The Army used to use the same general orders listed in the preceding section, but whittled them down to only three about four years ago:

1. **I will guard everything within the limits of my post and quit my post only when properly relieved.**

2. **I will obey my special orders and perform all of my duties in a military manner.**

3. **I will report violations of my special orders, emergencies, and anything not covered in my instructions to the commander of the relief.**

# *Getting the Lowdown on Customs and Courtesies*

The U.S. Military is comprised of five organizations that instill pride in their members because of history, mission, capabilities, and respect that has been earned in the service of the nation. A reflection of that pride is visible in the customs, courtesies, and traditions of military service.

## *Customs*

A *custom* is an established practice. Customs include positive actions — things you do — and *taboos*, or things you avoid. Some military customs are established by regulation, and you can be punished (even sent to jail) for disregarding them, while others are unwritten, but obeyed just the same.

The customs of the military services are their common law. These are a few:

- ✔ Never criticize your service or your leaders in public.
- ✔ Never go over the heads of superiors — don't jump the chain of command. (For more on the chain of command, see Chapter 5.)
- ✔ Never offer excuses.
- ✔ Never wear a superior's rank by saying something like, "The First Sergeant wants this done now" when in fact the First Sergeant said no such thing. Speak with your own voice.

✔ Never turn and walk away to avoid giving the hand salute.

✔ Never run indoors or pretend you don't hear (while driving, for example) to avoid participating in reveille or retreat (raising or lowering of the U.S flag).

✔ Never appear in uniform while under the influence of alcohol.

✔ If you don't know the answer to a superior's question, you will never go wrong with the response, "I don't know, sir (or ma'am), but I'll find out."

# *Courtesies*

Courtesy among members of the Armed Forces is vital to maintain discipline. Military *courtesy* means good manners and politeness in dealing with other people. Courteous behavior provides a basis for developing good human relations. The distinction between civilian and military courtesy is that military courtesy was developed in a military atmosphere and has become an integral part of serving in uniform.

Military courtesy is not a one-way street. Enlisted personnel are expected to be courteous to officers, and officers are expected to return the courtesy. Mutual respect is a vital part of military courtesy. In the final analysis, military courtesy is the respect shown to each other by members of the same profession.

## *Addressing military members*

Commissioned officers (and to a lesser extent, warrant officers) run the U.S. Military. They are the top dogs. As such, they're always addressed politely, using sir or ma'am.

In the Marine Corps, Air Force, and the first couple weeks of Coast Guard basic training, instructors are also addressed as sir or ma'am. Don't overuse these terms, though. In other words, don't say something like, "Sir, I have to go to the bathroom, sir." Otherwise, you're likely to hear a (very loud) speech about a sir sandwich.

If you're attending Army or Navy basic training, do not address your training instructor as sir or ma'am. This is guaranteed to result in a loud tirade about how they work for a living.

## The history of the salute

Some historians believe the hand salute began in late Roman times when assassinations were common. A citizen who wanted to see a public official had to approach with his right hand raised to show that he did not hold a weapon. Knights in armor raised visors with the right hand when meeting a comrade. This practice gradually became a way of showing respect, and, in early American history, sometimes involved removing the hat. By 1820, the motion was modified to touching the hat, and since then, it has become the hand salute used today. You salute to show respect toward an officer, the flag, or your country.

In the Army and Navy, drill instructors are addressed by using their military rank and often their last name — for example, Chief or Staff Sergeant Smith. In Marine Corps basic training, do not use personal pronouns such as "you," "I," or "we." These pronouns will send your Marine Corps basic training instructor into an absolute tizzy. Instead, speak in the third person: "Does the drill instructor want this recruit to inform the other recruits of his instructions?"

### Military salutes

The salute isn't simply an honor exchanged; it's a privileged gesture of respect and trust among military members. Remember: The salute is not only prescribed by regulation, but is also recognition of each other's commitment, abilities, and professionalism.

The salute is widely misunderstood outside the military. Some consider it to be a gesture of servility since the junior extends a salute to the senior, but this interpretation isn't true at all. The salute is an expression that recognizes each other as a member of the profession of arms — that they have made a personal commitment of self-sacrifice to preserve the American way of life. The fact that the junior extends the greeting first is merely a point of etiquette — a salute extended or returned makes the same statement.

The way you salute says a lot about you as a military member. A proud, smart salute shows pride in yourself and your unit and that you're confident in your abilities as a soldier. A sloppy salute can mean that you're ashamed of your unit, lack confidence, or, at the very least, haven't learned how to salute correctly.

You'll get plenty of practice saluting in basic training, but it wouldn't hurt to practice in front of a mirror several times before you leave so that you can do it correctly automatically.

All military enlisted personnel in uniform are required to salute when they meet and recognize a commissioned or warrant officer, except when it is inappropriate or impractical (for example, if you're carrying something using both hands). A salute is also rendered

- When the United States National Anthem, "To the Color," "Hail to the Chief," or foreign national anthems are played
- To uncased National Color outdoors
- On ceremonial occasions, such as changes of command or funerals
- At reveille and retreat ceremonies, during the raising or lowering of the flag
- When pledging allegiance to the U.S. flag outdoors
- When turning over control of formations
- When rendering reports
- On the stern of a ship when arriving or departing from the ship
- To officers of friendly foreign countries

Salutes are not required when

- Indoors, unless reporting to an officer or when on duty as a guard
- When you're in a combat zone
- When you're a prisoner
- Saluting is obviously inappropriate
- Either the senior or the subordinate is wearing civilian clothes

In any case not covered by specific instructions, render the salute.

### Other courtesies

Military courtesy shows respect and reflects self-discipline. While some of these courtesies seem to wane after basic, they're strictly adhered to during military basic training:

- When talking to an officer, stand at attention until ordered otherwise.
- When you're dismissed or when the officer departs, come to attention and salute.

✔ When speaking to or being addressed by a noncommissioned officer of superior rank, stand at parade rest until ordered otherwise.

✔ When an officer enters a room, the first enlisted person to recognize the officer calls personnel in the room to attention but does not salute. A salute indoors is rendered only when reporting to an officer.

✔ Walk on the left of and slightly behind an officer or NCO of superior rank.

✔ When entering or exiting a vehicle or boat, the junior ranking military member is the first to enter, and the senior in rank is the first to exit.

✔ The first person who sees an officer enter a dining facility gives the order "At ease," unless a more senior officer is already present. Many units also extend this courtesy to senior NCOs.

✔ When you hear the command "At ease" in a dining facility, remain seated and silent and continue eating unless directed otherwise.

# Following Reporting Procedures

In the military, you don't just walk into your boss's office, plop down on the couch, and put your feet up on the coffee table. This behavior may have been okay with your last boss, but in the military, it's a huge no-no.

*Reporting* is an official way of announcing your presence when asking permission to speak to your commanding officer, usually in her office.

In basic training, assuming that you don't get into huge trouble for doing something very stupid, you'll probably never have a chance to speak to your commanding officer in her office. Instead, you're required to report to your training instructor in her office.

To report, follow these procedures:

1. **Stand at attention and knock (just once) on the door.**

2. **When instructed to enter, march in a smart military fashion to a point three paces in front of the training instructor's desk (if she's sitting at her desk).**

   Whether or not you salute is up to your training instructor/rules of your service. Normally, you don't salute unless you're reporting to a commissioned officer, but some basic training instructors feel that since there are not enough commissioned officers in basic training for you to practice on, you should practice on them.

3. **While holding the salute (if required), say, "Sir or ma'am (if required), Private Jones reports."**

   If you were instructed to see your training instructor in his office, you'd say, "Private Jones reports as ordered."

4. **If you're told relax, at ease, or something to that effect, assume the position of parade rest.**

   See Chapter 9 for the parade rest position.

   When the conversation is finished, you'll be told, "Dismissed." That means the meeting is over, even if you have something else to say.

5. **When dismissed, snap to attention, salute (if required), and march in a smart military fashion (see Chapter 9) out the door.**

   Once outside the door, you can relax, sit down, throw up, or whatever.

# Making Sense of Military Time

Most Americans learn how to tell time using a 12-hour clock. In other words, at noon, the time starts all over again with 1, 2, 3, and so on. The U.S. Military tells time the same way most of the rest of the world does — using a 24-hour clock. After 12 noon (written 1200), the hours continue with 1300, 1400, 1500, and so on.

In basic training, you need to know how to tell time using the 24-hour clock. Table 6-1 tells you all you need to know about telling time the military way.

| Table 6-1 | Telling Time the Military Way |
|---|---|
| *American Time* | *Military Time* |
| 12 a.m. | 0000 hrs |
| 1 a.m. | 0100 hrs |
| 2 a.m. | 0200 hrs |
| 3 a.m. | 0300 hrs |
| 4 a.m. | 0400 hrs |
| 5 a.m. | 0500 hrs |
| 6:30 a.m. | 0630 hrs |
| 7 a.m. | 0700 hrs |
| 8 a.m. | 0800 hrs |

| American Time | Military Time |
|---|---|
| 9 a.m. | 0900 hrs |
| 10 a.m. | 1000 hrs |
| 11:35 a.m. | 1135 hrs |
| 12 p.m. | 1200 hrs |
| 1 p.m. | 1300 hrs |
| 2 p.m. | 1400 hrs |
| 3 p.m. | 1500 hrs |
| 4 p.m. | 1600 hrs |
| 5:20 p.m. | 1720 hrs |
| 6 p.m. | 1800 hrs |
| 7 p.m. | 1900 hrs |
| 8:40 p.m. | 2040 hrs |
| 9 p.m. | 2100 hrs |
| 10 p.m. | 2200 hrs |
| 11:55 p.m. | 2355 hrs |

# Chapter 7

# Mastering Military Law and Justice

*W*hen you enlist in the United States Military, you become subject to a whole new set of laws. That doesn't mean you get to ignore your old civilian laws; you just get to pile on a few more laws.

## Why a Separate Military Justice System?

So why does the military have its own justice system? Two reasons: portability and military discipline. Portability allows the military to assume legal jurisdiction over its troops if they commit a crime anywhere in the world. Otherwise, for example, if you commit a crime in Iraq, the Iraqi justice system handles it, and that wouldn't be much fun.

In addition, certain behaviors that aren't allowed in the military are not crimes in civilian life. For example, if you yell at your boss in civilian life, you simply may get fired. That same behavior in the military is a crime, and you may be sent to prison.

## Military criminal jurisdiction

A few years ago, the Supreme Court of the United States opinioned that there must be a *service connection* to an offense in order for the military to assume criminal jurisdiction. Otherwise, the crime is best handled by the civilian courts. For example, the court said that if a military member robs a bank while off duty, not in uniform, and off base, then the civilian justice system should handle the case.

The military has defined service connections (and so far the courts have not overturned this definition) as

- ✔ All offenses that occur on base or while on duty

- ✔ All drug-related offenses

- ✔ All offenses committed while a military member was supposed to be on duty

- ✔ All offenses committed when overseas due to military orders

- ✔ All offenses that are strictly of a military nature (for example, disobeying an order)

# The Uniform Code of Military Justice (UCMJ): The Basis of Military Law

The UCMJ is federal law, enacted by Congress. The UCMJ defines the military justice system and lists criminal offenses under military law.

The law requires the President of the United States, acting as commander-in-chief of the Armed Forces, to write rules and regulations to implement military law. The President writes these rules and regulations by issuing an executive order known as the *Manual for Courts-Martial* (MCM). The MCM details rules and regulations for military court-martials and provides for maximum punishments for each military offense listed in the punitive articles of the UCMJ.

## Military court-martials

Military court-martials are the most severe sanctions under military law. A court-martial conviction is the same as a federal conviction and can (depending on the offense) result in jail time (at hard labor) or a punitive discharge, such as dishonorable discharge, as well as fines and reduction in rank.

Military court-martials come in three levels:

- ✔ Summary
- ✔ Special
- ✔ General

The level chosen usually depends on the severity of the offense and the rank of the accused.

## Summary court-martials

*Summary court-martials* are relatively rare these days. Only enlisted personnel may be tried by a summary court-martial. A summary court-martial is very much like nonjudicial punishment (Article 15) proceedings, except it can result in a federal conviction. (See "Nonjudicial punishment: Article 15," later in this chapter.)

A commissioned officer (usually in the pay grade of O-3 or above) presides over summary court-martials; there is no panel (jury). Except in the Air Force, there is no requirement to provide the accused with a defense lawyer (although a lawyer is usually allowed).

The maximum punishment that can be imposed by a summary court-martial includes

- ✔ Confinement (or hard labor without confinement) for 30 days
- ✔ Forfeiture of two-thirds pay for one month
- ✔ Reduction to the lowest pay grade (E-1)

In a case where the accused is above the pay grade of E-4, a summary court-martial may not impose confinement, hard labor without confinement, or reduction except to the next lowest pay grade.

### Special court-martials

A *special court-martial* has jurisdiction over all personnel charged with any UCMJ offense. Special court-martials are generally used to try offenses of medium severity.

Special court-martials are composed of a military judge, prosecuting and defense attorneys, and a panel (jury) of at least three military members. If the accused is an enlisted member, he can demand that at least a third of the panel be enlisted members. (Otherwise, the panel usually consists of commissioned officers and warrant officers.) The accused can request to dismiss the panel and be tried by a judge alone if he wishes.

The maximum punishment that may be imposed by a special court-martial includes a combination of

- ✔ Confinement for 12 months
- ✔ Forfeiture of two-thirds pay for 12 months
- ✔ Reduction to the lowest pay grade (E-1)
- ✔ A bad conduct discharge

### General court-martials

A *general court-martial* is the most severe of the military court-martial types and is generally reserved for the most serious offenses, such as murder, rape, or robbery. A general court-martial has jurisdiction over all personnel charged with any UCMJ offense.

A general court-martial includes a military judge, the accused, prosecuting and defense attorneys, and a panel of at least five members. As with a special court-martial, if the accused is an enlisted member, he can request that at least a third of the panel be comprised of enlisted members. The accused can also choose to dismiss the panel and be tried by judge alone.

For both special and general court-martials, the accused can elect to be represented by a civilian attorney at his own expense, if he wishes.

A general court-martial may impose any sentence (including death) authorized by the Manual for Courts-Martial (for the offenses that the accused is found to have committed).

### Nonjudicial punishment: Article 15

Nonjudicial punishment is, by far, the most common type of proceeding under the military justice system. If a military member commits an offense covered by the UCMJ, the commanding officer may decide to offer him proceedings under Article 15. This is commonly referred to as *nonjudicial punishment.*

Nonjudicial punishment is often called *mast* in the Navy and Coast Guard, and *office hours* in the Marine Corps.

Article 15 proceedings are very much like a summary court-martial, except the commanding officer acts as judge and jury, and the proceedings do not result in a criminal record. Except aboard a ship at sea, military members do not have to accept nonjudicial punishment proceedings. They can turn down the Article 15 and demand trial by court-martial instead.

Unless you're innocent of the offense and know you can prove it, it's not usually a smart idea to turn down Article 15 and demand trial by court-martial. If you're found guilty by a court-martial, the possible punishments are much more severe, and you have a life-time criminal record.

Under Article 15, you have the following rights:

✔ Be informed of your right to remain silent under Article 31 of the UCMJ.

✔ Be accompanied by someone to speak on your behalf. However, there is no requirement that a military lawyer be made available to accompany you to the hearing. In fact, most nonjudicial punishment proceedings do not include military attorneys.

✔ Be informed of the evidence against you relating to the offense.

✔ Be allowed to examine all evidence upon which the commanding officer will rely in deciding whether and how much nonjudicial punishment to impose.

✔ Present matters in defense, extenuation, and mitigation, orally, in writing, or both.

✔ Have witnesses present if they're reasonably available. A witness is *reasonably available* if his appearance won't require reimbursement by the government, unduly delay the proceedings, or, in the case of a military witness, necessitate his being excused from other important duties.

✔ Have the proceedings open to the public unless the commanding officer determines that the proceedings should be closed for good cause.

The commanding officer acts as sole judge and jury. If she determines that you did commit the offense(s) alleged, then the punishment imposed depends on the rank of the accused and the rank of the commanding officer.

If your commanding officer is in grades O-4 or above, the maximum punishment may be

✔ Written admonition or reprimand (which may affect future promotions or assignments)

✔ Confinement on bread and water or diminished rations —imposable only on grades E-3 and below, attached to or embarked in a vessel, for not more than three days (U.S. Navy and U.S. Marine Corps only)

✔ Correctional custody (kind of a jail) for not more than 30 days

✔ Forfeiture of not more than half of one month's pay per month for two months

✔ Reduction of one grade, not imposable on E-7 and above (Navy, Army, and Air Force) or on E-6 and above (Marine Corps)

✔ Extra duties for not more than 45 days

✔ Restriction to the base or a specific area for not more than 60 days

If the punishment is imposed by a commanding officer in grades O-3 and below, possible punishments are

- Admonition or reprimand
- Confinement on bread and water or diminished rations — not more than three days and only on grades E-3 and below attached to or embarked in a vessel (U.S. Navy and U.S. Marine Corps only)
- Correctional custody for not more than 7 days
- Forfeiture of not more than 7 days of pay
- Reduction to next inferior pay grade; not imposable on E-7 and above (Navy, Army, and Air Force) or E-6 and above (Marine Corps), if rank from which demoted is within the promotion authority of the Officer in Charge (OIC):
- Extra duties for not more than 14 days
- Restriction for not more than 14 days

# Administrative Sanctions

In addition to judicial and nonjudicial actions, commanding officers can elect to choose among several administrative sanctions for those who break the rules.

## Counseling

Commanders and supervisors have the authority to counsel subordinates. Counseling can be both positive (atta-boy) or negative (don't ever do that again). Counseling can be either verbal or written. Unfortunately, in the military, positive counseling is usually verbal (creating no record), while negative counseling is often written (which can then be used against you later, if you don't change your behavior).

Written counseling is often called a *letter of counseling,* and a copy is usually filed in your military records, which may affect future promotions or assignments.

## Reprimands and admonitions

Reprimands and admonitions are basically a chewing out. They almost always appear in writing in order to create a record that can be used to justify future disciplinary action if your behavior doesn't improve.

# Administrative reduction in rank

It doesn't take a court-martial or Article 15 action for a commanding officer to take away a stripe. Commanders are the ones who approve enlisted promotions before you sew another stripe on, and they can also deny promotion, or — even worse — take rank away from you.

Administrative reductions are usually (although not always) a result of long-term problems, such as failing in training, being overweight, or failing to pass repeated fitness tests.

# Administrative discharge

The most serious administrative punishment is undoubtedly the administrative discharge. The civilian equivalent is "you're fired." However, when you're discharged from the military, you're given a *discharge characterization,* which can affect your future employment opportunities for the rest of your life. Possible discharge characterizations are

- ✔ **Honorable:** If you complete your military service or you're discharged early through no fault of your own, your characterization will probably be honorable. This type of characterization usually doesn't negatively affect future civilian employment and entitles you to veteran benefits, if you are otherwise qualified.

- ✔ **General (Under Honorable Conditions):** This is the second type of administrative discharge characterization. It means most of your service was okay, but some problems did occur. Usually, you're still entitled to many veteran benefits, but some employers may question you about why you "got fired" from the military.

- ✔ **Other than Honorable Conditions (OTC):** This discharge means you got "fired" from the military for doing something very, very bad and were probably lucky to escape a court-martial. Veteran benefits are usually not authorized, and you may find it hard to get a good civilian job.

- ✔ **Bad conduct:** This is a punitive discharge. By a punitive discharge, I mean it can only be imposed as a punishment by a military court-martial. This type of discharge can be imposed by either a special or general court-martial, following a finding of guilty for a military offense. Individuals with a bad conduct discharge are not eligible for most veteran benefits, and future employers may stare at them in disbelief.

- ✔ **Dishonorable discharge:** The most severe type of punitive discharge, it may be imposed only by a general court-martial, following a finding of guilty for a serious criminal offense. It's usually accompanied by a lengthy stay in a military prison. Those with dishonorable discharges are not entitled to veteran benefits and will definitely have problems finding a civilian job.

# Basic Training Punishments

You probably won't be court-martialed in basic training. It's also unlikely that you'll be punished under the provisions of Article 15 while in basic training (unless you commit a serious crime, such as stealing).

Because you're still learning in basic training, you're given a break. In most cases, documentation of any punishment is destroyed when you graduate, and nobody will even know it happened, unless you elect to tell them.

## Yelling

Yelling is, by far, the most common corrective action in military basic training. If you perform some bone-head stunt, your training instructor is going to let you know about it . . . loudly.

Don't discount being yelled at as a punishment. I've seen grown men reduced to a quivering bowl of jelly by a drill instructor's yelling. These military folks are professionals . . . far better at it than your parents ever were. When I was an Air Force First Sergeant, I was given the opportunity to revisit Air Force basic training as a guest. The ranting of the drill instructors scared me, even though they weren't yelling at me, and we First Sergeants are somewhat professional yellers ourselves.

## Getting dropped

*Getting dropped* is a very common punishment in basic training. It simply means being ordered to do some sort of physical exercise, usually push-ups.

The Marine Corps takes getting dropped one step farther in basic. In Marine Corps and Coast Guard basic training, you might get *quarter-decked*. The *quarter-deck* is a special place in the barracks where you're sent to do an amazing amount of physical exercises, all under the direct supervision and encouragement of a drill instructor.

In addition to quarter-decking in Marine Corps basic, there is also *pitting*. Pitting is incentive training for a large group of recruits, so named for the sandy pits set aside for such events.

# Recycling

*Recycling,* or getting *set back,* is by far the most feared punishment in military basic training. Recycling simply means being moved to a different military basic training unit that is in an earlier part of basic training than you are current in, which means you have to repeat training and spend additional time in basic.

Basic training instructors will lead you to believe that they have the power to recycle you for pretty much anything, but in actuality recycling is a very controlled administrative action that can be imposed by the only commanding officer, for very specific reasons.

You can be recycled without being punished. For example, if you're in week 2 of basic training and you get sick and put in the hospital for two weeks, when you get out, you won't be returned to your basic training unit (who are now in week 4). You'll be recycled to a different basic training unit who is presently in week 2 of training.

# Getting kicked out

Getting kicked out of the military while in basic training is not that easy, nor is it a very fast process. Training instructors are taught not to give up, and will try everything possible to turn someone around before recommending them for discharge.

Those who do get recommended for discharge often spend weeks, or even months, in a special discharge unit, waiting for their discharge to be processed and approved. During that time, they usually spend the day doing manual labor (cleaning buildings, cutting grass, sweeping sidewalks, and so on).

# Chapter 8

# Fit to Fight: Getting in Shape for Basic Training

*I*n the military, you have to be in shape at all times. Those who fail to maintain the required fitness standards are placed in a mandatory fitness program (to exercise with other fatties) until they get into shape. Those who fail to attain the standards while in the fitness program are subject to administrative disciplinary actions, including reduction in rank or discharge.

The good news is that you don't have to get into shape before military basic training. The instructors at basic won't let you fail for being out of shape. Instead, they'll exercise you every available second, until you do get into shape. However, this individualized attention isn't fun — your basic training experience will be much more pleasant if you arrive in some semblance of physical fitness.

But also think of it this way: If you're fit and prepared for the physical aspect of training before you arrive, the more time you have to focus on the academic side of basic training.

## The Importance of Being Fit

Being fit isn't just important for military basic training, but for your entire military career. While in the military, you'll take an official fitness test at least twice per year. If you fail the fitness test, you'll be entered into a mandatory fitness program and be destined to spend your precious off-duty time with a bunch of other out-of-shape folks sweating profusely, instead of relaxing at the enlisted club with a cold one. In extreme cases, you can even lose *stripes* (rank and pay) or even be *discharged* (kicked out of the military) for being overweight or out of shape.

Military members have been debating for years about which service members are in the best shape. If you talk to an Army Special Forces soldier, or an Air Force combat controller, he'll loudly tell you that Marines are all wimps. If you speak with a Navy SEAL, he'll assure you that the entire military (except SEALS) couldn't do a proper push-up to save their lives. Of course, if you talk with a Marine, he or she will drop down, crank out 50 quick push-ups, and say, "no contest."

My advice isn't to worry about which service personnel are tougher. Instead, spend your time making sure that you can meet the minimal basic training fitness standards for the branch of your choice. That's the only thing that counts.

## Army basic training fitness standards

Army fitness standards, even in basic training, are based on sex and age. You'll do a lot of different kinds of exercises during Army basic training, but the only ones that count for graduation purposes are push-ups, sit-ups, and timed running.

Interestingly, the Army is the only military branch whose basic training fitness standards are slightly less stringent than their normal semiannual fitness test standards. That means that you still have a little work to do, after basic training graduation, in order to be able to meet the standards of the normal semiannual Army fitness test.

You must be able to meet the normal Army fitness standard (see Tables 8-1 and 8-2) by the time you graduate from AIT (Army job school).

Tables 8-1 and 8-2 show the Army basic training fitness graduation standards for both males and females.

| Table 8-1 | Army Basic Training Fitness Standards for Males | | |
| --- | --- | --- | --- |
| *Age* | *Push-Ups* *(2 minutes)* | *Sit-Ups* *(2 minutes)* | *2-Mile Run* |
| 17–21 | 35 | 47 | 16:36 |
| 22–26 | 31 | 43 | 17:30 |

| Age | Push-Ups (2 minutes) | Sit-Ups (2 minutes) | 2-Mile Run |
|---|---|---|---|
| 27–31 | 30 | 36 | 17:54 |
| 32–36 | 26 | 34 | 18:48 |
| 37–41 | 24 | 29 | 19:30 |
| 42+ | 21 | 22 | 19:48 |
| **Fitness Standards After Basic** | | | |
| 17–21 | 42 | 53 | 15:54 |
| 22–26 | 40 | 50 | 16:36 |
| 27–31 | 39 | 45 | 17:00 |
| 32–36 | 36 | 42 | 17:42 |
| 37–41 | 34 | 48 | 18:18 |
| 42–46 | 30 | 32 | 18:42 |
| 47–51 | 25 | 30 | 19:30 |

**Table 8–2    Army Basic Training Fitness Standards for Females**

| Age | Push–Ups | Sit–Ups | 2–Mile Run |
|---|---|---|---|
| 17–21 | 13 | 47 | 19:42 |
| 22–26 | 11 | 43 | 20:36 |
| 27–31 | 10 | 36 | 21:42 |
| 32–36 | 9 | 32 | 23:06 |
| 37–41 | 6 | 29 | 24:06 |
| 42+ | 6 | 22 | 25:12 |
| **Fitness Standards After Basic** | | | |
| 17–21 | 19 | 53 | 18:54 |
| 22–26 | 17 | 50 | 19:36 |
| 27–31 | 17 | 45 | 20:30 |
| 32–36 | 15 | 42 | 21:42 |
| 37–41 | 13 | 38 | 22:42 |
| 42–46 | 12 | 32 | 23:42 |
| 47–51 | 10 | 30 | 24:00 |

# Air Force basic training fitness standards

The Air Force conducts a fitness test shortly after your arrival at basic training, just to see where you stand. If you fail to meet the minimum arrival standards, you can expect to receive some extra physical fitness one-on-one attention from your training instructor during the first few weeks of basic training. Trust me, extra attention from your drill instructor is not a good thing.

The arrival fitness standards aren't mandatory, but if you can't meet them, you're starting behind the power curve for meeting the graduation standards just a short few weeks later. As such, the instructor will give lots of extra physical fitness attention to those who fail to meet the following arrival standards:

Male recruits should be able to do 34 push-ups, 38 sit-ups, and run 1 ½ miles in 13:48 and 2 miles in 19:16. New female recruits should be able to perform 21 push-ups and 38 sit-ups. They should also be able to run 1 ½ miles in 16:01, as well as 2 miles in 22:43.

I've been told that the Air Force is toying with the idea of establishing a *fit flight* for Air Force basic training. If adopted, individuals who fail these standards on the initial fitness evaluation would be removed from their flight and placed into a special flight, doing pretty much nothing but exercising all day, until they meet the standards. After they meet the standards, these individuals would then be placed back into a normal flight, entering the first week of training. I have no idea whether the Air Force will ultimately implement this program, but it's best to be prepared.

Air Force basic training has three levels of physical fitness standards:

- ✔ **Liberator standards:** The Air Force calls their minimum basic training graduation fitness standards the *Liberator standards*. All recruits must meet these standards before they can graduate from Air Force basic training. Those who fail are "recycled" (set back to an earlier basic training day) for more practice.

  To graduate from Air Force basic training, males must be able to perform 45 push-ups, 50 sit-ups, and run 1 ½ miles in 11:57. Gals must accomplish 27 push-ups, 50 sit-ups, and a 1 ½ mile run in 14:21.

- ✔ **Thunderbolt standards:** To even have a shot at Air Force basic training's highest graduation award, Honor Graduate (see Chapter 20), recruits must meet physical fitness Thunderbolt standards. These standards are somewhat higher than the normal graduation standards and require pull-ups.

  To achieve Thunderbolt status, male recruits must run 1 ½ miles in 9:30. Female recruits must be able to run 1 ½ miles in 12:00. Additionally, male recruits must perform 55 push-ups, 60 sit-ups, and 5 pull-ups. Female recruits must accomplish 32 push-ups, 60 sit-ups, and 2 pull-ups.

✔ **War Hawk standards:** The *War Hawk physical fitness standards* are the highest fitness standards in Air Force basic training. Those who achieve these standards earn a special T-shirt, a recognition certificate, and an extra town pass on graduation weekend. (Trust me, after eight weeks of being locked up on base, that's a very big deal).

To achieve War Hawk status, males must perform 65 push-ups, 70 sit-ups, 10 pull-ups, and run 1 ½ miles in 8:55. Female recruits must do 40 push-ups, 60 sit-ups, 5 pull-ups, and run 1 ½ miles in 10:55.

## Navy basic training fitness standards

The Navy is the only military service that tests for flexibility. The Navy measures flexibility by means of a sit-reach test. You sit on the ground with your legs stretched out in front, knees straight, and toes pointed straight up. Without jerking or bouncing, you lean forward and touch your toes with your fingers. You must continue to touch your toes for at least 1 second. You get three tries.

Other than the sit-reach test, Navy basic training fitness standards are shown in Tables 8-3 and 8-4.

| Table 8-3 | Navy Basic Training Fitness Standards for Males | | |
|---|---|---|---|
| *Age* | *Sit-Ups* | *Push-Ups* | *1 ½–Mile Run* |
| 17–19 | 62 | 51 | 11:00 |
| 20–24 | 58 | 47 | 12:00 |
| 25–29 | 54 | 44 | 12:53 |
| 30–34 | 51 | 41 | 13:45 |

| Table 8–4 | Navy Basic Training Fitness Standards for Females | | |
|---|---|---|---|
| *Age* | *Sit–Ups* | *Push–Ups* | *1 ½–Mile Run* |
| 17–19 | 62 | 24 | 13:30 |
| 20–24 | 58 | 21 | 14:15 |
| 25–29 | 54 | 19 | 14:53 |
| 30–34 | 51 | 17 | 15:30 |

# Marine Corps basic training fitness standards

The Marine Corps is the only branch that requires recruits to pass a physical fitness test before they can even ship out to basic training. This Initial Strength Test (IST) occurs at MEPS before shipping out to Marine Corps basic training.

To pass the IST, male recruits must be able to perform 3 pull-ups and 35 sit-ups and run 1 ½ miles in 13:30. Female recruits must do 35 sit-ups, hang from a pull-up bar for 12 seconds, and run 1 mile in 10:30

### Initial fitness assessment

As a new recruit, you'll be given an initial fitness assessment within a few days of arriving at Marine Corps basic training. Those who don't pass this IST must spend time in a special physical fitness platoon until they can meet the standards and join a regular Marine Corps basic training platoon.

It's best to avoid any special platoons or units while in basic training. They're not designed for your enjoyment.

To pass the initial fitness assessment (and avoid the Physical Conditioning Platoon), males are required to do 2 dead-hang pull-ups, 44 sit-ups (in 2 minutes), and a 1.5 mile run in 13:30. Female recruits must run 1.5 miles in 15 minutes, perform a flex-arm hang of 12 seconds, and do 44 sit-ups in 2 minutes.

### Final fitness test

The final Marine Corps basic training fitness test, known as the PFT, has three events:

- ✔ Pull-ups (flexed-arm hang for females)
- ✔ Sit-ups (the Marine Corps call these *abdominal crunches*)
- ✔ A 3-mile run

All events are conducted in a single session, not to exceed 2 hours in duration. Tables 8-5 and 8-6 show the graduation standards.

| Table 8-5 | Marine Corps Basic Training Fitness Standards for Males | | |
|---|---|---|---|
| *Age* | *Pull–Ups* | *Sit–Ups (Crunches)* | *3–Mile Run* |
| 17–26 | 3 | 50 | 28:00 |
| 27–29 | 3 | 45 | 29:00 |

| Table 8–6 | Marine Corps Basic Training Fitness Standards for Females | | |
|---|---|---|---|
| *Age* | *Flexed Arm Hang* | *Sit–Ups (Crunches)* | *3–Mile Run* |
| 17–26 | 15 seconds | 50 | 31:00 |
| 27–29 | 15 seconds | 45 | 32:00 |

Keep in mind that the standards listed in Tables 8-5 and 8-6 are the bare minimums you must do to pass the PFT. These numbers total an overall score, which directly affect promotion standards.

### Combat fitness test

A couple of years ago, the Marine Corps developed a *Combat Fitness Test* (CFT) that all Marines (even troops in basic training) must pass, in addition to the standard Marine Corps Physical Fitness Test (PFT). The CFT consists of three activities:

- ✔ **880-yard run:.** Marines run for 880 yards while wearing boots and camouflage uniform (pants and t-shirt).

- ✔ **Ammo can lifts:** Marines must lift a 30-pound ammo can from the ground over their heads as many times as they can in 2 minutes.

- ✔ **Maneuver under fire:** Marines must move through a 300-yard course and perform the following designated tasks in the time limit authorized:

  - • Move in a quick scurry (run) for 10 yards and then a high crawl for another 15 yards.

  - • Drag a casualty for 10 yards while zigzagging through several cones. Then lift the casualty and carry him at a run for 65 yards.

- Carry two 30-pound ammo cans for 75 yards while zigzagging through a series of cones.

- Toss a dummy grenade 22 ½ yards and land it in a marked target circle.

- Perform three push-ups, pick up the two 30-pound cans, and sprint to the finish line.

Tables 8-7 and 8-8 show the minimum passing scores for the combat fitness test for both males and females.

| Table 8-7 | Marine Corps Combat Fitness Test Requirements for Males | | |
|---|---|---|---|
| *Age* | *880-Yard Run* | *Ammo Can Lifts* | *Maneuver Under Fire* |
| 17–26 | 3:48 | 45 | 3:29 |
| 27–29 | 4:00 | 45 | 3:55 |

| Table 8–8 | Marine Corps Combat Fitness Test Requirements for Females | | |
|---|---|---|---|
| *Age* | *880-Yard Run* | *Ammo Can Lifts* | *Maneuver Under Fire* |
| 17–26 | 4:34 | 20 | 4:57 |
| 27–29 | 4:40 | 19 | 5:27 |

## Coast Guard basic training fitness standards

Like the Air Force, the Coast Guard doesn't make fitness requirements easier for older basic trainees. The fitness graduation standards are the same for all trainees, regardless of age.

The Coast Guard uses only three exercises to measure your basic training fitness:

- **Sit ups:** In order to graduate, guys must perform 38 sit-ups in 1 minute. Females must do 32 sit-ups.

- **Push-ups:** Guys must do 29 push-ups in 1 minute. Ladies must do 15 push-ups.

> ✓ **A 1.5-mile run:** Men must run 1 ½ miles in 12:51, while women must run
> 1 ½ miles in 15:26

# Fitness Factor: Knowing What You Can Do to Get in Shape

It's hard to fail military basic training by being out of shape. They'll just keep you there as long as it takes in order for you to meet their standards. But, why spend even a single day longer in basic training unless absolutely necessary? Take my advice and get into shape before you leave. You'll be glad you did.

If you've never exercised regularly, you should have a physical exam by a doctor to ensure safety. Don't count on the entrance physical you had at MEPS. This physical isn't designed to diagnose medical conditions you may not know about.

## Stretch for success

Stretching your muscles is important in that they warm you up and help prevent exercise-related injuries. All basic training exercise sessions begin with a period of organized stretching exercises in order to increase flexibility and avoid injuries. You should perform each stretching exercise for at least three to five minutes.

When stretching, don't jerk. You're trying to loosen up your muscles, not rip them to pieces.

- ✓ **Bend and reach:** Begin with your hands above your head, palms facing in. Your feet should be about shoulder-width apart. On count 1, squat with the heels flat on the ground to allow straight arms to reach as far between the legs as possible. On count 2, return to the starting position. On count 3, repeat count 1. On count 4, repeat count 2.

- ✓ **Rear lunge:** Start with your feet approximately shoulder-width apart, hands on your hips. Take an exaggerated step back and touch the ground only with the ball of your left foot. On count 2, return to the starting position. On count 3, repeat count 1 with right side. On count 4, repeat count 2.

- ✓ **High jumper:** Start with feet shoulder-width apart and bend slightly at the waist with upper torso forward. Arms are straight to the rear and palms facing in. On count 1, jump a few inches and swing arms forward. On count 2, jump a few inches and swing arms backward. On count 3, jump forcefully into the air and swing arms overhead. On count 4, repeat count 2.

✔ **The rower:** Start by lying flat on your back, feet together, and toes pointed upward. Your hands should be stretched over your head. On count 1, sit up while swinging arms forward and bending at the hips and knees. On count 2, return to starting position. On count 3, repeat count 1, and on count 4, repeat count 2.

✔ **Squat bender:** Begin with your hands on your hips, feet shoulder-width apart. On count 1, bend at the knees and squat down. Your arms move straight out in front of you, with the palms facing each other. On count 2, return to the starting position. On count 3, bend over at the waist, keeping the knees slightly bent, and touch your ankles. On count 4, return to the starting position.

✔ **The windmill:** Stand with your feet approximately shoulder-width apart, arms outstretched at your sides, palms facing down. On count 1, bend over, twist your upper body and touch the outside of your left foot with your right hand, and look to the rear with your knees bent slightly. On count 2, return to the starting position. On count 3, bend over, twist your upper body, touch the outside of your right foot with your left hand, and look to the rear with your knees bent slightly. Return to the starting position for count 4.

✔ **Forward lunge:** Start by standing with your hands on your hips, feet about shoulder-width apart. On count 1, take a three- to six-inch step f orward with the right foot, bending the knee, in order to obtain a 90-degree angle with the forward leg. The hands remain on the hips. On count 2, return to the starting position. Perform the same movements with the right leg for counts 3 and 4.

✔ **Prone row:** Start by lying flat on the ground on your stomach, with your toes pointed to the rear and your head up. (Don't rest your head on the ground.) Your arms are extended in front of your head, with palms down. On count 1, raise your shoulder blades and upper body off the ground and move your hands to the side of your chest (like you were rowing a boat). Make fists with your hands while they move back toward your chest. Make sure that you lift your head up and look straight to the front. On count 2, return to the starting position.

✔ **Bent leg body twist:** Start by lying on your back with your hips and knees bent at a 90-degree angle with the knees together. Arms are out to the sides with palms on the ground. On count 1, rotate legs to the left side while keeping your upper body in place. On count 2, return to the starting position. On counts 3 and 4, repeat with the right side.

✔ **Push-up:** Start in the front leaning rest position with the hands placed directly beneath shoulder and fingers spread. On count 1, lower your body until your upper arms are at least parallel to the ground, arms are against your side, and elbows are back. On count 2, return to starting position. On count 3, repeat count 1. On count 4, repeat count 2.

## *Tighten your abs with sit-ups*

All the services do sit-ups in one form or another during military basic training. Additionally, sit-ups are part of every single basic training graduation requirements.

Sit-ups in the military are performed with the knees bent. This exercise measures abdominal muscular endurance.

To perform a proper military sit-up, lie on your back, knees bent, heels flat on the ground, and fingers interlaced behind your head. If necessary, have someone hold your feet for stability. Keep your lower back on the ground and raise your upper body approximately 90 degrees, before beginning a controlled descent back to the ground. Once your shoulder blades touch the ground, you can raise your upper body again. Do not tuck your chin into your chest as this causes strain on your neck. Your goal is to meet or exceed the physical fitness qualifications for graduation for your particular branch of service.

The Navy's version of the sit-up is a *curl-up.* Curl-ups are conducted by lying flat on your back with knees bent, heels about 10 inches from buttocks. Fold your arms across, touching your chest, with your hands touching your upper chest or shoulders. Your feet are held to floor by your partner's hands. A timer signals when to start and calls out 15-second time intervals until 2 minutes have elapsed. Curl your body up, touching your elbows to your thighs, while keeping your hands in contact with chest or shoulders. Then lie back, touching the lower edge of your shoulder blades to the deck (floor or ground). You may rest in either the up or down position. Repeat the process as many times as possible in 2 minutes. Your test ends (prematurely) if you lower your legs, raise your feet off the deck, lift your buttocks off the deck, fail to keep your arms folded across and touching your chest, and/or fail to keep your hands in contact with your chest or shoulders.

## *Pushing yourself with push-ups*

Like sit-ups (or curl-ups), all of the services require you to perform a minimum number of push-ups in order to graduate from basic training. Push-ups measure the muscular endurance of your upper body.

In order to perform a proper military push-up, start by placing hands where they're most comfortable, your feet together, or up to 12 inches apart, and your body forming a generally straight line from the shoulders to the ankles. Keep your body straight throughout the exercise. Lower your body until the upper arms are at least parallel to the ground and then push up to the initial position by completely straightening the arms.

Push-ups are often use as corrective action or an *incentive to remember* during basic training. If you do something wrong, an instructor may say something like, "Drop and give me 50." In that case, you're supposed to drop down and do 50 military push-ups.

In the military, there's no such thing as girl push-ups, where ladies do push-ups on their knees. In the military, women do push-ups exactly the same way as guys; they're just required to do fewer.

## Pulling up your standards

The Marine Corps is the only branch of military service that requires you to perform pull-ups (3 if you're a guy) in order to graduate. Ladies are required to hang from the pull-up bar for 15 seconds.

Although the other services don't require you to perform pull-ups in order to graduate from basic training, you'll get plenty of chances to do pull-ups during the daily exercise schedules.

The Air Force requires pull-ups in order to win a basic training fitness award. See "Air Force basic training fitness standards" earlier in this chapter.

Pull-ups are tough to do, but almost anyone can work up to a solid set of military pull-ups. To do a military pull-up, place your hands on the bar, shoulder width apart, with the palms facing out.

If your palms are facing in, it's called a *chin-up*.

To perform a proper military pull-up:

- ✔ Grasp the pull-up bar with your palms facing away from you. Straighten your back and relax your shoulders. Contract your abdominal muscles for support. Arms must be straight and elbows loose, not locked.

  In the Marines, you are required to lock out while doing pull-ups. If you perform pull-ups and keep your arms bent when coming down from the bar, they will not be counted.

- ✔ Pull yourself up slowly toward your hands until your head is above the bar and your elbows pass behind your torso. Contract your bicep muscles as you reach the top.

  A pull-up will count as long as your chin breaks the plane of the bar.

- ✔ Lower slowly back to the starting position. Keep your abdominal muscles tight and your back straight through the entire exercise to maintain form and isolate the bicep muscles.

## Run, fat boy, run

In these days where every teenager has a car, lots of young folks seem to have trouble getting around on their feet. Running is something you need to get over. You won't find cars in basic training (at least that recruits are allowed to use). You'll walk (march) everywhere you go, and when you're not marching, you'll be running.

Your basic training life will be much, much easier if you show up able to run without falling down and gasping for breath. Table 8-9 lists the goals you should strive for before boarding that plane for basic training.

| Table 8-9 | Running Goals for Basic Training | |
|---|---|---|
| *Branch* | *Guys* | *Gals* |
| **Army** | 2 miles in 16:00 | 2 miles in 19:00 |
| **Air Force** | 2 miles in 19:00 | 2 miles in 22:00 |
| **Navy** | 2 miles in 19:00 | 2 miles in 22:00 |
| **Marine Corps** | 4 miles in 37:30 | 4 miles in 41:00 |
| **Coast Guard** | 2 miles in 19:00 | 2 miles in 22:00 |

If you can achieve the goals listed in Table 8-9, you'll have no trouble at all with the running portion of military basic training.

## A simple exercise program

If you're planning on attending military basic training, the time to start getting into shape is now — not tomorrow, not next week, and certainly not next month. The more time you have to prepare, the easier the process will be on your poor, tired body.

If you join the Army or the Marine Corps, your recruiter will be very happy to help you get into shape. The following list outlines a viable program to get into shape. Remember to always begin with 10 to 15 minutes of easy stretching. Stretching will help limber you up and prevent workout injuries. You should exercise at least every other day (three to four days per week as a minimum).

 ✔ **Week 1:** Start easy. No need to kill yourself — yet. After you stretch, try to crank out a single pull-up, followed by about 15 push-ups and 25 sit-ups. Next, walk and jog for a mile. Don't worry about time at this point, but try to do more jogging than walking.

✔ **Week 2:** This week, try for 2 pull-ups. Follow the pull-ups with 20 push-ups and about 30 sit-ups. Hopefully, you're jogging the entire mile. If so, bump it up a notch and try to jog 1 ¼ miles.

✔ **Week 3:** Are you still sore every morning? Hopefully, you're over that phase and can start to crank it up a bit. See whether you can do 3 pull-ups. After your pull-ups, see whether you can crank out 25 push-ups (ladies, 20) and 35 sit-ups. Wrap up your session by jogging 1 ½ miles. Before you take a shower, walk for a mile to help cool down.

✔ **Week 4:** As usual, start your session with 10 to 15 minutes of stretching. Next, try for 30 push-ups (ladies, 20) and 40 sit-ups. Today, you should try to run 2 miles. It's okay at this point to walk a little, if you have to. After your run, walk for about 15 or 20 minutes. You'll feel better.

✔ **Week 5:** Pull-ups are hard for many people, but see whether you can do 5 of them. Then do 35 push-ups (ladies, 20) and 45 sit-ups. It's okay to ask a friend to hold your feet down when doing your sit-ups. Run for 2 miles without walking any of it. If you're joining the Marine Corps, try to run for 2 ½ miles. Remember to walk for 20 minutes or so afterward. A post-run walk gives you time to think about whether joining the military is really such a good idea.

✔ **Week 6:** See whether you can crank out six pull-ups. If you can't, do as many as you can. Try for 40 push-ups (ladies, 20), and 50 sit-ups. Wrap up your session with 2-mile jog. Try to achieve your target time (see the "Run, fat boy, run" section earlier in this chapter). Marine recruits, see whether you can do a 3-mile run without walking.

✔ **Week 7:** Keep practicing your pull-ups. If you can do more than six, go for it. If not, do as many as you can! Try for 45 push-ups (ladies, 20) and 55 sit-ups. Wrap up your session with a 2-mile timed run (Marine recruits, 3 miles) and then take a little walk.

✔ **Week 8+:** You're now at the point where you just have to maintain your fitness level until you finally ship out to basic training. However, if you can do more, go for it. Doing more than the minimum standards certainly can't hurt and may result in a basic training fitness award (see Chapter 20). As always, start by limbering up your body. Try to do 5 or more pull-ups, followed by at least 45 push-ups (ladies, 20) and 55 sit-ups. Time your run for 2 miles (Marine recruits, 3 miles). Have a nice, relaxing walk home.

# Nutrition Factor: Practicing Good Nutrition and Eating Habits

You can't get into shape if you eat garbage. Your body is a delicate piece of machinery that requires the right fuel to operate properly.

Good nutrition is vital to good health. Major causes of morbidity and mortality in the United States are related to poor diet and a sedentary lifestyle. Exercising every day isn't going to do you any good if you keep dumping cheeseburgers down your throat.

In basic training, you won't have to worry too much about it. The meals available in the chow halls are all scientific, nutritionally balanced, and designed to keep recruits in good health. Sugars (desserts) are limited. In fact, some drill instructors won't allow their recruits to have any sweets at all in the chow hall, except for nutritional sweets, such as fruit.

Get into the habit of eating properly long before you depart for basic training. Basic training is stressful enough without adding sugar withdrawal to the mix.

The U.S. Department of Health and Human Services has spent a lot of time and money trying to teach Americans how to eat right. But, nobody listens to them. They seem more interested in listening to McDonald's and Burger King, instead. However, if you want the food energy that will take you through the rigors of basic training, you should eagerly adopt their recommendations for a daily diet (see Table 8-10).

| Table 8-10 | Recommended Daily Diet | |
|---|---|---|
| *Food Group* | *Daily Recommended Amount* | *Examples* |
| Fruits | 2 cups (4 servings) | ½ cup equivalent is ½ cup fresh, frozen, or canned fruit, 1 medium fruit, ¼ cup dried fruit, or ½ cup fruit juice |
| Vegetables | 2.5 cups (5 servings) | ½ cup equivalent is ½ cup of cut-up raw or cooked vegetables, 1 cup raw leafy vegetables, or ½ cup vegetable juice |

*(continued)*

| Food Group | Daily Recommended Amount | Examples |
|---|---|---|
| Grain | 6 ounces | 1 ounce-equivalent is 1 slice bread, 1 cup dry cereal, or ½ cup cooked rice, pasta, or cereal |
| Meat and Beans | 5.5 ounce | 1 ounce-equivalent is 1 ounce of cooked lean meats, poultry, or fish; 1 egg, ¼ cup cooked dry beans or tofu, 1 T. peanut butter, or ½ oz. nuts or seeds |
| Milk | 3 cups | 1 cup equivalent is 1 cup lowfat/fat-free milk, yogurt, 1½ oz. of lowfat, fat-free, or reduced fat natural cheese, 2 oz. of lowfat or fat-free processed cheese |
| Oils | 27 grams (6 tsp) | 1 t. equivalent is 1 t. soft margarine, 1 T. low-fat mayo, 2 T. light salad dressing, 1 t. vegetable oil |

**Table 8-10** *(continued)*

# Medical Factor: Taking Care of Your Medical Needs

Hopefully, you won't have any medical needs. That's what those two trips to MEPS were all about — to make sure that you don't have any medical conditions that will impact on basic training or on your military career. If you do have a medical condition that will interfere with basic training, MEPS will not allow you to ship out.

When it comes to vitamins and nonprescription medication, I can make my advice real short and simply say, "Don't bring any, as they'll just be taken away from you." The basic training folks have no way of knowing that you're not trying to smuggle in illegal drugs, and they're certainly not going to take the time to send your One-A-Days out for testing. The training instructor will simply take them away from you and probably yell at you a bit for being stupid enough to bring them to basic with you.

From the military's point of view, if you eat balanced meals in the chow hall, you don't need supplements and vitamins.

## Basic training suicides

Suicide is the fourth leading cause of death among 25- to 44-year-olds in the United States, and basic training instructors are always on the lookout for recruits who exhibit signs of depression. For many, military basic training is the first time they've ever been away from family and friends, and some people simply can't handle the stresses associated with being separated from their loved ones. Unfortunately, there's no easy way to test for this at MEPS, so basic training instructors must remain ever vigilant. They seem to do a pretty good job; while suicide attempts are not unknown in basic training, successful suicides are rare.

Generally, prescription medicine isn't a problem because in most cases, MEPS won't approve your medical physical if you require prescription medication. However, approval for prescription medication at basic has been known to happen.

If you arrive at military basic training with prescription medication, it will be taken away from you, and you'll be sent to sick call (the military doctor), who will determine whether or not you really need that prescription. If so, you'll be given a military prescription that you can fill at the military pharmacy.

Depending on what the prescription is for and whether it's possible to overdose on it, your training instructor may hang on to your pills for you, and only dole out your daily dose. Suicide attempts are a big problem in basic training, and the instructors are trained not to take any chances.

# Chapter 9

# Hup, Two, Three, Four: Understanding Military Drill

*In This Chapter*

▶ Looking at the logic behind military drill

▶ Drilling while standing still

▶ Getting your march on

**M**ilitary drill is nothing more than methods that military folks use to walk together in a group. If you have experience in your high school marching band, you have an idea of what I mean.

The good news is, you can safely skip this chapter if you want. You'll get so much practice doing drill, beginning with your very first minutes in basic training, that it will become second nature within a few days.

However, if you want a shot at one of the basic training leadership positions (see Chapter 13), which could lead to a basic training award (check out Chapter 20), showing up knowing how to move in a group, without tripping over your own feet, may help your training instructor decide you would make an ideal basic training leader.

## The Importance of Drill

Drill is marching, plain and simple. In ancient times, the most powerful, efficient, and developed empires developed ways of moving troops from one place to another without them getting mixed up with other troops. So they marched together from one place to another, also known as *drill*.

The theory was, without drill, masses of soldiers would end up getting lost on the way to battle and have to fight with just any ol' unit they could find, instead of the unit they trained with.

As time went on, a system of flags developed. These flags allowed soldiers to find their own units (and side) on the battlefield if they got lost. However, the military quickly discovered that sticking to formed units worked better, as everyone was present when needed for battle.

Overall, the drill system worked: Soldiers stayed together and could be commanded as a group.

These days, military drill is mostly used for military ceremonies, such as military parades, and to instill pride and discipline during military training (such as basic training). In fact, the military drill manual (a book about 6 inches thick) confidently states that drill is the foundation of discipline in battle, and that its importance has been proven again and again.

For example, back in 2002 and 2003, when the North Koreans claimed that they were developing nuclear weapons, they conducted a huge number of public military parades, receiving lots of attention from the press, which commended them on how modern and disciplined their military was. The North Korean forces could clearly be seen to be skilled, which would act as a deterrent against many lesser military forces.

Today, regular parades in public display the military as a highly trained, disciplined, and professional force. Even though the parade itself doesn't provide any useful function on the battlefield, it instills public confidence in the nation's military forces. A rag-tag military is likely to be unable to put on parades, so it holds that larger and better military forces can display their discipline by means of public performances.

# Understanding How Drill Commands Work

Military drill is controlled by commands that are usually given in two distinct parts. The first part is the *preparatory command,* which serves to warn you what is coming, so that when you hear the second part, known as the *command of execution,* you'll be able to carry it out instantaneously.

No two military drill commands begin with the same preparatory command, so after you've learned the various commands, you'll know what is coming every time you hear a preparatory command.

For example, the command Right Face is given in two distinct parts. Right is the preparatory command, and because it's the only command that begins with the word "right," all members of the squad know that the next word they hear will be the command of execution "face," and they'll execute it together the instant they hear it.

This method ensures the precision that is essential in military drill. This is why you hear the single word "Attention" given as something like A-TEN (preparatory) HUT (execution). It's not just a way of sounding cool.

# Exploring the Different Types of Drill

There are two basic types of drill: stationary drill and marching drill. *Stationary drill* is just what it sounds like — drill while not moving (marching). *Marching drill* refers to drill movement while actually moving (marching) in formation.

Each branch does its drill just a little bit differently. If you read something in this chapter that conflicts with your drill instructions, you should, of course, go with what your drill instructor says.

## Stationary drill

Stationary drill consists of drill movements that are accomplished without marching. The drill positions of attention and parade rest are two perfect examples. Other stationary drill commands include parade rest, at ease, left (or right) face, about face, fall out. Some commands, such as present arms and order arms, can be accomplished while moving or while stationary.

If you don't remember anything else, do not forget to unlock your knees when you're participating in stationary drill. Bend your knees just enough so that it is not visible that you're doing so but enough to allow the blood to flow smoothly through your legs. Failing to unlock your knees will impede the blood flow to your brain so that, after a time (and you will find that stationary drill in the military often requires you to stand still for long periods), you'll grow faint and pass out. It's not a pleasant experience to suddenly find yourself abruptly kissing the asphalt of a parade grinder or the steel of a ship's deck.

### Attention

To come to the position of attention (see Figure 9-1), bring the heels together smartly (by moving the left foot only) and on line. Place the heels as near each other as the conformation of the body permits and ensure that the feet are turned out equally, forming a 45-degree angle. Keep the legs straight without stiffening or locking the knees. The body is erect with hips level, chest lifted, back arched, and shoulders square and even.

**Figure 9-1:**
Attention.

© iStock.

Arms hang straight down alongside the body without stiffness, and the wrists are straight with the forearms. Place thumbs, which are resting along the first joint of the forefinger, along the seams of the trousers or sides of the skirt. Hands are cupped (but not clenched as a fist) with palms facing the leg. The head is kept erect and held straight to the front with the chin drawn in slightly so that the axis of the head and neck is vertical; eyes are to the front, with the line of sight parallel to the ground. The weight of the body rests equally on the heels and balls of both feet, and silence and immobility are required.

To resume the position of attention from any of the rests (except fall out), the command is Flight/Squadron/Group, *(group name.)* Attention. On the preparatory command of Flight, or Squadron, or Group, the individuals assume the position of parade rest. At the command "Attention," assume the position of attention.

### Parade rest

This command can be given only when the formation is at the position of attention.

The Preparatory Command is "Parade," and the Command of Execution is "Rest." On the command "Rest," the recruit will raise the left foot just enough to clear the ground and move it smartly to the left so that the heels are 10 inches apart, as measured from the inside of the heels. Keep the legs straight, but not stiff, and the heels on line. As the left foot moves, bring the arms, fully extended, to the back of the body, uncupping the hands in the process, and extend and join the fingers, pointing them toward the ground. The palms will face outward. Place the right hand in the palm of the left, right thumb over the left, to form an X. Keep head and eyes straight ahead and remain silent and immobile (see Figure 9-2).

**Figure 9-2:**
Parade rest.

© iStock.

### At ease

The command is "At ease." On the command, you may relax in a standing position, but you must keep your right foot in place. Your position in the formation will not change, and silence will be maintained. Your arms may be relaxed, but your thumbs must also stay interlaced.

### Fall out

The command is "Fall Out." On the command, you may relax in a standing position or *break ranks* (move a few steps out of formation). You must remain in the immediate area, and return to the formation on the command "Fall In." Moderate speech is permitted.

### Right (or left) face

This command can be given only when the formation is at the position of attention.

The commands are "Right face" or "Left face." On the command "Face," raise the right (left) toe and left (right) heel slightly and pivot 90 degrees to the right (left) on the ball of the left (right) foot and the heel of the right (left) foot, assisted by slight pressure on the ball of the left (right) foot. Keep legs bent naturally, not stiff. The upper portion of the body remains at attention. This completes count 1 of the movement. Next, bring the left (right) foot smartly forward, ensuring that your heels are together and on line. Feet should now be forming a 45-degree angle, which means the position of attention has been resumed. This step completes count 2 of the movement.

### About face

This command can be given only when the formation is at the position of attention.

The command is "About, face." On the command "Face," lift the right foot from the hip just enough to clear the ground. While naturally bending the knees, place the ball of the right foot approximately half a shoe length behind and slightly to the left of the heel. Distribute the weight of the body on the ball of the right foot and the heel of the left foot. Keep both legs straight, but not stiff. The position of the foot has not changed. This step completes the first part of the movement. Keeping the upper portion of the body at the position of attention, pivot 180 degrees to the right on the ball of the right foot and heel of the left foot, with a twisting motion from the hips. Suspend arm swing during the movement and remain as though at attention. On completion of the pivot, heels should be together and in line and feet should form a 45-degree angle. The entire body is now at the position of attention.

### Hand salute

The command is "Hand, salute." On the command "Salute," you raise the right hand smartly in the most direct manner while at the same time extending and joining the fingers. Keep the palm flat and facing the body. Place the thumb along the forefingers, keeping the palm flat and forming a straight line between the fingertips and elbows. Tilt the palm slightly toward the face. Hold the upper arm horizontal, slightly forward of the body and parallel to the ground. Ensure that the tip of the right forefinger touches headgear to the right of the right eye. If wearing a nonbilled hat, ensure that the index finger touches the outside corner of the right eyebrow or the front corner of glasses. The rest of the body will remain at the position of attention.

This procedure is used (in some of the branches) for training purposes only. This command is not usually used in actual military ceremonies.

### Present arms and order arms

This procedure can be performed both during stationary drill and while marching.

When not under arms (carrying a rifle), the commands are "Present, arms" and "Order arms." On the command "Present, arms," the individual executes the hand salute. Then the hand salute ends when given the command, "Order arms." When under arms, to present arms, you bring your weapon up in front of you with the trigger facing away from your body; order arms is executed by returning the weapon to your side so that the butt is resting on the floor/ground/deck next to your right foot.

## Marching basics

Once you start getting the hang of stationary drill commands, your training instructor will take your unit to the next level and have you march. (You march everywhere you go in basic training.)

When performing marching drill, both the preparatory command and the command of execution are given as the foot in the direction of the turn strikes the ground. For single formations, the preparatory command is normally given as the heel of the left (or right) foot strikes the ground, and the command of execution is given when the heel of the left (right) foot next strikes the ground.

For multiple units, time is allowed for the subordinate commanders to give appropriate supplementary commands. The pause between commands is three paces.

When executed from a halt, all steps and marching begin with the left foot.

### Forward march

To march forward from a halt, the command of execution is "Forward, march." On the command "March," you smartly step off straight ahead with your left foot, taking a 30-inch step (measured from heel to heel), and place the heel on the ground first. When stepping off and while marching, you will use a coordinated arm swing — that is, right arm forward with the left leg and left arm forward with the right leg. The hands are cupped with the thumbs pointed down, and the arms hang straight, but not stiff, and swing naturally. The swing of the arms measures 9 inches to the front (measured from the rear of the hand to the front of the thigh) and 6 inches to the rear (measured from the front of the hand to the back of the thigh).

To halt from marching, the command is "Halt," given as either foot strikes the ground. On the command "Halt," you will take one more 30-inch step. Next, the trailing foot is brought smartly alongside your front foot. The heels are together, on line, and form a 45-degree angle. Coordinated arm swing ceases as the weight of the body shifts to the leading foot when halting.

### Mark time

Mark time is basically marching in place (without moving forward). The command is "Mark time, march." When marching, the command of execution, "March" is given as either foot strikes the ground. You take one more 30-inch step with the right (or left) foot. You then bring your trailing foot to a position so that both heels are on line. The cadence is continued by alternately raising and lowering each foot. The balls of the feet are raised 2 inches above the ground. Normal arm swing is maintained.

At a halt, on the command of execution "March," you raise and lower first the left foot and then the right. The halt executed from mark time is similar to the halt from forward march.

To resume marching, the command "Forward, march" is given as the heel of the left foot strikes the ground. You then take one more step in place and then step off in a full 30-inch step with the left foot.

### Half step

The command "Half step, march" is given as either foot strikes the ground. On the command "March," you take one more 30-inch step followed by a 15-inch step (measured from heel to heel) in *quick time* (double normal marching speed), setting your heel down first without scraping the ground. Make sure that you maintain a coordinated arm swing and continue the half step until marched forward or halted.

## Column right (left), march

This movement can be rather confusing to read about, but trust me – with a few minutes of practice with your drill instructor, you'll be turning as a group in no time.

To keep confusion to a minimum, I describe the movement to the right. Turning the left is the same (just exactly opposite).

On the command "Column right, march," the fourth element leader (the person in front of the far-right line of troops) takes one more 30-inch step, pivots 90 degrees to the right on the ball of the left foot, and suspends arm-swing during the pivot. Following the pivot, step off in a 30-inch step and resume coordinated arm-swing. Beginning with the second step after the pivot, take up the half step. Each succeeding member of the fourth element marches to the approximate pivot point established by the person in front of her and performs the same procedures as the element leader (lead person).

The third element leader (the person to the immediate left of the fourth element leader) takes one 30-inch step (maintaining coordinated arm swing throughout), pivots 45 degrees to the right on the ball of the left foot, and takes two 30-inch steps prior to pivoting 45 degrees to the right on the ball of the left foot. Continue marching in 30-inch steps until even with the fourth element leader. Then begin half-stepping and establish interval and dress (alignment). Each succeeding member of the third element marches to the approximate pivot point established by the person in front of her and performs the same procedures as the element leader.

The second person (the person to the immediate left of the third element leader) takes one more 30-inch step (maintaining coordinated arm swing throughout), pivots 45 degrees to the right on the ball of the left foot, and takes four 30-inch steps prior to pivoting 45 degrees to the right on the ball of the left foot. Continue marching in 30-inch steps until even with the person who marches on the right. Then begin half-stepping and establish interval and dress. Each succeeding member of the second element marches to the approximate pivot point established by the person in front of her and performs the same procedures as the element leader.

The first element leader (the person in front of the far-left line of troops) takes one more 30-inch step (maintaining coordinated arm swing throughout), pivots 45 degrees to the right on the ball of the left foot, and takes six 30-inch steps prior to pivoting 45 degrees to the right on the ball of the left foot. Continue marching in 30-inch steps until even with the person who marches on the right. Then begin half-stepping and establish interval and dress. Each succeeding member of the first element marches to the approximate point established by the person in front of him or her and performs the same procedures as the element leader.

Once the entire formation has changed direction and dress, cover, interval, and distance are reestablished, "Forward, march" is given. On the command "March," take one more 12-inch step with the right foot and then step off with a full 30-inch step with the left foot. When performing column left, the responsibility of dress reverts to the left flank on the preparatory command "Column left."

### To the rear, march

The command "To the rear, march" is given as the heel of the right foot strikes the ground. On the command of execution "March," you take a 12-inch step with the left foot, placing it in front of and in line with the right foot and distributing the weight of the body on the balls of both feet. Then pivot on the balls of both feet, turning 180 degrees to the right, and take a 12-inch step with the left foot in the new direction, with coordinated arm swing, before taking a full 30-inch step with the right foot. While pivoting, do not force the body up or lean forward. The pivot takes a full count, and the arm swing is suspended to the sides as the weight of the body comes forward while executing the pivot, as if at the position of attention.

### Change step

The command is "Change step, march." On the command "March," given as the right foot strikes the ground, you take one more 30-inch step with the left foot. Then in one count, place the ball of the right foot alongside the heel of the left foot, suspend arm swing, and shift the weight of the body to the right foot. Step off with the left foot in a 30-inch step, resuming coordinated arm swing. The upper portion of the body remains at the position of attention throughout.

Sometimes, when marching, you'll notice you're out-of-step with everyone else. A simple change step movement of your own will fix that.

### Right (left) step

The command is "Right (left) step, march," given only from a halt and for moving short distances. On the command of execution "March," you raise your right (left) leg from the hip just high enough to clear the ground. The leg will be bent naturally, and not stiff, throughout the movement. You place the right (left) foot 15 inches, as measured from the inside of the heels, to the right (left) of the left (right) foot. Transfer the weight of the body to the right (left) foot and then bring the left (right) foot (without scraping the ground) smartly to a position alongside the right (left) foot as in the position of attention. The upper portion of the body remains at attention, and arms remain at the sides throughout.

Cadence may be counted during this movement. Counts 1 and 3 are given as the right (left) foot strikes the ground. Counts 2 and 4 are given as the heels come together.

To halt from the right (left) step, the preparatory command, and command of execution are given as the heels come together. The halt from the right (left) step is executed in two counts. On the command, "Halt," one more step is taken with the right (left) foot, and the left (right) foot is placed smartly alongside the right (left) foot as in the position of attention.

### Right (left) flank

The command is "Right (left) flank, march," given as the heel of the right (left) foot strikes the ground. On the command of execution "March," you take one more 30-inch step and pivot 90 degrees on the ball of the lead foot, keeping the upper portion of the body at the position of attention. Then step off with the right (left) foot in the new direction of march with a full 30-inch step and coordinated arm swing. Arm swing is suspended to the sides as the weight of the body comes forward on the pivot foot. The pivot and step off are executed in one count. This movement is used for a quick movement to the right or left for short distances only. Throughout the movement, maintain proper dress, cover, interval, and distance.

# Part III
# Heading to Basic Training

The 5th Wave                    By Rich Tennant

©RICHTENNANT

"Remember men, when you're out there, be ready for the unexpected — booby traps, snipers, CBS camera crews..."

## In this part . . .

$B$efore you can begin your adventures with the United States Military, you have to get to basic training. This journey is a little more complicated than simply getting on a plane and then getting off again. First, you must make one final visit to MEPS to make sure you're not ill and complete a ton of more paperwork. Then, you actually have to get to your basic training location, the military way, not your way.

# Chapter 10

# Packing Right by Packing Light

. . . . . . . . . . . . . . . . . . . . . . . . . . . . . . . . . . . . . . . . . . . . . .

## In This Chapter

▶ Making a (packing) list and checking it twice

▶ Keeping your packing list short and simple

▶ Deciding to pack it — or not

. . . . . . . . . . . . . . . . . . . . . . . . . . . . . . . . . . . . . . . . . . . . . .

*Y*ou're not allowed to bring very much with you to military basic training. Your storage space at basic training is very, very limited — possibly just one small wall locker and a foot locker (trunk). These lockers must hold not only the things you bring with you, but your entire military uniform issue. That's the bad news.

The good news is, you won't need much. Everything from your reading material to your underwear is provided for you.

## Your First On-Base Shopping Trip

Within your first few days on base, you'll be given your initial military uniform issue and make a supervised shopping trip to the exchange to purchase anything you need, such as toiletries. The exchange center is located at military installations worldwide and resembles a large department store or strip mall. You don't even need to bring money. Whatever you purchase at the exchange is deducted from your first military paycheck!

Don't get too excited about this first shopping trip. There will be a training instructor with you at all times to make sure that you purchase only the items on your authorized list of basic training essentials, such as toothpaste and shaving cream. You'll have to wait to purchase your new stereo system and computer until after you graduate from basic training. The services have different names for their retail area. The exchange is known to the Army as the *Post Exchange* (PX), the Air Force calls it the *Base Exchange* (BX), the Marine Corps call it the *Marine Corps Exchange* (MCX), the Navy calls its store the *Navy Exchange* (NEX), while the Coast Guard calls its exchange center the *Coast Guard Exchange* (CGX).

Anyone with a military ID card is authorized to enter almost any base and shop at the exchange. A military exchange is known to offer considerable discounts when compared to civilian stores.

# Essentials to Never Forget

Although most things are provided for you in basic training, you do need to bring some items with you, as they're simply not available for purchase or to be issued to you.

The items you probably should bring with you include important paperwork, such as your marriage license and children's birth certificates (necessary to get your family members a military I.D. card), your enlistment contract, banking information, all prescription information, and college transcripts.

You're also able to bring essential toiletries, such as deodorant, shampoo, and shaving equipment. Don't worry if you forget or run out of these items; you can purchase them at the exchange. If you're female, you should bring hair accessories, brushes, undergarments, and feminine hygiene products with you.

Lastly, you're able to bring items such as batteries, calling cards, stamps, and nail grooming equipment. Your recruiter should give you a list of required and recommended items to bring before you report to basic.

## ID

Shortly after arrival, you'll be issued a brand-new military identification card, which will be the only ID you will need for the rest of your basic training stay. This ID may very well be the only form of identification you'll need for the rest of your time in the military.

However, you'll need your civilian ID for the first couple of days of basic training and in order to prove that you're who you're supposed to be in order to receive your military ID.

## Important paperwork

Your recruiter will give you a packet containing your important military enlistment paperwork, including your enlistment contract, which you'll turn in to the administrative folks when you arrive at basic. However, you also need to remember to bring other important paperwork with you as well, if you want to take advantage of the available military pay programs:

- ✔ **Banking information:** Everyone in the military is paid by direct deposit. In order to be paid, you need your bank account number, and — if it's a checking account — the bank routing number. (Both are on your checks, so bringing a blank check with you is a good idea.)

- ✔ **Marriage certificate and children's birth certificates:** Everyone in the military receives a *base pay,* a minimal monthly pay amount just for being in the military. Those who have dependents (spouse and/or children) are entitled to additional pay, such as a housing allowance and family separation allowance ($250 per month!). In order to receive this extra pay, you must prove you have legal dependents.

   Your spouse and children over the age of 13 are also entitled to obtain a military dependent identification card. If entitled, you fill out the paperwork for it at basic training, but you'll need proof of your relationship. The military ID card entitles them to enter military bases, receive military medical care benefits, and shop at the BX/PX and on-base commissary.

- ✔ **College transcripts:** If you have any college, you may be entitled to a higher enlistment rank (and therefore more pay). Your recruiter should take care of required paperwork to upgrade your rank, but the ball has been known to drop in the past. If you have a certified copy of your college transcripts with you, you can easily fix any errors you may have with your rank-paperwork while in-processing at basic training.

   If you're entitled to advanced enlistment rank due to other factors, such as JROTC, or the Girl Scout Gold Award, you'll want to bring proof of these achievements as well.

## Civilian clothes

It may be a few days after arrival before you receive your first military uniform issue. During that time, you'll need something to wear, but don't overdo it. Casual clothing to last two or three days should be sufficient. If something happens and your first uniform issue is delayed, washers and dryers are available in basic, so you can keep your civilian clothing supply going.

Make sure that your civilian clothing is noncontroversial — no "word" shirts. What may be funny or entertaining to you may not be funny to others (including your training instructors). You most certainly don't want to wear a shirt that says, "No Nukes" or "Ban all War," in front of people who have dedicated their lives to combat (especially when those people have the power to make your life miserable, if they take a dislike to you).

Training instructors like to give nicknames to recruits who stand out from the crowd during the first days of basic training. While many times these nicknames are based on doing or saying something stupid, they are just as often based on first impressions derived from your appearance. These nicknames tend to stick throughout the entire basic training period, even if they no longer apply. You don't want to go through the entire basic training period known as "Pacifist" or "Wimp," based on what you chose to wear during the first day of basic, do you?

When I went through basic, we had a guy who showed up with extremely long hair. For the entire six weeks, he was called "hippy." I bet he wished he had spent a couple of bucks on a haircut before he shipped out.

## Keepsakes: Favorite family photos

Sorry, you won't be able to plaster the walls with pictures of your girlfriend or boyfriend. However, a very small (about 4 inches by 4 inches) photo album is perfectly okay (usually kept in a locker). There will be times during basic training that you feel ready to give up, to throw it all away. Taking a few minutes in the evening to look at your loved ones can do a lot to help you remember why you decided to take this plunge in the first place. In fact, I recommend asking your family members to send current photos to you while you're in training. Advise your girlfriend, however, that others may see these photos, so make sure they're appropriate.

Photos in your wallet would be even better because that way they would be with you at any time the drill instructor gives you a few minutes breather between marching, push-ups, and shooting rifles.

I recently had a person ask me whether he could bring his journal with him to basic. He had written in this journal every single day since he was 10 years old. I told him that it was certainly allowed, and he may even have a few minutes of spare time each evening to write in it. However, he needed to remember that everything you have in basic training is subject to inspection by your drill instructors at any time, and some drill instructors may find it humorous to share interesting tidbits of information with other members of your unit. I advised this person to leave the journal at home, send his daily experiences home via letter, and then catch up the diary after graduation.

## Bible or religious medallion

The only things you're allowed to read in military basic training are the basic training study materials issued to you by your training instructor (I'm sorry, but this book doesn't count) and religious reading material, such as the Bible or Koran. I have to warn you, however, that your available reading time will be extremely limited. What little time you have will probably be taken up by studying your basic training manuals for the upcoming test. (It seems like a test is always coming up shortly.)

Religious medallions are also permitted, as long as they can be worn without being seen (such as under the shirt).

## Calling card

In basic training, you'll get one mandatory phone call to family and loved ones. By mandatory, I mean that the military has to give you the opportunity to call, not that you have to make the call, if you don't want to.

The first call is during the first week after arrival. The purpose of this call is to let your loved ones know that you arrived safely and are doing well and to give them your new mailing address.

Warn your loved ones before you leave that you won't sound well during this first phone call, for a couple of reasons. First, your voice will be shaking: You're scared every second during the first week that your training instructor will see you doing something wrong and will yell at you.

When my twin daughters attended basic training, I was prepared for their shaky, frightened voices over the phone, having gone through it myself . . . I thought.

Three days after they left home, the first phone call finally came. My little babies could barely speak, their voices were shaking so much. They had just enough time to tell me they were okay (I could hear they were not) and give me their basic training mailing address. Then I heard someone yelling at them that their time was up. The whole call lasted about three minutes.

I was very upset when I hung up the phone. I was ready to jump on the next plane and teach some military drill instructor about the consequences of making my babies upset. Fortunately, cooler heads prevailed, and my family tied me to a chair.

Months later, during their basic training graduation, I brought this reaction up to my daughters. Both of them laughed and told me I was imagining things — that they were never scared. I know better.

Recruits are allowed very, very little time for that first phone call home — only about three minutes. This is just about enough time for them to spit out their new mailing address and say they love you, and that's about it.

The second mandatory phone call is a week or so before graduation. The purpose of this call is to give loved ones information about the graduation events and invite friends and family to the big moment.

All other phone calls during basic training are earned — not by the individual, but by everyone in the basic training unit. You may be the best soldier since Kubla Khan, but if the rest of your basic training unit messes up, there will be no phone calls home.

You can choose to call home collect, but that process uses up precious minutes of your available calling time. Plus, what if nobody wants to talk to you and refuses to accept the charges? Embarrassing.

Most troops elect to use a calling card. You can choose to purchase a calling card at the BX/PX during your initial shopping trip there, but you may not get the best rates, and why spend your available paycheck on something that you can bring with you? Get a card with lots of minutes. While you may not use them all during basic training, you'll have opportunities to use them later. (I can guarantee your cellphone probably won't work if you're on a Navy/Coast Guard ship or deployed to someplace in the desert.)

## Essential toiletries

While you'll be given the opportunity for a shopping trip to the BX/PX, it may not happen until a couple of days after arrival. You'll want a few days' supply of essential toiletries, such as shampoo, toothpaste, toothbrush, razors/shaver, shaving cream, deodorant, dental floss, and so on.

Don't bring more than a few days worth, unless you use some special brand or type that you just can't live without. In basic training, everything is subject to inspection, and that means everything must be kept operating-room clean. Before your BX/PX shopping trip, your drill instructors will pass out experienced advice about what brands/type of items are the easiest to keep clean and are available in the BX/PX. Listen to their advice — they've been there, done that.

## Cellphone use in Army basic

Cellphones in Army basic training? Yes. Under a standard program, some Army basic combat training platoons are allowing soldiers to call home on their cellphones.

Don't get too excited. That doesn't mean you get to carry your cellphone with you throughout basic training. Cellphones are kept by the drill sergeants and given out only during the times when phone calls home would otherwise be authorized.

Benefits to the soldiers? Well, first of all, most cellphone plans include free long distance, so you don't have to worry about calling collect or purchasing a calling card. Second, you can call home immediately (when authorized), instead of waiting in long lines at the available pay phones. That leaves you extra time to talk. Third, all your important phone numbers are usually in your cellphone's memory, so you don't have to memorize numbers, write them down on a scrap of paper carried in your wallet, or keep a phone number notebook.

For the other branches, cellphones are still not allowed during basic training. However, I think this rule will probably change — it just makes sense. One reason the US Military is so successful is that it's willing to take full advantage of new technology. Most adult members of society carry a cellphone these days. New military recruits generally have a cellphone with them all the time, following basic training. Some military members even use cellphones to call home from overseas assignments. There have even been cases of military members in Iraq and Afghanistan using personal cellphones to pass on vital military information to their commands, when military communication means failed.

## *Shower shoes*

Shower shoes (flip-flops) are mandatory in basic training. Because a lot of people are living in a confined space, you're not allowed to run around barefoot, spreading your evil germs all over the nice, clean floor. If you don't have shower shoes, you'll be running around the barracks in your underwear and combat boots, which looks sort of silly.

Shower shoes are usually readily available at the BX/PX, but why take chances? When I went to basic training, the BX was out of my size, and my training instructor told me I would just have to wear my boots. Fortunately, another basic trainee had brought two pair with him (I still don't know why) and offered to give one pair to me.

Make sure that your shower shoes are conservative, preferably plain white, black, or gray. Military basic training is no place to be running around with pink or blue shower shoes displaying images of Scooby Doo. I guarantee that would get you a nickname.

# Items to Avoid Bringing

You're not going away to college, and you're certainly not going on a vacation to the tropics. Certain items have no place at military basic training, and you should leave them at home.

## Excess civilian clothes

You don't get to wear civilian clothes at basic, except for the first couple of days or so, before you get your first uniform issue. Don't bring more than two or three days' worth. You don't need civilian clothes, you can't wear them, and you won't have the storage space at basic to keep them. You'll just wind up mailing them home (at your expense).

## Alcohol and illegal drugs

Don't laugh. Every year or so, somebody tries to bring alcohol or illegal drugs. They always, always get caught. I guarantee there are no hiding places in basic training that the drill instructors don't know about.

When I went through basic, someone (I don't know how) was able to sneak in some paste wax for shining shoes. We were supposed to use liquid wax because, apparently, paste wax is flammable (although in 23 years of service, I've never seen someone's boot burst into flames). In any event, our squadron thought we were pretty smart and hid the paste wax above one of the removable ceiling tiles. It wasn't even there a full day when the drill instructor walked in, called us all to attention, walked directly under our wax-tile, and poked at it with his baton. All that paste wax came crashing to the floor, and he simply looked at us and said, "Nothing, absolutely nothing happens in this squad bay without me knowing about it." The next seven days were not pleasant.

## Electronics

Except for certain Army locations, which are allowing cellphone use for recruits, leave your cellphones, palm-top computers, and hand-held video games at home. You can't keep them. You'll either wind up mailing them home (at your expense), or they'll be locked away for the duration of your stay.

## Excess money

Shortly after arrival, you'll be issued a debit card, which is used to purchase anything you need during basic training. The amount you spend is deducted from your first military pay check.

To discourage theft, you're required, in most cases, to record the serial numbers of all of your paper money in your basic training notebook and keep the list up-to-date at all times. This requirement is just another opportunity to make a small error and give a drill instructor the chance to use you as an example of what happens when you don't follow the rules to the letter.

## Other no-no's

Your recruiter will give you an official list of what to bring with you to basic training. If it's not on the list, don't bring it. It's that simple. These lists are continually updated by the drill instructors who will actually be in charge of you. If the official list conflicts with something in this chapter, go with the official list. Don't try to tell your drill instructor, "But Rod Powers said . . ." She just won't care. It's amazing but true that some people in life don't care a bit about what I say, and drill instructors fall into that group.

Take care with what you pack. One of the very first things that is going to happen when you first meet your training instructor is that he is going to dump out your precious belongings in front of everyone, and then he and his buddy instructors are going to make fun of anything "unusual" you may have brought — even items as innocent as a book or magazine ("What do you think this is, a library? Answer me!") If you bring a book or magazine to read on the flight, leave it in the reception area of the airport. Try to pack clothes that have no writing, slogans, or pictures on them. This includes that neat Air Force t-shirt the recruiter gave you. ("How dare you wear a shirt that indicates you're a member of my beloved Air Force? You have *not* earned the right to wear that yet, and you probably never will. Answer me!")

# Chapter 11

# One Last Trip to the Military Entrance Processing Station (MEPS)

· · · · · · · · · · · · · · · · · · · · · · · · · · · · · · · · · · · · · · · · · · · · · · · · · · · · · ·

*In This Chapter*

▶ Making your way to MEPS

▶ Completing a final checkout

▶ Flying away to basic training

▶ Getting paid

· · · · · · · · · · · · · · · · · · · · · · · · · · · · · · · · · · · · · · · · · · · · · · · · · · · · · ·

*Y*ou can't just leave your warm, comfy bed at home and hop directly onto a plane bound for basic training. First, you have to make one more trip to the Military Entrance Processing Station (MEPS).

You remember MEPS. It's that place where you spent a 10- to12-hour day, standing and waiting most of the time. It's that evil place where doctors made you do strange things, such as the duck-walk, where you spent several hours taking a written test (ASVAB), and where that guy told you that you couldn't have your first choice of military jobs, for one reason or another.

Now, the good news. This trip to MEPS will be totally different. This time, you've already passed the ASVAB test, and you've already been accepted for a military job or enlistment program. All that's left is to finalize things and give you another medical exam. I can hear you groaning, but this medical exam is quite different.

## Getting the Scoop on MEPS

Officially, MEPS is the Military Entrance Processing Station, but nobody ever calls it that. Everyone calls it MEPS. MEPS is managed by the U.S. Army, but it's not owned by the Army. It's owned by the Department of Defense and the

Department of Homeland Security. MEPS' job is to ensure that you're mentally and physically eligible for military service, according to military regulations and federal law.

Other people who work at MEPS aren't actually a part of the MEPS command. These recruiting personnel are in charge of your actual enlistment process. They work directly for your service's recruiting command (just like your recruiter does), not for the folks at MEPS. They just share the same building as the MEPS folks because the process works easier that way.

# Getting the Medical Okay

Another physical? Yes, but not to worry — this one is much, much simpler than the physical you went through the last time you visited this puzzle palace. Like the last time, you will complete a bunch of medical history forms, and you'll see the MEPS doctor. However, this time, MEPS is concerned only about medical problems that have surfaced since your last visit to MEPS. You don't have to remember what childhood diseases you've had or the name of your doctor when you were in the third grade. All you have to do is remember what medical conditions you've had since your last visit, which was probably less than eight months ago.

If you have had a medical condition (especially a serious one) occur since your last MEPS visit, make sure that you tell your recruiter about it; don't surprise everyone by bring it up for the first time at MEPS. Many medical conditions require a waiver to be issued by the recruiting command, and this process can take several days. If you tell your recruiter in advance, then she can get the ball rolling, reducing the chance of any delays in getting to basic training.

# Signing a New Contract

First, almost immediately upon arrival at MEPS, if you enlisted for full-time active duty, you'll be discharged from the military Delayed Enlistment Program (DEP). Enjoy your first military discharge while it lasts (about 30 seconds!). You'll immediately sign a new enlistment contract, placing you on full-time active duty. If you enlisted in the Reserves or the National Guard, you don't have to be discharged and then enlist all over again.

If you're enlisting on active duty, this second enlistment contract is the one that counts. It doesn't matter a hill of beans if you were promised an enlistment bonus or a specific job in your DEP contract. The only contract that the military will honor is the final enlistment contract.

Make sure that your final enlistment contract includes everything the recruiter promised you. This contract is the one the military will enforce, not the DEP contract, and certainly not any verbal promises given by your recruiter. I should mention that this contract includes only the items that are special for your enlistment, such as enlistment rank, guaranteed assignment, enlistment period, guaranteed military job, extra college money, or enlistment bonus. It does not include entitlements that are guaranteed under federal law, such as your military pay amount (it's based on rank), G.I. Bill education benefits, or shopping and medical benefits. Everyone in the military is entitled to these benefits, so they won't be in the contract.

# Taking the Final Oath

After the paperwork is all done, you'll be sent back to the main waiting room to wait. You may have to wait here for awhile, while they get everyone else through the process.

Then it's time to gather all your family and friends, if they came with you, and proceed back to the auditorium to swear in. Again, if you previously enlisted in the Reserves or National Guard, you won't be swearing in again. You swore in (for the final time) the last time you were at MEPS.

While your family and friends are certainly invited to this final swearing-in ceremony, they're not welcome to hang out with you during the rest of the process. They'll have to kill time in the waiting room or coffee shop (if available) until it's time to swear in.

At some point, a commissioned officer will enter and give a little speech. He will probably tell you (and everyone else) what a big step this is in your life, and not to waste it, and so on, and so on.

Then, he will ask you to raise your right hand, and repeat these words:

> *I, (NAME), do solemnly swear (or affirm) that I will support and defend the Constitution of the United States against all enemies, foreign and domestic; that I will bear true faith and allegiance to the same; and that I will obey the orders of the President of the United States and the orders of the officers appointed over me, according to regulations and the Uniform Code of Military Justice. So help me God.*

Congratulations. You're now in the U.S. Military. You're subject to legal orders and entitled to military pay and benefits. In other words, as the song goes, "You're in the Army now. You're not behind a plow."

From now on, if you're early, you're on time. If you're on time, you're late. If you're late, you're dead.

# Saying Farewell to Family and Friends

If your family and friends accompanied you on this final MEPS trip, after the swearing-in is a good time to say goodbye because you won't see them again for a few months.

At most MEPS locations, you can sit with your loved ones at a coffee shop where you can spend your last minutes before you ship out to basic.

Make sure that you don't leave MEPS or lose track of time. The MEPS recruiting personnel should have told you what time to be out front to catch the bus or shuttle to the airport. Don't miss that bus or shuttle.

Your friends and family are not allowed to ride with you on the bus or shuttle, so this last time together is a good time to say your final goodbyes. When you arrive at the airport, you'll go through airport security to the departure gate immediately, so I don't recommend that your family and friends go to the airport on their own because they won't be able to spend any time with you there.

# Figuring Out Who's in Charge

Who's in charge of this goat-rope? Quite possibly, you are. Before you leave MEPS, each service branch will appoint one recruit to be in charge of all other recruits of your branch, until you arrive at your basic training location. The person-in-charge is responsible to watch everyone in their group, to make sure that they don't get into trouble, and to make sure that they get on the flight they're supposed to.

Actually, I don't recommend volunteering for this duty. First of all, you're babysitting a bunch of kids, many of whom have never been away from home. Trying to get them where they need to be at the time they need to be there can be a daunting task.

If someone gets misplaced, you can be sure that you will be the very first person in your basic training unit to get chewed out upon arrival, even if you did everything right. It doesn't sound fair, but welcome to basic training!

Finally, if everything does go right, don't expect any kudos or even a "good job" by anyone. Once you arrive at basic, nobody will know, or even care, that you were the person who was responsible for the group. This responsibility will be the first of many thankless jobs you will experience in the military. Serving in the military is about service, not about making you feel warm and fuzzy.

# Leaving on a Jet Plane

Finally, at the airport, they'll call your flight, and it's time to board the plane. If you've made it to this point, give yourself a pat on the back. Unless your aircraft gets hijacked, or over-run with rabid squirrels, you've got it made. Next stop — military basic training.

The military branches have several basic training locations. Your destination depends on several factors, including the branch you joined, the location of your MEPS, your sex, and even what military job you're going to do.

## Army basic combat training locations

The Army has five basic training locations. The Army plans to change this number to four. In many cases, where you go depends on what your Army job is going to be. For many military jobs, the Army has a program called OSUT, or one-station unit training, which combines basic training and Army job school all into one course. Locations are

- **Fort Jackson:** Columbia, South Carolina
- **Fort Knox:** Louisville, Kentucky (armor OSUT). The Army plans to close basic training at Fort Knox, effective October 1, 2011, and move armor OSUT to Fort Benning in Georgia.
- **Fort Leonard Wood:** Waynesville, Missouri (combat engineers, military police, and chemical warfare OSUT)
- **Fort Sill:** Lawton, Oklahoma
- **Fort Benning:** Columbus, Georgia (infantry OSUT)

## Air Force basic training locations

The Air Force has only one basic training location: Lackland Air Force Base, located in San Antonio, Texas.

### Navy basic training locations

Like the Air Force, the Navy has only one location for boot camp: The Great Lakes Naval Training Center, which is located on the western shore of Lake Michigan, halfway between Chicago and Milwaukee.

### Marine Corps basic training locations

Two locations turn men into Marines:

- The Recruit Training Depot at Parris Island, South Carolina
- The Recruit Training Depot at San Diego, California

Where you go depends largely upon where you enlist. Those who enlist west of the Mississippi will likely go through boot camp in San Diego, while those in the east will attend at Parris Island. There is only one boot camp to turn women into Marines — Parris Island.

### Coast Guard basic training locations

Like the Air Force and the Navy, the Coast Guard has only one location for enlisted boot camp: Cape May, New Jersey.

## Figuring Out How Long You'll Be at Basic Training

Not all military basic trainings are created equally, and how long you'll have drill instructors yelling at you depends on your service branch:

- Army Basic Combat Training (BCT) lasts nine weeks. This length of time doesn't count time spent in reception (see Chapter 12), nor does it count the time spent for job training if you attend an OSUT unit, which combines basic training and job training into one combined course.

✔ Air Force basic training at Lackland AFB in Texas is eight weeks, plus one week of in-processing, called *zero week*. Until recently, Air Force basic training was only six weeks, the shortest basic training of any of the military branches. However, the Air Force recently redesigned their basic training program, tacking on two extra weeks in the process.

✔ Navy basic training is seven weeks, plus one week at the beginning called *processing week,* which isn't officially part of basic training, but because you will still have drill instructors yelling at you and telling you what to do, it might as well be.

✔ The Marine Corps has the longest basic training — 12 weeks, not including 4 days of in-processing time.

✔ Counting the half week you spend in *forming* (in-processing), you'll spend a total of seven and a half weeks in Coast Guard basic training at Cape May, the shortest basic training of all the services.

---

# When do I get paid?

You're in the military and entitled to receive military pay at the time you take the final oath at MEPS. However, don't expect anyone to hand you any money yet. In order to get paid, the military has to establish your military pay records, and that won't happen until you in-process during the first few days of basic training.

Military members are paid twice each month — on the 1st and 15th of each month. You get one-half of your monthly pay on the 1st and the second half on the 15th.

Remember, this is the government, so getting paid isn't instantaneous. It takes a few days for the gears to grind. If you arrive at basic training before the 10th of the month, you'll get paid on the 15th. If you arrive after the 10th of the month, you won't see your first paycheck until the 1st of the following month, but it will include all pay you're entitled to, as of that date.

Everyone in the military is entitled to base pay, which depends on your rank and the number of years of military service you have had. If you have family members (dependents), you're also entitled to receive a monthly housing allowance. The exact amount depends on where your family members live. Also if you have dependents, you'll receive a monthly separation allowance any time you've been separated from your family for longer than 30 days.

You can view specific pay amounts at `http://usmilitary.about.com/od/ militarypaycharts/a/paycharts. htm`.

---

# Chapter 12

# Arriving at the Base

. . . . . . . . . . . . . . . . . . . . . . . . . . . . . . . . . . . . . . . . . . . . . . .

## In This Chapter

▶ Getting from the airport to basic

▶ Meeting with basic training instructors

▶ Playing instructor games

▶ Getting a "good" night's sleep

. . . . . . . . . . . . . . . . . . . . . . . . . . . . . . . . . . . . . . . . . . . . . . .

*A*rriving at base is the moment you've been waiting for. It's the point where your life, as you know it, is now over. From this moment on, everything you do, everything you say, and sometimes (it seems) everything you think, belongs to the military.

Basic training drill instructors aren't really psychic. (I don't think.) However, they've seen a thousand kids just like you, and they know how you feel. They know how you think, and often they will head you off at the pass. If you're hungry, they know it. If you're tired, they know it. If you're scared, they know it (and will take advantage of it for their purposes).

What is their purpose? You may be tempted to believe that their purpose in life is to make you miserable. While they do a very good job at this, that's not their goal. Their goal is to "knock the civilian out of you." What you say, how you think, how you act, is no longer your business. It's now the business of the United States Military, and — through them — your drill instructors.

Although the Army calls their drill instructors drill sergeants (and each branch uses a different term for its drill instructors), I refer to them as drill instructors throughout this book.

# The Big Arrival

Your plane will land at a designated airport, and you'll be instructed to pick up your checked bags (if any) and make your way to a designated area. This place is usually in the airport, such as the USO (United Service Member's Organization) Lounge, where a noncommissioned officer will meet you. Here, you'll wait until the basic training bus arrives. Your wait may be a few minutes, or it may be a couple of hours. The USO attendant isn't going to call for the bus until enough new recruits are waiting to fill it up.

# Bus to Basic: In-Processing

When your bus to basic arrives, you'll meet a drill instructor for the first time. This person probably won't be "your" drill instructor, just one who has been detailed to get the new recruits to the base and give them a brief introduction to their new lifestyle.

This meeting will not be pleasant. Don't expect the instructor to walk up to you, shake your hand, and kindly welcome you to the military. She will march smartly up to your group, stop, and then suddenly begin screaming at you to get in line at the door. A few people in your group will not move fast enough to satisfy the instructor and will be rewarded with her personal attention (not pretty).

After everyone is lined up, the instructor will give a short speech, welcoming you to basic training. It doesn't really matter what the instructor says at this point, what she really means is, "You're mine now, maggot!"

After you arrive at basic training and the drill instructor is tired of playing games (see the sidebar), you'll be lined up in front of an in-processing building.

In-processing is nothing more than turning in the packet your recruiter gave you and filling out around 7,000,000 forms. Some believe the military runs on its stomach, but I firmly believe it runs on paperwork.

In the military, your Social Security number is your military serial number. In basic training, you'll write your Social Security number on every single form you complete. It's a good idea to have this number memorized before you leave for basic training.

# Games instructor(s) like to play

Many instructors like to start playing their games right there at the airport.

**Bus boarding:** One favorite instructor game is called, "get on the bus/get off the bus." When you are ordered to get on the bus, you're expected to board the bus quickly and quietly and sit down without hesitation or confusion. Of course, it never works this way, so the instructor may (loudly) order everyone to get off the bus.

After everyone is back in formation, the instructor spends a few minutes describing your bad habits and the bad habits of your ancestors and then orders everyone to board the bus again. This game continues until everyone can board the bus quickly, quietly, and efficiently.

**Entering/exiting the barracks:** You probably won't get to play this game until a little later in the day. At some point during this first day, in-processing will be complete, and it will be time to retire to the barracks to unpack and enjoy a good night's sleep.

Your group is expected to enter the barracks quietly, quickly, and efficiently. I can guarantee that won't happen the first time. So, the instructor will order everyone out, line them up, and give everyone the opportunity to try it again. This game continues until the instructor is satisfied.

Now, this doesn't sound too bad, except when you realize that you're carrying your luggage (aren't you glad you packed light?) and that many barracks' bays are on the fourth floor (sorry, no elevators in basic training).

**Fire drill:** This game is the same as the entering/exiting the barracks game, except it usually occurs after day 1. The instructor enters the barracks, looks around for a second, and then suddenly yells, "Fire!"

Recruits must exit the barracks, quickly, quietly, and efficiently and then form up (line up in military formation) on the drill pad outside of the barracks. Repeat as necessary.

**What did you say?** Drill instructors will never pass up a chance to prove that they're smarter than you. In my experience, some drill instructors are dumber than dirt, but the rules are such that they always prove to be smarter than unseasoned recruits.

After a while, the instructor will get tired of playing games, and everyone will (finally) board the bus to basic training. This is not a tour bus. Throughout the trip, make sure that you sit still and don't talk with anyone. Remember, that nice drill instructor will be aboard as well, just looking for an opportunity to further instruct you in proper basic training etiquette.

It's important to remember at this point that this type of specialized attention only occurs during basic training. When I first arrived at basic training, I remember thinking, "Oh wow! I signed up for four years of this???" That was a scary, scary thought.

Initial in-processing will take between two and three hours. Except for Army recruits, once it's complete, you'll be turned over to your permanent drill instructor, who will take you to the barracks and get you settled in.

## Army reception

You won't start Army basic training immediately upon arrival. First, you have to wait your turn in a special program called *reception*. Believe it or not, for many, this reception is the hardest part of Army basic training. Desert Shield/Desert Storm proved that much of war for the Army is "hurry up and wait." The United States moved thousands of Army troops and tons of equipment, weapons, and ammunitions in a few weeks, and then the deployed troops waited for months and months for the first sign of action. The Reception Battalion gives you a chance to practice waiting . . . and waiting . . . and waiting. When you get bored with waiting, you'll be allowed to practice more waiting. If efficiently organized, the actual processing that goes on at the Reception Battalion would probably take 8 to 10 hours. You get to do it the Army way, however, which means doing just a little bit of "processing" each day for anywhere between one and three weeks.

The good news is that while you're at reception, the drill sergeants assigned to watch over you don't yell at you very much. At least they don't for the first half of your stay, while you're still running around everywhere wearing your official Army physical training (PT) sweats, (You won't get your uniforms until several days into processing,). It's almost as if they don't notice you until you're just about ready to depart for official boot camp. Then they seem to wake up and say to themselves, "Oh yeah . . . I'd better yell at these guys some before they leave."

There's one exception, however: the initial physical fitness test. For males, this test consists of 13 push-ups, 17 sit-ups, and a one-mile run in under 8:30. For females, the test consists of 3 push-ups, 17 sit-ups, and a one-mile run in under 10:30. If you fail this test, you'll get to spend some time at "Fat Camp," where brand-new drill sergeants get to practice on you for awhile.

# Settling In: To the Barracks You Go

After you complete your initial in-processing paperwork, you'll be told to fall in outside. At this point, unless you've joined the Army, you'll meet your real drill instructor, and he will get acquainted with you by lining you up and attempting to march you to your new barracks. This sight is rather amusing because nobody knows how to march yet. If you've joined the Army, you'll be taken over to the reception barracks and settled in there.

If you joined one of the other branches, you may be thinking to yourself, "This isn't too bad. It's only 8:00. I'll be able to get to bed early." However, you forgot about the evil ways of drill instructors.

On the way to the barracks, it's very probable that your instructor will try to get to know you by playing a few games (see "Games Instructors Like to

Play"). It's quite possible that your drill instructor may be disgusted with your first attempt at marching and decide to stop off at the drill pad to give you first lesson in drill basics.

Sooner or later, the drill instructor will get tired of playing, order everyone to enter the barracks, and tell everyone to choose a bunk (called *rack* in the Navy, Coast Guard, and Marine Corps).

Next, the drill instructor will call everyone together for *orientation.* For the next several hours, the instructor will go over basic training basics and impart important information, such as how to make your bunk (rack) in the morning, what needs to be done each morning to keep the barracks ship-shape, and how to fold your underwear correctly. Pay extremely careful attention to this briefing. You'll be using this information every single day of your basic training life.

You can watch an excellent video about how to make a proper basic training bed (with hospital corners) on my website at: `http://video.about.com/ usmilitary/How-to-Make-Military-Corners.htm`.

## *Finally, lights out*

Finally, just when you think you can't keep your eyes open any longer, your drill instructor will tell everyone to hit the rack. It's now 3 or 4 a.m.

After the drill instructor shuts off the lights and leaves the room, don't waste time gossiping with your new squad-mates. Before you know it (around 5 a.m.), your drill instructor will come back in, yelling and screaming for everyone to get up, get dressed, and get their butts on the drill pad.

You never exit the barracks unless your bunk is properly made and the area around your bunk is neat, clean, and orderly. This first morning will be used as an example because not everyone will think about making their bunk neatly after only two hours of sleep. I can guarantee everyone will be yelled at and ordered back to the barracks to do the job right.

Many instructors like to throw a tantrum at this point, running around the barracks, ripping apart bunks, taking your clothing out of the drawer, and throwing them around, while screaming throughout the process. Don't get scared — the drill instructor hasn't lost his mind. They learned this routine in drill instructor school.

## A little drill in the morning

This first morning will probably be taken up with drill practice. That's what the military often calls marching. I can guarantee your drill instructor was not impressed by your marching abilities the night before and will be anxious to fix that problem right away.

You can get a head start about the basics of drill by taking a look at Chapter 9.

## Chow down

After a couple of hours of drill practice, your drill instructor will figure that you've finally learned enough so that she can march you to the chow hall without embarrassment. The chow hall (excuse me, military dining facility) is very much like the cafeteria where you ate lunch in high school. It serves nutritionally balanced meals at least three times per day. When you finish basic training, you can also get snack food, such as hamburgers and hot dogs (with fries) in the chow hall, but those choices won't be available to you in basic training.

The chow hall is set up very much like a buffet. You move down the line, adding food items to your tray as you choose. At basic training chow, you can take whatever you want and how much you want.

You would think the chow hall would be a pleasant experience. However, the chow hall is a favorite place for other instructors to sit and mess with the recruits, especially the new ones. It's almost like they have a contest to see who can rattle the new recruits the most. Most basic training graduates I've talked to list the chow hall experience as their most stressful experience of basic training.

## Settling into the routine

After chow, and for the rest of the week, there will be more instruction. You'll attend some classroom training, but most of it will be direct instruction from your drill instructor about barracks standards, drill (of course), barracks rules and cleanliness, discipline, and — of course — physical fitness.

# Shots, Dental, and Drug Testing, Oh My

The doctors at MEPS certified that you were well. However, the military wants to make you "weller," in the way of giving you vaccinations, fixing your teeth, and making sure that you're drug free.

## Shots: You get 'em whether you need 'em or not

During the first week, you'll get more vaccinations than you've gotten in your entire life. Military members live in close quarters, and they're subject to deployment to anywhere in the world. Some of these places harbor diseases that you've never even heard of, and a military that is sick in bed isn't much good.

If you bring accurate and legible shot records from home, you may be able to avoid some shots. Make sure that the records are signed by a doctor.

Table 12-1 details the vaccinations you'll receive during the first week of basic training.

| Table 12-1 | Military Basic Training Vaccinations |
|---|---|
| *Immunizing Agent* | *Remarks* |
| Adenovirus (Type I) | Given in basic training to all new recruits after October 2006. |
| Adenovirus, Types 4 and 7 | Air Force recruits receive adenovirus vaccination only when there is evidence of active disease transmission. Coast Guard Recruits receive it only when specifically directed by the Coast Guard Commandant. Army, Navy, and Marine Corps recruits do receive this vaccination at basic training. |
| Influenza (Flu Shot) | Navy and Marine Corps officer and enlisted accessions receive the influenza vaccine year-round in basic training. Other service recruits receive this shot in basic only during the designated flu season (October – March). |

*(continued)*

**Table 12-1** *(continued)*

| Immunizing Agent | Remarks |
| --- | --- |
| Measles, Mumps, and Rubella | Measles, mumps, and rubella (MMR) is administered to all recruits regardless of prior history. |
| Meningococcal | Quadrivalent meningococcal vaccine (containing A, C, Y, and W-135 polysaccharide antigens) is administered on a one-time basis to recruits. |
| Polio | A single dose of trivalent Oral Poliovirus Vaccine (OPV) is administered to all enlisted accessions. |
| Tetanus-diphtheria | A series of tetanus-diphtheria (Td) vaccinations is given to all recruits lacking a reliable history of prior immunization. |

## Open wide: Dental checks

You'll undergo a complete dental exam during the first week of military basic training. However, unless you need emergency or very urgent dental work, any dental procedures will wait until after basic training. The dentist will thoroughly examine your teeth and establish a dental plan (for after basic training) to restore your teeth to perfect health.

After basic training, you'll be given dental appointments to take care of all of your dental needs. After that, you'll be scheduled for a complete military dental exam once per year.

## Drug testing in the military

The military doesn't mess around when it comes to illegal drugs. You'll undergo a urinalysis drug test within a day or two of arriving at basic training, and then you're subject to periodic (random) urine tests for the remainder of your career.

If your drug test is positive in basic training, you'll be discharged, plain and simple. If you enlisted in the Army, Navy, or Marine Corps, you have a small chance that you could apply for a waiver after one year and get back in. If you come up positive during Air Force or Coast Guard basic training, you're barred from those two services for life.

After basic training, if you test positive for drugs on any military random or medical urinalysis test, you're subject to disciplinary action, including court-martial (see Chapter 7). In fact, according to the military's No Tolerance policy regarding illegal drugs, if you test positive, you will be discharged.

# Chapter 13

# Getting Picked for a Basic Training Job

## In This Chapter

▶ Deciding whether to volunteer

▶ Mopping the floor (or telling others how to do so)

▶ Leading the way to success

▶ Getting specific about basic training jobs

*Y*ou may be tempted to think that your only job in military basic training is to find out how to be a military member. While becoming a military member is your primary duty, it probably won't be your only job.

In this chapter, I tell you everything you need to know about the jobs you'll encounter in the military basic training program.

## Discovering the Pros and Cons of Leadership Jobs

Basic training jobs fall into two broad categories: leadership jobs and other jobs. All branches select recruits to perform basic training leadership jobs. Some services also assign other wide-ranging duties to recruits in basic training.

If you want to earn one of the basic training awards (see Chapter 19), your chances are much higher if you hold (or have held) one of the basic training leadership jobs. Recruit leaders must possess or cultivate a variety of leadership and problem-solving skills. Holding a leadership position, which helps you develop those skills, is bound to impress your basic training instructors, and you'll be the first one they think of when considering names for various awards.

If you hold a basic training leadership position for longer than a week without getting fired, you're far ahead of the power curve. Basic training student leaders are in the limelight, and the instructors scrutinize every single thing they do and say. On the down side, basic training leaders are also held responsible every single time one of the other recruits screw up.

I used to think that the reason so many recruits got fired from leadership jobs in a short period of time was because the jobs are so hard, and new recruits are unlikely to have direct leadership experience and therefore probably make a lot of mistakes.

However, a basic training instructor friend of mine set me straight. Sure, the leadership jobs are challenging, and instructors give zero room for mistakes. But the primary reason so many student leaders get fired is to allow as many recruits as possible a chance to get a little leadership experience. This attitude makes sense in a "military" sort of way.

# To Volunteer or Not to Volunteer: That Is the Question

You may wonder whether you should step up and volunteer for a basic training job. And, this question is a tough one. Some drill instructors don't allow recruits to volunteer for specific basic training jobs, preferring to just assign the duties to those they think are the most suited to them. Others will happily ask for volunteers, knowing that most recruits have no idea what they're getting into. Still others will ask for volunteers, with the express intention of making sure that no recruit gets the job(s) that he is interested in.

Any way you look at it, getting assigned a basic training job that interests you, gives you important extra study time, and doesn't get you chewed out for something you didn't really do, is a crap shoot.

If the drill instructor asks for volunteers, you may want to lay low for a bit to see how he does it. If other recruits appear to be getting the job(s) they actually volunteer for, it's probably safe to raise your hand when the job(s) you like come up. On the other hand, if the drill instructor simply laughs when someone volunteers or gives them a different (undesirable) job instead, you may want to keep your hand down and your mouth shut.

Whatever you do, don't try to volunteer for a leadership job. If you do, the drill instructor will immediately label you as a kiss-up, and your chances of ever getting selected for a leadership position (or winning an award) drop to zero.

# Figuring Out How Instructors Choose Their Leaders

Different instructors have different methods for selecting recruits for the various student leadership positions. Many instructors will select recruits based on informal leadership traits they may display during the first couple of days of basic training. For example, the recruit who routinely helps out another recruit who is having problems with a particular task is likely to be an initial leadership selectee.

Other instructors will select their student leadership recruits based on prior leadership or military experience, such as high school ROTC, Boy Scouts, high school sports (especially leadership positions, such as team captain), and presidents/officers of scholastic organizations.

Still other instructors will select leaders based on age, subscribing to the theory that older recruits are more responsible, wiser, and less affected by emotional issues (maturity).

Some instructors base their selections by simply watching the recruits for the first couple of days, and selecting those who seem to have the most "on the ball."

Don't worry if you don't get selected for a leadership position right off the bat. The initial leaders are very likely to be fired within a week or so, and new leaders will be selected to replace them.

While it helps to hold a basic training leadership job in order to be chosen for an award, it's not absolutely necessary. A substantial number of recruits are selected for basic training awards without ever having held a position of responsibility during basic training.

# Looking at Leadership Jobs

You may be surprised to find out that much of the military basic training program isn't managed by the instructors, but is instead led by the students (recruits).

All the branches use recruits as student leaders during military basic training. When an instructor wants something done, he won't assign the job directly to a recruit. Instead, he will tell the recruit leader and hold him responsible for making sure that the job gets done.

The program is organized this way because it's the same way the military operates on a day-to-day basis after basic training. Four-star generals don't issue orders directly to one-stripers. Instead, the four-star tells her second-in-command what she wants done, and that individual then passes the order down the chain until it finally gets to the person who is actually going to do it.

## Army basic training leadership jobs

The Army has three leadership jobs that are assigned to recruits during basic training:

- ✓ **Platoon Leader:** The *Platoon Leader* is the recruit in charge of the day-to-day operations of the basic combat training platoon. He ensures that the barracks are kept up to standard, recruits are where they're supposed to be when they're supposed to be there, and recruits have all of their problems and issues addressed.

- ✓ **Squad Leader:** Depending on the size of the basic training platoon, between four and six recruits will be selected as *Squad Leaders.* Squad leaders are in charge of 10 to 20 recruits and work directly for the Platoon Leader, making sure that everything that needs to get done during the day actually gets done.

- ✓ **First Sergeant:** The Platoon Leader is assisted by the recruit *First Sergeant.* The First Sergeant ensures that all the Platoon Leader's instructions and requests are passed onto the Squad Leaders, and that the Squad Leaders actually get the job done. The First Sergeant is also the recruit who is responsible for ensuring that all the recruits understand and practice all the drill (marching) movements.

## Air Force basic training leadership jobs

The top student leader in an Air Force basic training flight is called the *Dorm Chief.* Dorm Chiefs report directly to the TI for everything that happens in the basic training flight.

To assist the Dorm Chief in this enormous responsibility, the flight is divided into elements, with an Element Leader" in charge of each one. The Element Leaders are responsible to the Dorm Chief to make sure that members of his element comply with orders and instructions. The bad news is that being a Dorm Chief or an Element Leader means that in addition to getting chewed out for things you do wrong, you also get the added pleasure of getting chewed out for things that members of the flight (or your element) do wrong.

The TI will also choose a flight *Guideon*. Although the Guideon is not exactly a leadership position because he doesn't get to tell people what to do, the position is very important, none the less. The Guideon carries the flight flag and marches in front of the flight. When the TI commands the flight to march to the left, the Guideon turns first, and the other members of the flight align themselves on the Guideon.

The bad thing about being the Guideon is that you have to carry the unit flag, every time your flight marches somewhere (which is most of the time). The good news is that the Guideon really stands out from the crowd. Your parents, friends, and loved ones will have no problem picking you out during the Airman's Run or graduation parade at the end of basic training.

## Navy and Coast Guard basic training leadership jobs

Recruits who have positions of authority in Navy and Coast Guard basic training are called *Recruit Petty Officers* (RPO). The Navy and Coast Guard have several RPO positions so that recruits can display and practice their leadership skills:

- ✔ **Recruit Chief Petty Officer (RCPO):** The RCPO is the top dog among recruits in the division. When the drill instructors aren't around, the RCPO is in charge. She makes sure that recruits obey all standing orders and regulations and reports any violations to the instructors. She also implements instructions or orders issued by the instructors.

- ✔ **Recruit Leading Petty Officer (RLPO):** The RLPO is the second in command among recruits. He assists the RCPO to ensure that orders are properly carried out. When the RCPO isn't available, the RLPO takes over.

- ✔ **Recruit Master at Arms (RMAA):** The RMAA is third in the line of student command. When the RCPO and RLPO aren't around, the RMAA takes over. She is also responsible for organizing and supervising the work details when it's time for the recruits to clean the division spaces.

- ✔ **Recruit Section Leaders (RSL):** RSLs are responsible for the day-to-day supervision of the recruits. Depending on the size of the division, between four and six RSLs are usually selected.

## Marine Corps basic training leadership jobs

Two recruit leadership positions are assigned to new recruits during Marine Corps basic training:

- **Guide:** Unlike the other branches, where the Guide simply marches in front of the formation to show recruits where to turn, in Marine Corps basic training, the Guide is the recruit leader, responsible for everything in the unit. When the drill instructor has something he wants the platoon to do, he tells the Guide and holds the Guide responsible for it getting done.

  Of course, like the other branches, the Guide also marches in front of the formation and carries the unit flag.

- **Squad Leader:** Depending on its size, a basic training platoon will be divided into four to six squads, with a Squad Leader in charge of each one. If the Guide wants something done, he tells one of the squad leaders, who then orders recruits in his squad to actually accomplish the task.

  The Squad Leaders are also responsible to ensure that the barracks exceed the daily cleanliness standards, before the recruits are released to go outside and form up.

# Scouting Out the Other Basic Training Jobs

In addition to leadership jobs, most of the branches also assign recruits to be responsible for day-to-day duties that are necessary to keep basic training flowing smoothly.

## Army

The Army is the only branch that doesn't seem to assign responsibility for almost every single task in basic training to specific recruits. Whereas the other branches will, for example, assign a specific recruit (or recruits) the task of washing everyone else's dirty underwear, the Army leaves such tasks up to the individual.

One nonleadership job that the Army does assign during basic training is the *CQ Runner.* The CQ Runner is the go-for for the instructor. If the instructor needs the daily schedule from the headquarters building, she'll send the CQ Runner to go and get it. If the instructor wants to know what's on the menu in the chow hall, she'll send the CQ Runner to go and find out. The CQ Runner is sort of a telephone with legs.

# Air Force

After observing the flight for a few days, the TI assign flight duties. Most TIs ask for volunteers for these duties, but some assign them using method(s) known only to themselves.

The Air Force flight duties are

- ✔ **House Mouse:** The *House Mouse* is primarily responsible for being the go-for for the TI If the TI needs something picked up from the headquarters building, she'll send the House Mouse. If the TI wants to speak to the assistant TI or the Dorm Chief, she'll send the House Mouse to fetch them.

- ✔ **Dorm Guard Monitor:** Often (but not always), the House Mouse and the *Dorm Guard Monitor* are the same person. The Dorm Guard Monitor makes and maintains the dorm guard schedule. This job is not fun job. Everyone will hate you when you schedule them for a middle-of-the-night two-hour dorm guard shift.

- ✔ **Bowling Team:** Members of the *Bowling Team* (which consists of several recruits) clean the latrine (bathroom) every morning after everyone is done with their showers. Generally, the recruits on the Bowling Team are divided into subteams, each responsible for a different area of the latrine.

- ✔ **Latrine Queen:** The *Latrine Queen* is in charge of the Bowling Team, making sure that the job is done right. If you're thinking that it's better to be in charge of cleaning the bathroom instead of actually cleaning it yourself, remember that the person in charge is the person who gets chewed out if the job is not done perfectly.

- ✔ **Laundry Team:** The *Laundry Team* (consisting of 10 to 15 recruits) gather everyone's dirty clothes each evening and hauls them downstairs to the washers/dryers to run them trough the machines. Members of the team then gather up the clean laundry and return them to their proper owners. The only good thing about this duty is that team members don't have to fold the clean clothes. The individual is responsible to fold her own clothes when the laundry team member brings it back.

✔ **Dayroom Team:** Members of the *Dayroom Team* ensure that the barracks dayroom is kept spotless. The dayroom is a large room in the dormitory used for special events, group meetings, and group classes.

✔ **Bed Aligners:** While individuals are responsible for making their own beds every morning, it's the *Bed Aligners* responsibility to ensure that all the beds are arranged in a perfect line.

✔ **Shoe Aligners:** The *Shoe Aligners* are usually the last people to exit the dormitory each morning. On their way out the door, they double-check to make sure that everyone's shoes and boots are perfectly aligned under the bunks.

✔ **Chow Runner:** The *Chow Runner* gets to announce that your flight is ready to enter the dining hall. While this job sounds easy, it's not a very desirable duty, and it's often assigned to the biggest screw-up in the flight. The reason is that the Chow Runner is the first recruit to see the other TIs who are sitting at the TI table in the chow hall, which makes him a huge target. TIs seem to hold a contest each day at chow to see which one can abuse the Chow Runners the most.

✔ **Road Guards:** If you're close to your weight limit or are having problems with the physical fitness requirements, the TI will very likely assign you as one of the flights four *Road Guards.* If you're assigned as a Road Guard, you'll get plenty of exercise. Two Road Guards march at the front of the flight, and two Road Guards march at the rear of the flight. When the flight approaches an intersection or needs to cross the street, the two front road guards step ahead to block traffic. As the flight finishes crossing the street, the two rear road guards jog up to the front of the formation and take the place of the two Road Guards who are blocking the street. Once the flight makes it all the way across, the two who are blocking the street run to take their place at the rear of the flight.

## Navy and Coast Guard

The Navy and Coast Guard use recruits to perform many day-to-day tasks that usually need to be accomplished in any large military organization. These jobs aren't called jobs or duties but rather are referred to as *billets.*

Navy and Coast Guard basic training billets are

✔ **Recruit Yeoman:** The *Recruit Yeoman* is basically the secretary of the basic training division. If the instructor needs any logs kept, notes made, or forms filled out, the job falls to this individual.

✔ **Recruit Medical Yeoman:** These recruits are responsible for assisting the RDCs in preparing and maintaining recruit medical documentation, coordinating appointments with the Medical Liaison, tracking the status of all special physicals, and attending the medical/dental brief.

✔ **Recruit Dental Yeoman:** What the Recruit Medical Yeoman does for medical issues, the *Recruit Dental Yeoman* does for dental issues.

✔ **Division Laundry Petty Officer:** The *Division Laundry Petty Officer* makes sure that laundry items are correctly processed to the cleaners and also is responsible for maintaining the division cash box and expense log, for incidental expenses.

✔ **Recruit Athletic Petty Officer:** This recruit is responsible for making sure that all the other recruits are ready for the final fitness evaluation and to lead additional fitness sessions for those who need a little extra fitness assistance.

✔ **Recruit Religious Petty Officers:** The *Recruit Religious Petty Officer* helps ensure that all recruits are given the opportunity to observe their religious beliefs. They attend a religious services briefing in order to gather information about available services to brief the other recruits. If a division has three or more recruits of the same faith, a Recruit Religious Petty Officer must be selected to represent that faith.

✔ **Recruit Mail Petty Officers:** The MPO is responsible for pickup and delivery of all mail.

✔ **Recruit Damage Control Petty Officer:** The Recruit Damage Control Petty Officer is responsible for checking and maintaining the service ability of all the fire extinguishers assigned to the recruit division.

## Marine Corps

Like the Navy and the Coast Guard, the Marine Corps calls their basic training jobs billets. You may be assigned to several billets during your stint in Marine Corp basic training:

✔ **Scribe:** The *Scribe* is the administrative assistant (secretary) for the platoon. He's responsible for scheduling medical appointments and doing any paperwork necessary for the platoon.

✔ **Artist:** In each platoon, the drill instructor will seek out the most artistically talented to perform the duties of the *platoon artist.* This individual will design the platoon's guideon (flag) for the motivational run.

- ✔ **Lay Reader:** This individual is the religious leader for the platoon. He will lead other recruits in prayer at night and be available to council them about their religious views.

- ✔ **Gear Locker Recruit:** The *Gear Locker Recruit* is responsible for organizing the platoon's cleaning supplies, making sure that all supplies are accounted for, and requisitioning new supplies when needed.

- ✔ **Laundry Recruits:** *Laundry Recruits* ensure that an adequate supply of laundry detergent is always available in the laundry room and that recruits are scheduled for appropriate "laundry times" each week.

- ✔ **Knowledge Recruit:** These are usually the eggheads in the platoon. Their primary job is to assist other recruits with study. Often, this duty is given to those with prior military experience or ROTC classes.

# Part IV

# Basic Training Life, Branch by Branch

"Oh, this? It's just a little souvenir my son brought back from Basic Training."

# In this part . . .

While each military basic training program has the same purpose — to turn you into a disciplined member of the U.S. Military — they all go about it a little bit differently.

In this part, you find out what to expect during your time in basic training at each branch. I describe the details in-depth in each branch's very own chapter.

If you like to be in the know, then you're in the right place!

# Chapter 14

# Army Basic Combat Training

*F*inally the day will arrive when you will leave the Army basic combat training reception battalion (see Chapter 12), and your real basic training experience will begin.

Reception gave you a (very small) taste of Army basic training life. Now the Army will bump it up about 7,000 notches. You may have gotten a small sense of relief in reception, thinking this was what Army basic combat training was all about. You ain't seen nothing yet.

# Red Phase: Training Week 1 Through Week 3

Officially, the Army separates the Army basic combat training into three phases. The first phase is called *Red Phase,* and it includes the first three weeks of Army basic combat training. The second phase is called *White Phase* and also lasts for three weeks. The final three-week phase is called *Blue Phase*.

If you get confused, simply remember the red, white, and blue of the American flag.

Weeks 1 through 3, called the Red Phase, is best characterized by a term known as *total control*. Total control is where the soldiers only do what they're told to do by their drill sergeants — nothing less, nothing more.

While the Army actually likes initiative and innovation, drill sergeants hate it (at least during the first three weeks). The first few weeks of basic training is definitely not the time to find a better way of doing things. Soldiers arrive to the basic training unit from the reception battalion and are immediately immersed into an environment where every move they make is scrutinized by the drill sergeant.

## Meeting your real drill sergeant

Finally the day will arrive when you will be told to pack up all your gear and form up on the drill pad with a bunch of other folks who have been waiting with you in reception.

This occasion is when you'll meet, probably for the first time, the drill sergeant who will be in charge of every aspect of your life for the next several weeks. Describing this first meeting is hard because no two Army drill sergeants do it the same way. Perhaps your drill sergeant will greet you with one or more of the games that drill instructors like to play. Maybe your drill sergeant will decide that the best way to get to know you would be to have you drop your bags on the drill pad and go for a little run (just three or four miles). Or, perhaps calisthenics on the drill pad may be more his style. In any event, the drill sergeant will be using the opportunity to scope the group out, to see what he has been given to work with.

First impressions last a long, long time. Your new drill sergeant will be using this opportunity to gauge your abilities and attitude.

Although some of the other branches want their recruits to address instructors as sir or ma'am, don't try this with an Army drill sergeant unless you want to witness a one-hour tirade (shouted, of course) about how he "works for a living." Said tirade is normally followed by the unfortunate sir-sayer demonstrating the definition of work. The correct way to address an Army drill sergeant is as *drill sergeant*, such as "Yes, Drill Sergeant" or "No, Drill Sergeant," shouted at the top of your lungs.

## Training for physical fitness

The Army calls their fitness program the *Army Physical Readiness Program*. The official program actually consists of several different phases, but in Army basic combat training, you only have to worry about the toughening phase. Sounds a little scary, doesn't it?

The Army has released a brand-new fitness manual designed for Army fitness instructors to help get troops into shape. The manual is TC 3-22.20, Army Physical Readiness Program, and you can find it (in PDF format) at several places on the Internet.

In the toughening phase, you'll become an expert with jumping, landing, climbing, lunging, bending, reaching, and lifting. The toughening phase lasts throughout Army basic combat training and is designed to turn you into a lean, mean, fighting machine. The following programs are assigned to your regimen five to six times per week in variation:

- **Preparation drill (PD):** You perform this drill as a warm-up. It consists of ten general stretching activities, such as lunges, windmills, jumps, body twists, and push-ups.

- **4 for the core (4C):** These four exercises are designed to stabilize and strengthen the pelvis, lower spine, and abdomen. They consist of the bent leg raise, side bridge, back bridge, and quadraplex.

- **Hip stability drill (HSD):** These five exercises train your hip and upper thigh areas. Exercise one is the lateral leg raise, followed by a medial leg raise, into a bent leg lateral leg raise, followed by a single leg tuck, and ending with the single-leg-over leg raise.

- **Conditioning drills 1 and 2 (CD 1 and CD 2):** Conditioning drills stimulate proper balance, strength, and coordination. These exercises generally consist of one-leg push-ups, jumps, the V-up, the mountain climber, and the leg tuck-and-twist.

- **Climbing drill 1 (CL 1):** These activities consist of exercises performed on a high bar or climbing bars. This drill develops upper body and trunk strength and mobility while manipulating body weight off the ground.

- **Strength-training circuit (STC):** This circuit consists of various sequenced climbing and strength training exercises performed in a designated time.

- **Push-up and sit-up drill (PSD):** You do 30 to 60 second sets each of alternating push-ups and sit-ups during this drill to improve muscular strength and endurance.

- **30:60s and 60:120s:** You're required to do six or eight repetitions of speed running in 30 or 60 seconds, with recovery walking in 60 to 120 seconds.

- **300-yard shuttle run (SR):** This run enables you to repeatedly sprint with sustained agility after changing direction (basically running in circles).

- **Ability group run (AGR):** You're assigned to one of four groups for your group run based on a 1-mile timed assessment. Your group then runs together when assigned in a timed manner intense enough to enable improvement.

- **Release run (RR):** You run in formation for up to 15 minutes and then are released to run as fast as you can back to your starting point.

- **Foot march with fighting load (FM-fl):** You're trained to march successfully while your body adapts to various terrain, frequency, load, distance, visibility, halts, and rest.

- **Conditioning obstacle course (CDOC):** Your strength, endurance, and mobility are challenged in a timed obstacle course with various conditioning exercises.

- **Combatives (CB):** You're trained to successfully defeat opponents using grappling, striking, and weapons training.

- **Recovery drill (RD):** This drill safely ends your intense training for the day, by walking after running, cooling down, and getting proper hydration, nutrition, and rest in preparation for training the next day.

## Getting fired up for fire guard and CQ duties

Fire guard and charge of quarters (CQ) duties are extra duties that will begin immediately and will be your first real taste of responsibility during Army basic training.

Fire guards patrol the barracks at night. Their primary duty is to watch for fires (which never happen), clean anything they notice that needs cleaning, and watch for recruits attempting to leave the barracks. Shifts are generally one-hour long, and the recruit getting off duty is responsible to wake up his replacement.

Fire guard stems back to the days of wooden barracks and wood-burning stoves. The fire guard would watch the stoves to make sure that the barracks would not catch fire. Because open flames aren't generally used to heat sleeping areas anymore, present-day fire guard during basic training is more an exercise in discipline than a practical necessity.

The CQ duty rotates through the entire basic training company, not just the individual platoon. Technically, the actual CQ (charge of quarters) is a drill sergeant. The two recruits who pull CQ duty are runners assigned to the CQ to perform tasks for the CQ. For example, only the CQ on duty may open the barracks doors, and the runners must alert the CQ if someone else attempts to enter or leave the barracks.

# Living the core values

For the past few years, the biggest buzzwords around Army basic training have been *core values*. The Army has seven core values that will be continually hammered into you during your nine-week stay. You'll sleep, eat, and um . . . eat some more about Army core values until you think they're part of the Constitution and wonder how your high school history class could have missed them.

Memorizing these seven core values before you arrive at basic training may give you a little extra breather time while others are trying to commit them to memory:

An acronym for the core values is LDRSHIP.

### Loyalty

> *Bear true faith and allegiance to the U.S. Constitution, the Army, your unit, and other soldiers.*

Bearing true faith and allegiance is a matter of believing in, and devoting yourself to, something or someone. A loyal soldier is one who supports the leadership and stands up for fellow soldiers. Wearing the uniform of the United States Army is a highly visible means of expressing your loyalty. You show your loyalty to your unit by doing your share.

Any time you choose one individual's actions — right or wrong — over the safety and welfare of the rest of the unit, or over your own interest and commitment, you are eroding the value of loyalty.

### Duty

> *Fulfill your obligations.*

Doing your duty means more than carrying out your assigned tasks. The work of the United States Army is a complex combination of missions, tasks, and responsibilities — all in constant motion. And the work, inevitably, is a matter of building one assignment or task on work that has been done previously. Doing your duty is a very important responsibility.

Duty also means being able to accomplish tasks as part of a team. You must fulfill your obligations as a part of your unit. Examples include voluntarily assuming your share of the workload, willingly serving as a member of a team, or assuming a leadership role when appropriate. You demonstrate the value of duty when you complete a task even when no one is looking, or when you resist the temptation to take shortcuts that might undermine the integrity of the final product. You do your duty as a soldier every time you do something that needs to be done — without being told.

### Respect

*Treat people as they should be treated.*

Respect to a soldier simply means treating people as they should be treated. It means giving others the same consideration we would like or expect to be given. The Army is one huge team, made up of hundreds of component parts. There must be connections — ground rules — so that when one soldier approaches, works with, or talks to another, you treat him with immediate and unquestioned cooperation and respect. The Army mirrors this country's diversity. Each person has something to contribute.

Respect is what allows you to appreciate the best in other people. Respect is trusting that all people have done their jobs — fulfilled their duty. Self-respect is a vital ingredient within the Army value of respect that results from knowing you have dug down deep to put forth you best effort. Your self-respect is shown by taking care of yourself physically, keeping fit, and not using drugs or tobacco products (smoking, chewing, and so on).

Finally, respect for other people includes not using profanity and obscene gestures. You're now in the military. What may have been acceptable in your civilian life may not be acceptable in the Army.

### Selfless service

*Put the welfare of the Nation, the Army, and your subordinates above your own.*

In serving your country, you're doing your duty loyally, without thought of recognition or gain. The reward of selfless service is the satisfaction of a job well done — a successful accomplishment that reflects on the soldier and his unit.

The greatest means of accomplishing selfless service is to dedicate yourself to the teamwork that is the underlying strength of the Army. It is when thousands of soldiers work together as a team that spectacular results arise. The basic building block of selfless service is the commitment of each team member to go a little further, endure a little longer, and look a little closer to see how he can add to the effort of the unit, platoon, or company.

Selfless service is larger than just one person. With dedication to the value of selfless service, each and every soldier can rightfully look back and say, "I am proud to have served my country as a soldier."

## Honor

*Live up to all Army values.*

When I talk about living up to something, I mean being worthy of it. You must make choices, decisions, and actions based on the Army core values.

Nowhere in your values training does it become more important to emphasize the difference between knowing the values and living them than when you discuss the value of honor. Honor is a matter of carrying out, acting, and living the values of respect, duty, loyalty, selfless service, integrity, and personal courage in everything you do. Noticing a situation and deciding to take action to assist another involves respect, duty, and honor.

It was a matter of honor that soldiers, at great risk to themselves, distributed food in Somalia and kept the peace in Bosnia, while managing to protect the communities. There are hundreds of examples of soldiers who have distinguished themselves with honorable actions and lives.

The Nation's highest military award is named The Medal of Honor. This award goes to soldiers who make honor a matter of daily living — soldiers who develop the habit of being honorable and solidify that habit with every value choice they make.

## Integrity

*Do what is right, legally and morally.*

When I say that someone has integrity, I mean that person respects the rules of an organization, the country, and life. Such persons can be counted on to do the right thing, live honestly, and relate to others without playing games or having false agendas. Integrity is a quality you develop by adhering to moral principles. It requires that you do and say nothing that deceives others.

As your integrity grows, so does the trust others place in you. It's integrity that requires you to pay your debts on time, turn in items that someone else has lost, and follow rules as laid out in the law or in the code of human ethics and morality. The Soldier's Code says,

> *"No matter what situation I am in, I will never do anything for pleasures, profit, or personal safety that will disgrace my uniform, my unit, or my country."*

The more choices you make based on integrity, the more this highly prized value will affect your relationships with family and friends, and, finally, the fundamental acceptance of yourself.

### Personal courage

*Face fear, danger, or adversity (physical or moral).*

Personal courage has long been associated with the U.S. Army. Accounts of the dangers and hardships that soldiers face are legendary. With physical courage, it is a matter of enduring physical duress and, at times, risking personal safety.

Facing moral fear or adversity may be a long, slow process of continuing forward on the right path, especially if taking those actions is not popular with others. When considering personal courage, physical or moral, there is one important point to be made. Nowhere does the value say that fear must disappear — or that you should not feel fear.

Some great instances of courage are those carried out by the soldiers who have never seen a battlefield. You can build your personal courage by daily standing up for and acting upon the things that you know are honorable.

## Memorizing the Soldier's Creed

You'll barely have time to absorb the Army core values, when you'll be required to memorize the Soldier's Creed:

*I am an American Soldier.*

*I am a Warrior and a member of a team. I serve the people of the United States and live the Army Values.*

*I will always place the mission first.*

*I will never accept defeat.*

*I will never quit.*

*I will never leave a fallen comrade.*

*I am disciplined, physically and mentally tough, trained and proficient in my warrior tasks and drills. I always maintain my arms, my equipment and myself.*

*I am an expert and I am a professional.*

*I stand ready to deploy, engage, and destroy the enemies of the United States of America in close combat.*

*I am a guardian of freedom and the American way of life.*

*I am an American Soldier.*

## Studying up on Army rank

One of your first classroom lessons will be about Army enlisted, warrant officer, and officer rank insignias. You'll be able to save yourself a lot of worry by memorizing Army rank and insignia before you get to basic. Chapter 5 will make you an expert on military rank and insignia in no time.

## Singing the Army song

"The Army Goes Rolling Along" is the official Army song and is played on many occasions. You should stand at attention when it's played or sung, and you will have to memorize the song in basic training.

The song was dedicated on Veterans Day, November 11, 1956. The music was composed in 1908 by Lieutenant (later Brigadier General) Edmund L. Gruber and was known originally as the "Caisson Song."

**Verse**

*March along, sing our song*
*With the Army of the free*
*Count the brave, count the true*
*Who have fought to victory.*
*We're the Army and proud of our name!*
*We're the Army and proud to*
*proclaim:*

**First Chorus**

*First to fight for the right*
*And to build the nation's might.*
*And THE ARMY GOES ROLLING ALONG.*
*Proud of all we have done.*
*Fighting till the battle's won.*
*And THE ARMY GOES ROLLING ALONG.*

**Refrain**

*Then it's hi! Hi! Hey! The Army's on its way.*
*Count off the cadence loud and strong:*
*For where're we go, you will always know*
*That THE ARMY GOES ROLLING ALONG.*

**Second Chorus**

*Valley Forge, Custer's ranks,*
*San Juan Hill and Patton's tanks,*
*And the Army went rolling along.*
*Minutemen from the start,*
*Always fighting from the heart,*
*And the Army keeps rolling along.*

**Refrain**

*Then it's hi! hi! hey!*
*The Army's on its way.*
*Count off the cadence loud and strong:*
*For where're you go, you will always know*
*That THE ARMY GOES ROLLING ALONG.*

**Third Chorus**

*Men in rags, men who froze,*
*Still that Army met its foes,*
*And the Army went rolling along.*
*Faith in God, then we're right*
*And we'll fight with all our might*

**Refrain**

*Then it's hi! hi! hey!*
*The Army's on its way,*
*Count off the cadence loud and strong:*
*(Two! Three!)*
*For where're we go, you will always know*
*That THE ARMY KEEPS ROLLING ALONG!*
*(Keep it rolling)*
*And THE ARMY GOES ROLLING ALONG!*

## Gassing up: The gas chamber

Chemical defense equipment, such as the gas mask, is important in the military because it allows you to continue to do your job even if the enemy lobs chemical weapons at you. The problem is that this equipment is extremely uncomfortable, so nobody wants to wear it. That's where the gas chamber in basic training comes in. Its purpose is not to teach you how to wear the gas mask (that's pretty simple). The gas-mask training in basic is often called *confidence training* (although many recruits call it *practice bleeding*) because the purpose of the training is to give you confidence that your gas mask actually works.

For most people, worrying about the gas chamber is actually much worse than the actual training session.

The *gas chamber* is a room with vents and valves that allow a controlled concentration of tear gas (orto-chlorobenzylidene-malononitrile) to be administered. Tear gas is an irritant; specifically, it irritates mucous membranes in the eyes, nose, mouth and lungs, causing tearing, sneezing, coughing, and so on. Tear gas is the active ingredient in Mace and is used for self-defense and for riot control by the police.

There is no set procedure for the gas chamber. Different drill sergeants do it a little bit differently. However, the following process appears to be about average:

1. **You line up in a group (usually 5 to 15 recruits) outside of the gas chamber door.**

2. **Your group is instructed to enter the gas chamber.**

3. **Once inside, you're joined by a drill sergeant (or two or three).**

   You will see a drill sergeant with a coffee can next to a table. This coffee can will have a flame inside, which is the gas burning.

4. **A drill sergeant will touch your shoulder and instruct you to lift your mask and state your name, rank and Social Security number.**

   Many recruits get nervous and forget the answers to these simple questions. If you remain calm, you will do fine. (You can replace the mask after you state your answer).

   You will inhale some of the gas, and you will get some in your eyes. Don't worry. That's the whole point — to show you that the gas mask works.

Eat a light meal on the day you're scheduled for the gas chamber. Taking a few breaths of tear gas on a full stomach is not a fun experience.

## *Receiving your rifle*

During the first week of basic training, you'll be issued a standard M-16 military rifle. Don't get too excited — you won't be allowed to shoot it yet. You just get to learn how to take it apart, clean it, and put it back together. You do get to carry it around with you everywhere you go.

The actual shooting of the rifle will have to wait until later in basic training. You can find out more about the M-16 rifle and actually shooting it in Chapter 4.

## *Meeting your battle buddies*

For several years, the Army has used a *battle buddy system* during basic training, which is designed to keep recruits from getting into trouble. In fact, the system works so well that the Army has expanded the battle buddy system to units other than basic training as well.

Under the battle buddy system, you're issued a friend. One of your fellow basic trainees is assigned to go everywhere with you, and you with him, to support each other and to keep each other out of trouble.

You don't get to choose your battle buddy. The drill sergeant will select your best friend for you. By regulation, buddy teams must be made up of same-gender soldiers. Additionally, soldiers who do not speak English well are paired up with English-speaking soldiers who can help them understand instructions and orders. Finally, soldiers are paired so that their strengths and weaknesses complement and balance each other.

The battle buddy system works by following the system's simple rules:

- ✔ To the maximum extent possible, never go anywhere without your battle buddy.

- ✔ If you must go somewhere without your battle buddy (such as an x-ray room at the hospital or a one-stall porta-potty), make sure that your battle buddy knows where you are.

- ✔ Pass on any information that may affect your battle buddy, such as appointment times or a change of schedule.

- ✔ Battle buddies will discuss each day's training and plans for the next day.

- ✔ Battle buddies will help each other to solve problems.

- ✔ Battle buddies will encourage each other to complete all training.

- ✔ Check your battle buddy's appearance and conduct.

- ✔ Inform the drill sergeant of any changes or problems with your battle buddy.

- ✔ Assist your battle buddy in living up to the Army's core values.

# White and Blue Phases (Training Week 4 through Week 9)

The good news is that the second half of Army basic combat training, known as the white and blue phases, is the most fun. Drill sergeants aren't yelling at you as much, Army and basic training routine is starting to become second nature, and you get to do cool military stuff such as fire the rifle and run the obstacle course.

By this time, you should be fairly sure that you're going to complete the course and graduate, as long as you don't do something very, very stupid.

## Practicing on the firing range

As a result of lessons learned in both Iraq and Afghanistan, the Army revamped its basic combat training schedule to include much more time on the firing range. During basic combat training, infantry basic trainees and non-infantry basic trainees fire about 500 rounds. Before the change, all Army basic trainees fired only about 300 rounds.

The Army takes marksmanship training very seriously. In basic training, you spend 103 hours firing the M-16 or M-4 rifles. You can also qualify for marksmanship awards in basic training — your very first military awards. These marksmanship awards can be worn on your military uniform after basic training graduation.

Somewhere around week 1of basic combat training, you'll be issued your baby. This rifle is yours, and no one else's, during the rest of your stay. At night, you will sleep with your weapon or store your weapon in a weapon's rack in your barracks.

Every morning you will sign out your rifle, and it will be your responsibility for the rest of the day. Make sure that you follow these simple rules any time your weapon is in your possession:

- ✔ Never leave your weapon unattended, even for a second.
- ✔ Never point your weapon at anyone, or anything that you don't intend to shoot.

🖊 Never call it a gun; it's your rifle.

🖊 If you're doing push-ups, place the rifle across the backs of your hands so that it won't touch the floor/ground.

If you've never fired a rifle, I don't recommend that you spend time on a range practicing before you depart for Army basic combat training — you'll only learn bad habits that will then have to be unlearned.

You can read much more about the basic training firing range and weapons training in Chapter 4.

## Cruising through the Army obstacle course

In Army basic combat training, there is a separate obstacle course called a *confidence course*. That's because most complete this obstacle course without significant problems, and — once you do — you feel, well . . . confident.

There is no standard Army basic training confidence course. Each Army basic training location has its own variation. However, each course is similar in that it has approximately 25 obstacles and usually includes the following:

🖊 Climbing towers

🖊 Swinging on a rope (often over a pond of dirty water)

🖊 Walking across rolling logs

🖊 Scaling a cargo net

🖊 Walking a *weaver* (a series of wood planks placed at an incline and then a decline (resembling an upside down V)

The confidence course is a timed event, and you'll get at least two chances to run it during Army basic combat training. Two or three soldiers generally run the obstacle course together, although it's not a competition. Most Army basic training graduates remember the confidence course as one of the most fun events during their entire basic training experience.

## Getting from point A to point B with field navigation

An Army that gets lost on the battlefield isn't much good, so a substantial number of Army basic training days are dedicated to traveling without getting lost. The Army calls this exercise *land navigation,* and it's something that all soldiers need to master.

The Army uses a building block approach when it comes to teaching land navigation. In basic combat training, you learn the basics — how to get from point A to point B without getting lost. During future Army leadership training, the Army will build on what you learned in basic combat training until — ultimately — you're able to lead a team across any terrain and arrive at your intended destination at your intended time.

### Military maps

Military maps are produced by the National Geospatial-Intelligence Agency (NGA)". The NGA's mission is to provide mapping, charting, and all geospatial support to the armed forces and all other national security operations. DMA produces four categories of products and services: hydrographic, topographic, aeronautical, and missile and targeting. Military maps are categorized by scale and type.

#### Map scales

Because a map is a graphic representation of a portion of the earth's surface drawn to scale as seen from above, you need to know what mathematical scale has been used. You must know the scale so that you can determine ground distances between objects or locations on the map, the size of the area covered, and how the scale may affect the amount of detail being shown. The mathematical scale of a map is the ratio or fraction between the distance on a map and the corresponding distance on the surface of the earth. Scale is reported as a representative fraction with the map distance as the numerator and the ground distance as the denominator:

> Scale = map distance/actual distance

As the denominator of the representative fraction gets larger and the ratio gets smaller, the scale of the map decreases. National Geospatial-Intelligence Agency maps are classified by scale into three categories: small-, medium-, and large-scale maps.

The terms *small scale, medium scale,* and *large scale* may be confusing when read in conjunction with the number. However, if the number is viewed as a fraction, it quickly becomes apparent that 1:600,000 of something is smaller than 1:75,000 of the same thing. Therefore, the larger the number after 1:, the smaller the scale of the map. The following provides detailed information about NGA maps:

- ✔ **Small:** Those maps with scales of 1:1,000,000 and smaller are used for general planning and for strategic studies. The standard small-scale map is 1:1,000,000. This map covers a very large land area at the expense of detail.

✔ **Medium:** Those maps with scales larger than 1:1,000,000 but smaller than 1:75,000 are used for operational planning. They contain a moderate amount of detail, but terrain analysis is best done with the large-scale maps. The standard medium-scale map is 1:250,000. Medium-scale maps of 1:100,000 are also frequently encountered.

✔ **Large:** Those maps with scales of 1:75,000 and larger are used for tactical, administrative, and logistical planning. As a soldier or junior leader, you're most likely to encounter these maps. The standard large-scale map is 1:50,000. However, many areas have been mapped at a scale of 1:25,000.

### Map types

The map of choice for land navigators is the 1:50,000-scale military topographic map. It is important, however, that you know how to use the many other products available from the NGA as well. When operating in foreign places, you may discover that NGA map products have not yet been produced to cover your particular area of operations, or they may not be available to your unit when you require them. Therefore, you must be prepared to use maps produced by foreign governments that may or may not meet the standards for accuracy set by NGA. These maps often use symbols that resemble those found on NGA maps but that have completely different meanings. There may be other times when you must operate with the only map you can obtain. This map may be a commercially produced map run off on a copy machine at higher headquarters. In Grenada, many American troops used a British tourist map.

The following list provides information about different types of maps:

✔ **Planimetric map:** This map presents only the horizontal positions for the features represented. It's distinguished from a topographic map by the omission of relief, normally represented by contour lines. Sometimes, it's called a line map.

✔ **Topographic map:** This map portrays terrain features in a measurable way (usually through use of contour lines), as well as the horizontal positions of the features represented. The vertical positions, or *relief,* are normally represented by contour lines on military topographic maps. On maps showing relief, the elevations and contours are measured from a specific vertical datum plane, usually mean sea level.

✔ **Photomap:** This reproduction of an aerial photograph contains added grid lines, marginal data, place names, route numbers, important elevations, boundaries, and approximate scale and direction.

✔ **Joint operations graphics:** These maps are based on the format of standard 1:250,000 medium-scale military topographic maps, but they contain additional information needed in joint air-ground operations. Along the north and east edges of the graphic, detail is extended beyond the standard map sheet to provide overlap with adjacent sheets. These maps are produced both in ground and air formats. Each version is identified in the lower margin as either Joint Operations Graphic (Air) or Joint Operations Graphic (Ground). The topographic information is identical on both, but the ground version shows elevations and contour in meters and the air version shows them in feet. Layer (elevation) tinting and relief shading are added as an aid to interpolating relief. Both versions emphasize air landing facilities (shown in purple), but the air version has additional symbols to identify aids and obstructions to air navigation.

✔ **Photomosaic:** This assembly of aerial photographs is commonly called a *mosaic* in topographic usage. Mosaics are useful when time doesn't permit the compilation of a more accurate map. The accuracy of a mosaic depends on the method employed in its preparation and may vary from simply a good pictorial effect of the ground to that of a planimetric map.

✔ **Terrain model:** This scale model of the terrain shows features, and in large-scale models, it shows industrial and cultural shapes. It provides a means for visualizing the terrain for planning or indoctrination purposes and for briefing on assault landings.

✔ **Military city map:** This topographic map (usually at 1:12,550 scale, sometimes up to 1:5,000) shows the details of a city. It delineates streets and shows street names, important buildings, and other elements of the urban landscape important to navigation and military operations in urban terrain. The scale of a military city map depends on the importance and size of the city, density of detail, and available intelligence information.

### Colors used on a military map

By the 15th century, most European maps were carefully colored. Profile drawings of mountains and hills were shown in brown, rivers and lakes in blue, vegetation in green, roads in yellow, and special information in red. A look at the legend of a modern map confirms that the use of colors hasn't changed much over the past several hundred years.

To facilitate the identification of features on a map, the topographical and cultural information is usually printed in different colors. These colors may vary from map to map. On a standard large-scale topographic map, the colors used and the features each represent are

✔ **Black:** Indicates cultural (manmade) features, such as buildings and roads, surveyed spot elevations, and all labels.

✔ **Red and brown (combined):** Identify cultural features, all relief features, nonsurveyed spot elevations, and elevation, such as contour lines on red-light readable maps.

✔ **Blue:** Identifies water features, such as lakes, swamps, rivers, and drainage.

✔ **Green:** Identifies vegetation with military significance, such as woods, orchards, and vineyards.

✔ **Brown:** Identifies all relief features and elevation, such as contours on older edition maps, and cultivated land on red-light readable maps.

✔ **Red:** Classifies cultural features, such as populated areas, main roads, and boundaries, on older maps.

✔ **Other colors:** Occasionally, show special information. These colors are indicated in the marginal information as a rule.

### Orienteering

There is much, much more involved in land navigation than I can cover in this chapter. So, how can you gain the necessary skills to navigate from point A to point B in the woods, with just a map and a compass, before leaving for Army basic training? That's easy — join an orienteering group and attend some orienteering competitions.

*Orienteering* is a competitive form of land navigation. It's for all ages and degrees of fitness and skill. Orienteering provides the suspense and excitement of a treasure hunt. The object of orienteering is to locate control points by using a map and compass to navigate through the woods. The courses may be as long as 10km.

You can find an orienteering club in your area by visiting Orienteering USA organization at http://orienteeringusa.org.

## This is not my drill sergeant — attitude changes

Sometime around week 4 or week 5, you'll notice that someone switched drill instructors on you. This one doesn't yell as much as the last one. This one doesn't enter the barracks each morning screaming. He enters and quietly says, "Get up." You can even approach this one and ask a question without getting dropped. What's happened?

I'll tell you what my own drill instructor told me many years ago: The drill instructor hasn't changed — you have. You're starting to get it. You're not doing stupid little things, and the drill instructor no longer has to yell at you or hand out push-ups like candy in order to get you to pay attention. You find that you actually like learning how to do something new the Army way.

# Exodus

The Army closes down basic combat training and Army job schools for about two weeks around the Christmas and New Year's timeframe. During this time, Army soldiers are given the opportunity to take leave (vacation time) and go home.

The Army is the only military branch that closes down basic training during the Christmas holidays. They call this program *Exodus.*

Keep in mind that Exodus is not free time off. Military members earn leave (vacation time) at the rate of 2.5 days per month (30 days per year). If you decide to go home during Exodus, your time away is subtracted from your current and future leave (vacation) time. The Army also doesn't pay for travel during this time. However, you will be allowed to book a flight at the discount travel office on base at a substantial savings. Or, if your family lives close to your basic training location, they can pick you up.

Keep in mind that if you take advantage of Exodus, you will likely not have any leave time saved up when you finish Army job training and will likely have to go directly to your first duty assignment, without any time off. Usually, new soldiers are allowed to take two weeks of leave after graduating Army job school before reporting to their first duty assignment. You need to make the choice if you would rather visit home during Christmas or after you finish your Army training.

Soldiers who choose not to take leave at the time of Exodus are normally assigned to do details (answer phones, cut the grass, clean buildings, and so on) because most of the instructors and drill sergeants will be away on leave themselves, and classes are not conducted during this time.

The exact dates of Exodus change from year to year, and even from Army basic combat training post to post. The Army Basic Training Post Commander determines the exact dates for that post each year, months in advance.

If you're planning to attend Army basic combat training during the Christmas timeframe, check with your recruiter to ensure that the Exodus program still exists. For the past few years, the Army has been considering eliminating the program. Many recruits have problems getting back into the basic training mode after two weeks off, and some soldiers fail to return at all (go AWOL).

## Taking your final PT test

Around week 7, you take the final physical fitness test. By this time, you should have no problem passing the test. The final basic training PT test is the exact same test you'll be subject to twice each year during your Army career, except the graduation standards are slightly less than the normal Army PT standards.

See Chapter 8 for the Army Basic Training PT standards that you'll have to achieve in order to pass this event.

## Camping army-style

After you complete your final physical fitness test, you'll get to go camping! You find out how to set up tents, go on night patrols, and perform night operations. You learn to appreciate Army chow halls, as all your meals in the field will consist of MREs (Meals, Ready to Eat).

If you'd like to experience an MRE prior to basic training, you can pick them up at nearly any military surplus store. Many people use them for camping.

Sometime during your stay in the field, I can almost guarantee that your platoon will receive *incoming* (somebody will be pretending to shoot at you). It's a very good idea (and looks impressive) for the squad leaders and platoon leader to discuss this "attack" in advance and assign specific duties. Don't let the drill sergeants hear you planning a strategy, however; they're very good at making their own plans to thwart any plans you may devise.

## Tying everything together with the final event

During the second week of Phase 3 (week 8 of basic training), you'll culminate the field training experience with a special tactical "Field Training Exercise (FTX)". This exercise is basically a "play war in the woods" exercise. This exercise ties everything you've learned in basic together. The drill sergeants will advise (and keep you from getting hurt), but tactical decisions will be made by the platoon leaders and squad leaders. While they differ in names, all Army basic combat training programs include this final event. As an example, Fort Jackson's basic training calls their final event *Victory Forge*.

At the end of the field event, you return to a short, informal ceremony that marks your transition from civilian to soldier. You then return to Army basic to spend the final week preparing for the graduation ceremony.

Basic combat training in the Army is designed to lay a foundation for discipline and basic combat. Your real training, however, will begin after basic when you transition to Advanced Individual Training (Army job school).

# Chapter 15

# Air Force Basic Training

*W*hen the Air Force completely revamped its basic training course a few years ago, it divided the course into four distinct phases:

✔ Introduction phase, designed to get you into the basic training routine

✔ Predeployment phase, which continues to enhance your military skills and builds on skills that an average airman will need to prepare to deploy to a combat zone

✔ Post-deployment phase, which simulates deploying to an Air Force bare-bones combat operation

✔ Final phase, designed to give you the knowledge you need for after the deployment

## Introduction Phase: Zero Week and Week 1

Until a few years ago, Air Force basic training at Lackland Air Force Base in San Antonio, Texas was 6 ½ weeks long. The Air Force completely revamped its basic training program in November 2008, extending the course by two weeks. New recruits are now learning the basics for 8 ½ weeks.

Unlike the Army basic training (see Chapter 14), Air Force basic training has no reception period in. You start the official basic training program immediately upon arrival. Assuming that you pass all the requirements, figuring out your graduation date is pretty simple. If you make the cut, you'll graduate exactly 8 weeks from the Friday after your arrival at Lackland.

Most new recruits arrive at Lackland on Tuesday, Wednesday, or Thursday. These first few days are called *zero week* by the Air Force basic training folks because the official basic training doesn't start until the first Friday, which is called *training day 1*. However, from the recruit's perspective, training begins immediately: You're assigned to an instructor, you're being yelled at, you're doing PT, you move into your dormitory (barracks), and you begin marching and learning other Air Force military subjects.

## Arrival at the airport

When you arrive at the San Antonio airport, you should pick up your bag, make your way to the A Terminal, and report in to the Air Force Receiving Station. For the first time, you meet some Air Force Military Training Instructors (MTIs, or more commonly, TIs) who will take a copy of your orders and direct you to a waiting area.

You'll note that these TIs are pretty nice folks, and you'll think to yourself, "Wow! This isn't so bad." Just wait . . . you're not on the bus yet. Instilling discipline is not a matter for public display, so the real show doesn't start until you're well away from the public airport.

Depending on what time you arrive, you may have to wait a long time for your bus to leave. Take advantage of the time and relax; it will be your last good relaxation time for a while. Take the opportunity to chat with the others waiting. There's a very good chance that those arriving at the same time will wind up being your flight mates.

Pretty soon, the TIs will line you up (your first formation!) and march you out to the bus. The ride to Lackland AFB takes about an hour. You'll still be feeling pretty good; while the TIs on the bus (if any are with you) don't seem quite as kind as the ones you met in the airport, you probably won't hear any significant yelling . . . yet.

The bus delivers you directly to the welcome center, where you turn in your records and do a little preliminary *in-processing* (Air Force speak for paperwork). After the preliminary in-processing, the bus takes you straight to your dormitory. (For more on your dormitory, see the section "Your basic training dormitory," later in this chapter.)

## Meeting your training instructors

You'll meet your official training instructors on the very first day, right after the in-processing bus drops you off at the barracks. After you get off the bus, you'll be herded into a building for a couple of hours of paperwork. When you come out, your assigned training instructors will be there waiting for you.

The Air Force calls their basic training units *flights*. Most flights get two training instructors, called MTIs (Military Training Instructor, or TIs for short.) In some instances, you may have more than the regulation two TIs, such as when a new TI is in training.

Always (and I mean *always*) address your training instructors, who are noncommissioned officers (NCOs), by sir or ma'am, depending on gender. Basic training doesn't have enough commissioned officers for you to practice on, so the TIs lovingly allow you to practice this etiquette on them. After you leave basic training, your technical school instructors will be quick to inform you that, as they are NCOs and thus "work for a living," you do not call them sir or ma'am. However, in basic training, you should call everyone who outranks you (pretty much everyone except other trainees) sir or ma'am.

So far, Air Force basic training hasn't been so bad. This sentiment is about to change. Suddenly, the skies will darken, your ears will ring, and all heck will break loose. You'll say to yourself, "What have I gotten myself into?"

When I went through Air Force basic training, I remember thinking at this point, "Oh, no! I signed up for four years of this?" Don't worry. TIs are a very special breed and live only at Air Force basic training. After you graduate from Air Force job training, and move on to your first duty station, you'll find that your superiors are very much like civilian bosses.

Before leaving home, make sure that you don't stand out in your personal appearance. When you meet your training instructor for the first time, trust me — you'll not want him to remember you for your long hair, earrings (male), handlebar mustache, or pants that are four sizes too big. Ladies, while you're not required to cut your hair for basic, you will be required to keep it off your collar at all times when in uniform (which is most of the time in basic), so you may want to consider cutting your hair short enough so that it doesn't have to be put up.

The very first thing you'll discover is that even if you're 6 foot, 2 inches and 190 pounds, and your TI is 5 foot 4 inches and 120 pounds, she is the biggest, meanest thing you've met in your life. You'll soon realize that your TI does not like you, doesn't like your friends, and absolutely hates your family. Air Force TIs don't use profanity (at least, they're not supposed to), nor will they put hands on you. But, they are very, very good at scaring people. *Very good.*

The second thing you'll discover about basic training is that nobody in your flight can do anything right. Everything you do during the first couple of days will be wrong. You'll stand wrong, you'll walk (march) wrong, you'll talk wrong, you'll look wrong, and possibly you'll even breathe wrong. Hopefully, if you read this chapter, you'll have a few minutes of respite while the TI concentrates on the person next to you with the purple hair. If so, do not giggle, do not smile. If you do, you'll discover just how short a TIs attention span can be, as he shifts attention to examine and comment (loudly) about your particular deficiencies.

# An MTI experience

Years ago, when I was an up-and-coming young staff sergeant, I attended a supervisor's course at Chanute AFB in Illinois. One of my classmates was a small, petite woman who had just returned to the "real Air Force" from four years of TI duty. One evening, while walking back to billeting (the base hotel) from a study group meeting at the NCO Club, we passed a young airman, walking down the street with his field jacket unzipped. (This is a uniform no-no.) My former TI friend said, "Watch this."

She braced the very large young man, ordered him to stand at attention, and — standing 6 inches in front on him, looking up at his frightened face — proceeded to discuss his family's work ethic and disgusting personal habits for ten minutes straight, all without a single word of profanity escaping her lips. When she was finished, the young man was 6 inches shorter and bleeding from the ears. I was very much impressed (and, from that moment on, slightly afraid of her).

Keep in mind that TIs hate the word yeah. They also hate the words nope and un-uh. They especially hate any sentence that doesn't begin or end with the word *sir* or *ma'am*.

When I went through Air Force Basic Training (several centuries ago), each and every sentence had to begin and end with *sir* or *ma'am*, as in "Sir, can I go to the latrine, sir?" However, this custom changed several years ago. These days, TIs hate this *sir sandwich* (or ma'am sandwich), which is when you use "sir" or "ma'am" at the beginning and ending of a sentence. Sir sandwiches are another notorious pet peeve of those kind gentle souls.

TIs are also notoriously hard of hearing. No matter how loudly you say, "Yes sir!" or "No, ma'am!" your TI will probably politely ask you to speak up. Because of this implied hearing problem, the TI will probably assume that that you're similarly inflicted and will make a special effort to speak loudly — right next to your ear. Moving or showing any evidence of discomfort is considered to be impolite and will be commented upon (loudly).

Before long, it will dawn on you that somewhere between the welcome center and your dormitory, someone stole your first name. You'll probably never hear your first name throughout your entire time in basic. For your time there, everyone (TIs, flight mates, and so on) will be addressing you by your last name. If a TI doesn't know your last name, she will call you trainee or recruit (loudly). If you're female, often she'll yell, "Hey, you! Female!" (My daughters, who went through Air Force basic training just a few years ago, hated this.)

## In-processing: A multiday affair

During your first couple of days of zero week, your TI will spend most of the day marching your flight from building to building so that you can stand in line for in-processing." You'll be measured for military uniforms (you don't get them just yet), establish your military finance records (so that you can start getting paid), receive about a billion shots (see Chapter 11), and visit the dentist (also in Chapter 11).

During in-processing, you receive your basic training debit card. You use this card to pay for anything you need at basic training (toiletries, haircuts, and so on). The amount you charge is deducted from your first military paycheck.

Between in-processing functions, your TI will give you lots of drilling practice (see Chapter 9). If you desire a leadership position such as flight chief, look and act sharp during this period. Your TI is still getting to know you and is evaluating the flight to determine which one of you may make the best flight leaders.

Like most of the branches, leadership within the Air Force basic training squadron is accomplished mostly by using the recruits. During the first week, your TI will appoint recruits to various basic training leadership positions, called *flight leadership.* Chapter 13 gives you an overview of these jobs.

During in-processing, you'll also undergo a urinalysis to test for illegal drug use. Like the Marines, if you test positive for illegal drugs in Air Force basic training, you're immediately discharged, and you can never, ever rejoin the Air Force.

## Rainbow, rainbow, shining bright

Until your first uniform issue, which doesn't happen until around day 3, you'll be lovingly known by everyone at basic as *rainbows.* This nickname is because you'll be wearing the civilian clothes you brought, and — compared to all the other trainees — you are oh, so colorful and bright.

Everyone at basic training, from the instructors, to the staff, to the other trainees, will instantly know that you are brand, brand new, and you'll receive absolutely no respect at all.

You'll actually look forward to the day when the barber cuts off all of your hair (males), and you get to put on your first Air Force uniform.

## Don't ask to keep the hair

When I went through basic, one of the (stupid) recruits in my flight asked the TI if he could keep his hair. It seems his recruiter had told him that the Air Force no longer required hair to be cut short in basic training.

The TI looked at him, gave him a kindly smile (that should have been his first hint that something bad was going to happen), and said, "Sure. Let me talk to the barber."

When it was his turn in the chair, the barber quickly cut off all his hair, put it into a small trash bag, handed it to the recruit, and said, "Here, keep it." The TI made him carry that bag with him at all times during the first two weeks of basic. He also earned the nickname, "Harry."

## *Just a little off the top: Haircuts*

Guys, on the very first day of zero week, you meet your first civilian at Lackland AFB. He will introduce himself by cutting off all your hair (well, most of it, really). To add insult to injury, you have to pay for the haircut. The good news is that it will probably be about the fastest haircut you've ever had in your life. There's hardly any waiting! Don't bother saying, "Just a little off the sides." He's heard it a hundred times.

After the first haircut, you'll receive a haircut once every other week while in Air Force Basic Military Training (AFBMT).

Ladies, while in uniform (which is 90 percent of the time in basic training), you must wear your hair in such a manner that it does not protrude past the bottom of the collar. You can braid it and/or put it into a bun, but at no point can the bulk of your hair (including any "bun") exceed 3 inches. Any pins or barrettes you wear must be the same (approximate) color of your hair. Your bangs cannot touch your eyebrows, and your hair cannot interfere with the proper wear of military headgear. (For your Battle Dress Uniform, or BDU, the uniform you will wear most days, your *headgear* is kind of like a small baseball cap.)

## *Getting in touch with home*

A day or two after arrival, you'll learn your mailing address. On the Sunday or Monday following arrival, you should get a chance to call home and let your loved ones know your new address. You'll also fill out a postcard to mail to your loved ones, as soon as you get your address.

Seven Recruit Training Squadrons (TRS) are at Lackland. Your mailing address depends on your squadron, the flight you're assigned to, and the dormitory number your flight is assigned to.

If all else fails, a week (or so) after arrival, your address is listed at the Lackland AFB Basic Training Reception Center. Your family can call the center at (210) 671-3024 and get your address. Family members will need to know your Social Security number and full name.

## Your basic training dormitory

The Army and Marines call them *barracks.* The Navy calls them *ships.* In the Air Force, your sleeping quarters in Air Force Basic Military Training are called *dormitories,* (or dorms, for short). (Don't let the name fool you and don't confuse this with college campus dormitories. In Air Force basic training, like the other services, the dorms are large rooms with a whole bunch of bunks and lockers in them.)

Don't worry if you accidentally forget and call it a barrack (Army terminology). Your MTI will be happy to remind you that the Air Force doesn't have any barracks — more than happy to remind you, in fact.

The dorms are housed in large buildings. While these buildings are now more than 40 years old, they are very, very, very clean. Why not? They've had years and years of recruits going through who have spent a substantial number of hours keeping them that way. Most dormitory buildings are three stories tall. The drill pad, chow hall, laundry, and administrative offices are located on the first floor, and the dorm bays are located on the second and third floors.

Each dorm consists of two bays (two very large rooms), with bunks and lockers aligned along two walls. The dorm also has an office for the staff, a large bathroom/shower (called a *latrine*), and a dayroom. Don't get excited about the dayroom. You don't get to spend any time relaxing in it. It's used by the TI for flight events, such as training demonstration, and during mail-call.

You and your flight mates will keep the dorm spotless at all times. Each morning, you'll make your bunks the military way, using hospital corners.

See the online video at: `http://video.about.com/usmilitary/How-to-Make-Military-Corners.htm` to see how to make a military bunk with hospital corners.

Your shoes will be shined and aligned under your bunk, and your drawers and lockers will have everything placed in them just right.

## 341s

During zero week, the TIs will explain what happens to those who are not quite cutting it. You won't be cutting it if you haven't learned to march, have failed some tests, received too many demerits, and so on. Recruits are all given little forms (designed to keep in your breast pocket), affectionately known as *341s.* If you goof up significantly and your TI (or another TI) catches you at it, he will demand that you give him a 341. Getting too many 341s pulled can cause you to be recycled.

## Initial fitness test

The final fitness test in Air Force basic military training is accomplished during the end of the seventh week of training. That's not very much time to get into shape, even though you'll be working out six days per week during your time at basic. As such, Air Force officials highly recommend that you be able to meet certain minimum fitness standards, known as the *initial fitness standards,* when you arrive at basic. You don't have to meet these requirements, but it'll make your life much easier.

The initial fitness standards are the minimum recommended for when you first arrive at basic training. They're not the graduation standards, which are much harder — see Chapter 8.

On the Saturday or Sunday after your arrival, you'll undergo an initial fitness evaluation. If you fail to meet these standards, you can expect some additional attention from your TI and extra time dedicated to physical training each day.

The Air Force is toying with the idea of establishing a *fit flight* for Air Force basic training. If adopted, individuals who fail the standards on the initial fitness evaluation would be removed from their flight and placed into a special flight, doing pretty much nothing but exercising all day, until they meet the standards. After they meet the standards, they would then be placed back into a normal flight, entering the first week of training. I have no idea whether or not the Air Force will ultimately implement this program. The other services have similar programs for their basic training.

## Classroom training

Throughout week 1, you attend several Air Force basic training classes on various introductory topics to the Air Force:

- Entry control procedures
- Career guidance

✔ Dorm preparation

✔ Code of conduct and core values

✔ Law of armed conflict

✔ Chain of command

✔ Air Force rank insignia

✔ Weapons parts identification

✔ Human relations and cultural sensitivity

# Predeployment Phase (Weeks 2 Through 5)

Everything you've experienced during the first 1 ½ weeks of Air Force basic training has been designed to get you into a military mindset. The real military training begins in week 2 when you begin discovering the knowledge that you'll use if you're ever deployed to a combat zone.

All the training during this phase is geared toward teaching you the necessary skills to fight and survive in an actual combat area.

## Weapons issue

Before the Air Force changed its weapons training program, you saw a military weapon only twice during Air Force basic training — once to learn how to clean, load, and shoot it and again when you qualified with the weapon on the firing range.

One of the biggest changes that the Air Force made when they revamped basic training was that you're now issued an M-16 rifle during week 2. That rifle becomes your baby throughout the rest of the basic training course.

After your weapon is issued, you'll carry it with you throughout the remainder of basic training. You'll be required to treat this rifle just as if it were a loaded weapon, at all times.

In the Air Force, your M-16 rifle is always called your *weapon.* You can sometimes get away with calling it your rifle, but never, ever call it your gun.

These M-16 rifles have been rigged so that it's impossible to shoot them, just in case some recruit might think it would be fun to take out his TI. When it's your turn to visit the firing range, you'll exchange your rifle for one that really does shoot, for as long as it takes you to qualify.

So, why doesn't the Air Force use real M-16s (other than on the firing range) in Air Force basic? It's because real M-16s are a high-priority theft threat, and Air Force regulations require M-16s to be guarded by an armed guard any time they're outside of an alarmed armory.

During weeks 2 and 3 of Air Force basic, you'll undergo extensive training with your M-16 weapon. You learn and practice the rules for safe use and handling of the weapon. You also receive training in how to assemble, disassemble, clean, and repair the M-16.

During week 2, you use the M-16 to practice integrated base defense, tactical movement, firing positions, and force protection. You don't actually get to fire a real weapon until week 5 when you visit the weapon's range (see Chapter 4).

At the end of week 4, you undergo your first Air Force test. This test isn't written, but it's a demonstration test, where you take apart your M-16 replica rifle and put it back together again.

## Obstacle course

The Air Force used to call the obstacle course the Confidence Course in Air Force Basic Military Training (AFBMT). These days, if you take a drive through Lackland AFB (not that you'll be driving during your stay at basic), you'll note that signs show the direction to the obstacle course. This terminology reflects the change in attitude among Air Force officials to toughen up Air Force basic training. The philosophy is no longer to build your confidence, but rather test your ability to overcome obstacles placed in your path.

In any event, the obstacle course is a lot of fun. Lots of folks worry about this aspect of training, but they don't need to. I've never seen or even heard of anyone who has failed the obstacle course. During a recent trip to Lackland AFB, I asked a bunch of new basic training graduates which part of basic training they would be most be willing to repeat. Almost to a person, everyone answered, "The obstacle course!"

For a period of time, recruits got to visit the obstacle course twice during their stay at basic. Unfortunately, with so much additional training items, despite the extra two weeks added to basic, recruits now visit only once, during week 4.

The Air Force obstacle course is 1.5 miles long and consists of 17 obstacles that are designed to test your strength, endurance, and will power. On average, completing the course takes about 45 minutes.

The course also encourages team-building, as the recruits waiting to tackle an obstacle cheer for their flight mates. Recruits climb over, under, and around obstacles. Some of the course is over water, so you'll get very wet if you lose your grip. Strangely, the number of butterfingers always seems to increase in the summer, when Texas temperatures are very hot. I wonder why that is?

You can see an excellent interactive video of the Air Force basic training obstacle course online at www.airforce.com/interactive/obstacle-course.

## Pugil stick fighting

Following your crack at the obstacle course, you'll have a chance to work out your basic training frustrations with a little pugil stick fighting session. Figure 15-1 gives you an idea of what pugil stick fighting is all about.

Air Force basic military training isn't going to turn you into a black belt, by any means, but you will be trained to defend yourself, appropriately react to contact, and strengthen your body to its optimum potential

**Figure 15-1:**
Air Force basic trainees at Lackland AFB, Texas enjoy an afternoon of pugil stick fighting.

Don't like the dorm guard schedule? Here's your chance to show the dorm guard monitor what you really think of him. Unfortunately, you probably won't get a chance to beat up your TI.

Seriously, though, you don't stand much of a chance of getting hurt. The TIs will be watching closely, and you're wearing protective equipment.

However, pugil stick fighting was added to Air Force basic training in 2005. The Air Force introduced pugil stick fighting into the Air Force academy way back in 1980, and the students there have nothing but good things to say about the lesson. Also, the Army and Marine Corps have had pugil stick fighting as part of their basic training programs for years and years.

## More time in the classroom

Basic training classroom instruction really gears up during the predeployment phase. During this phase, you'll attend classroom training on

- ✔ Weapon handling and maintenance
- ✔ Field tent erection
- ✔ Defensive fighting positions
- ✔ Challenge procedure
- ✔ First aid
- ✔ Anti-terrorism
- ✔ Security programs
- ✔ The code of conduct
- ✔ Mental preparation for combat
- ✔ Basic leadership
- ✔ Basic situational awareness
- ✔ Public relations

Your first written test occurs during week 5 and covers all the subjects you've studied so far. The test is multiple choice, and you must score a 70 percent or better to pass.

If you fail the rifle assembly/disassembly test (see the "Weapons issue" section) or the written test, you're given one more chance to retest. If you fail the retest, you'll be *recycled*, which means that you must go through the training all over again — this is never fun.

## The gas chamber

Chemical warfare training and the gas chamber are relatively new additions to Air Force basic training. Before the change, Air Force personnel didn't get a chance to go through the gas chamber until they arrived at their first duty assignment, following Air Force technical training (job school).

You now go through the gas chamber during week 4 of Air Force basic training. The Air Force operates its gas chamber training using the exact same methods as the Army. See Chapter 14 for a preview of what you are in for during this portion of your Air Force training.

## PT assessment

At the end of week 5, you undergo a PT assessment. You won't have time to do daily PT while you're out in the field pretending to fight bad guys, so your TI needs to make sure that you'll be able to pass the final PT test when you return to basic following the BEAST.

This particular PT evaluation has no set standards, but if your TI doesn't feel you'll be able to pass the final PT test, he'll recommend that you be recycled (see Chapter 8) to give you more time to get into shape before going on to the next phase of training.

# Deployment Phase and the BEAST

The deployment phase of Air Force basic training takes everything that you've learned in the first two phases and puts you to the test of a mock Air Force combat deployment.

Before Iraq and Afghanistan, the Air Force deployed to relatively safe areas, well outside of the combat zones, where it would launch aircraft to fight. Times have changed. At any given time, between 4,000 and 5,000 airmen are deployed to Iraq and Afghanistan to jobs intended to be filled by soldiers and Marines, and airmen are increasingly responsible for patrolling the areas around their expeditionary bases. Air Force basic training's new emphasis on combat training, as well as a deployment to a mock combat zone, known as the BEAST, is a reflection of that reality.

The *BEAST* is an acronym for *Basic Expeditionary Airman Skills Training*. That's fancy Air Force talk for play war. That's exactly what this final exam portion of Air Force basic is — it's a mock war, fought by guess who?

The BEAST has four zones: Reaper, Predator, Vigilant, and Sentinel. Each zone simulates self-contained forward operating bases. The zones consist of a ring of 12 Army field tents — 10 for barracks, plus a command post and hospital tent — centered on a three-story observation tower and a hardened briefing facility that serves as an armory and bomb shelter. The zone is defended by five sandbag defensive firing positions, and trainees control access to the zone through an entry control point.

At the beginning of week 6, the entire Air Force basic training class, consisting of about 800 recruits, is marched to the BEAST, which is a field training site on the Medina Annex at the west end of Lackland. It's not a long march — only about 4 miles — but you'll be carrying all your field gear (chemical warfare equipment), and combat gear with you, so it'll feel like 50 miles.

## Preparing for combat

The BEAST starts on a Monday, and you'll spend that day with your instructors, setting up camp and reviewing all the combat lessons and procedures that you learned during the previous five weeks.

It took the Air Force four years to design and build the BEAST. The first 750 recruits went through the BEAST in December 2008. Almost to a person, what they hated the most was the amount of gear they were required to wear/carry with them at all times, and wearing chemical warfare suits and mask for hours at a time. Each recruit is required at all times to wear body armor and a helmet and carry a rucksack loaded with three MREs (Meals, Ready to Eat), MOPP (Mission Oriented Protective Posture) Gear (chemical suit, gloves, boots, and gas mask), as well as carry two canteens and an M-16 rifle. You must wear or carry this gear for 24 hours per day, for 4 days.

## Chowing down at the BEAST

As much as people tend to complain about chow hall cooking, you'll learn to miss it during the BEAST. Instead, you'll satisfy your hunger pains with MREs. An MRE is a self-contained, individual field ration in lightweight packaging bought by the United States Military for its service members for use in combat or other field conditions where organized food facilities aren't available. The MRE replaced the canned MCI (Meal, Combat, Individual) rations in 1981 and is the intended successor to the lighter LRP (Long Range Patrol) ration developed by the United States Army for Special Forces and Ranger patrol units in Vietnam.

## Who's in charge of this circus?

While most field exercises are conducted by your instructors, the mock combat conducted during the BEAST is entirely in the hands of the students.

During the war, the instructors don't teach. Before departing for the BEAST, instructors choose one zone leader and ten small unit leaders for each zone. These student-leaders are responsible for the day-to-day war operations in their zone and schedule manning for the defensive firing positions and entry control points (ECPs). Student leaders and trainees are expected to complete assigned tasks on their own and respond (on their own) to the various attack scenarios that are thrown at them. Instructors then debrief (yell) about what you did wrong and (more quietly) praise about what you did right.

## The war starts

During the very next day, the four-day war begins. During the war, you'll sleep in your tent and wake up at 0445 each morning, when you're given an intelligence briefing on the current threat.

Throughout the remainder of the day, you'll experience simulated attacks and take action accordingly. Some attacks are chemical/biological, and others are conventional attacks. Attacks can come from the air, hostile ground forces, or suicide bombers. Attacks can take place at any time, day or night. Sometimes the bad guys will use chemical weapons, and at other times, they'll use conventional weapons and bombs. TIs and folks in the 3E9 Emergency Management career field act as the bad guys, and throw everything they have at your team.

Throughout the day and night, recruits pull two-hour shifts as camp guards in the ECP. Don't expect to get much sleep during The BEAST, kiddies.

In order to know how to protect yourself, you must know the attack alarm signals and the MOPP level (chemical threat).

### Attack warnings

The Air Force uses standard attack warning signals to let you know the current attack threat. You should commit these warning signals to memory:

- ✔ **Alarm Green:** All clear. Attack is not probable or expected. The simulated war usually begins and ends with an Alarm Green. This condition is normally identified by green flags flying over the base.

- ✔ **Alarm Yellow:** Attack is probable and usually expected within 30 minutes. The majority of the war exercise is under Alarm Yellow. During Alarm Yellow, mission essential personnel continue to do their jobs. Non-essential personnel and those off-duty remain under cover. Alarm Yellow is signified by the display of yellow flags.

- ✔ **Alarm Red:** Attack is imminent or in progress. A wavering tone on a siren means it's an air or missile attack, and a call to arms signal with a bugle indicates an attack by ground forces. All forces, except emergency and mission-essential defense forces, must take cover immediately.

> ✔ **Alarm Black:** Indicated by a steady tone on the siren, Alarm Black means the attack is over, and now is the time for post-attack actions, such as checking for unexploded ordinance (UXO) hazards and battle-damage assessment.

On European bases, the warning Alarm Blue is used instead of Alarm Red because Alarm Red conflicts with European disaster response warnings.

### MOPP levels

MOPP stands for *Mission Oriented Protective Posture*. In plain speak, MOPP means the level of threat for chemical attack. Each of the five MOPP levels indicates what chemical protective gear you should be wearing in order to protect yourself:

> ✔ **MOPP 0:** Chemical warfare gear is issued to and inspected by the individual and prepared for use. Personnel carry their protective masks strapped on their waste. The standard issue over-garment and other chemical protective gear are carried or are readily available. To be considered readily available, equipment must be carried by each individual, stored within arm's reach, or be available within 5 minutes — for example, within the work area, vehicle, or fighting position.

> ✔ **MOPP 1:** When directed to MOPP1, personnel immediately don the over-garment. (In hot weather, the over-garment jacket can be left open and the over-garment can be worn directly over underwear) All other protective gear (footwear cover, mask, gloves, and so on) must be readily available or carried.

> ✔ **MOPP 2:** In MOPP2, you wear the over-garment and footwear covers. You also place the protective cover on your combat helmet. As with MOPP1, the over-garment jacket may be left open, but trousers remain closed. The mask with mask carrier and gloves are carried.

> ✔ **MOPP 3:** Personnel wear the over-garment, footwear covers, protective mask, and protective helmet cover. In hot weather, you can open the over-garment jacket and roll the protective mask hood for ventilation, but the trousers remain closed. The protective gloves are carried.

> ✔ **MOPP 4:** All chemical protective equipment is worn.

When at MOPP 1, 2, or 3, you must immediately transition to MOPP 4 during any Alarm Red.

### Improvised Explosive Devices (IEDs)

IEDs are explosive devices used extensively by terrorists in Iraq and Afghanistan. They're generally made of common materials, such as a cellphone, and have killed hundreds of Americans in both countries. They're tricky because they don't always look like bombs.

## Air Force Challenge Coin

A Challenge Coin is a large coin or small medallion that bears the organization's emblem and is carried by the organization's members. Like many aspects of military tradition, the origins of the challenge coin are a bit murky. While many organizations and services claim to be the originator of the challenge coin, most historians believe it originated with the Air Force, back when the Air Force was the Army Air Service.

As the most common legend goes, the tradition originated in flight training during World War I. According to legend, a wealthy lieutenant ordered small bronze medallions for all of his classmates as a memento of their time together. The gold-plated medallion bore the squadron's insignia and was quite valuable. One of the pilots in the squadron came from a poor family and had never owned such luxury. He placed it in a leather pouch, which he wore around his neck for luck when flying. After graduating from flight training, the pilot was shot down behind enemy lines. He was then captured by the Germans, but escaped before they could transport him to a POW camp.

During his capture, all of his identification was taken by the Germans, but they somehow missed the coin. After his escape, the pilot avoided German patrols and made his way to the front lines, where he came into contact with the French army. Unfortunately, the French mistook him for a German saboteur and prepared to execute him. With no ID, the pilot pulled out his gold coin and showed it to his captors. One of the Frenchmen recognized the unit insignia on the coin and delayed the execution long enough to check out his story.

After the young pilot returned to his unit and told his story, it became a tradition for all aircrew to carry their coins with them at all times. To check on compliance, the pilots would challenge each other to produce the coin. If the challenged couldn't produce the coin, he was required to buy a drink of choice for the challenger; if the challenged could produce the coin, the challenger would purchase the drink.

This tradition spread to other military units in all branches of service. Today, it's given to all Air Force enlisted members, upon completion of the BEAST, as a symbol of their achievement.

The BEAST site includes a 1.5-mile improvised explosive device (IED) trail littered with simulated roadside bombs. (Can you tell an IED from an old soda can?) Here you learn to spot IEDs. You also use the trail in training scenarios. For example, under one scenario, you make your way down the lane in tactical formation (ready for combat), trying to identify IEDs from the other debris. Get too close to an IED, and it goes Bang!, and you're dead. (The instructor will emphasize this point with plenty of yelling.)

WARNING!

If you end up dead, you can't rejoin the exercise until the TI tells you to. Sometimes you'll have to lay there until you're taken to the morgue by a fellow airman. The good news, though, that the odds of making it through the BEAST "alive" are in your favor; a vast majority of recruits make it through.

At the end of the IED trail, assuming that you didn't make too many mistakes and are still alive, you're broken into teams of two wingmen and negotiate a combat-obstacle course.

The course is similar to the obstacle course (see the "Obstacle course" section, earlier in this chapter), except this time you're wearing about 40 pounds of combat gear, and the course is designed to simulate difficulties you might find on a battle field. The obstacles include

- ✔ Low-crawling under netting
- ✔ Hiding behind walls to avoid enemy fire
- ✔ Rolling behind bushes and timbers
- ✔ Striking dummies with the butt of your rifle
- ✔ High crawling through deep sand up a 40 percent grade

This is a team effort, not a competition. Do not advance ahead of your wingman, and whatever you do, do not stick the barrel of your rifle in the sand!

## Winning the war

Like most military war games, this game is rigged. Assuming that you don't do something really stupid and get sent back early to be recycled, you'll ultimately be declared the winners of the war and be told to pack up your gear and get ready to march back to basic training.

Once you arrive back at the base, it's not bedtime yet, even though you're extremely tired. First, you'll attend retreat, where they play the National Anthem and lower the flag, but this time there is a small ceremony where you're presented with your Air Force Challenge Coin, or Airman's Coin (see Figure 15-2). This coin indicates that you're no longer considered to be an idiot who can't be trusted not to poop on the floor, but rather an official trusted member of the greatest Air Force in the world!

Front

Reverse

**Figure 15-2:**
The Air
Force
Challenge
Coin.

# Post-Deployment Phase
# (Weeks 7 and 8)

Basic training isn't over yet, but your last two weeks after returning from the
BEAST won't quite feel like basic training anymore. For one thing, you feel
like you're now a member of the United States Air Force. Most importantly,
your TIs don't seem to yell at you anymore, unless you do something
monumentally stupid.

Now that you've learned how to fight a war and have proven yourself by surviving the BEAST, the final two weeks consist of getting ready for graduation and lots of time in the classroom, learning other topics that you need to know to enter the real Air Force.

Much of the last two weeks of Air Force basic training is spent in the classroom. Sorry, still no sleeping in class!

Week 7 classroom training covers the following:

- Air Force history
- Enlisted heritage
- Joint warfare
- Combat stress recovery
- Sexual assault prevention and reporting
- Suicide awareness and prevention
- Financial management
- Sexually transmitted diseases
- Ethics

At the end of week 7, you take the second written test. As with the first test, this test is multiple choice, and you need to score a 70 percent or better to pass.

At the beginning of your last week of basic training, you take your final written test, consisting of multiple choice questions covering everything you've learned during Air Force basic training. As with all Air Force basic training written tests, you must score a 70 percent or better to pass. If you fail the final test, you get one chance for a retest the very next day. If you fail the retest, you'll be recycled in order to give you a chance to "relearn" the information.

During your last week of basic training, you'll do more drill — lots of it. However, this is drill with a purpose: You're practicing the drill movements required for your final graduation parade.

The final fitness test is conducted during week 7, a few days after returning from the BEAST. For the graduation and award standards, see Part V.

If you fail the final fitness test, you'll meet with your TI and your basic training commander to determine whether you should be recycled or if it's possible for you to pass the test if you're given a few more days. Much depends on your attitude and how close you were to meeting the standards.

# Chapter 16

# Navy Boot Camp

. . . . . . . . . . . . . . . . . . . . . . . . . . . . . . . . . . . . . . . . . . . .

## In This Chapter

▶ Getting to basic

▶ Cruising through the confidence course

▶ Understanding ships and aircraft

▶ Putting out fires the Navy way

. . . . . . . . . . . . . . . . . . . . . . . . . . . . . . . . . . . . . . . . . . . .

*Y*ou'll pick up a lot of information during your eight weeks at Navy basic training. You discover not only how to be in the U.S. Military, but how to sail on ships and other Navy vessels as well. Many people pay big bucks for this instruction. In the Navy, you get paid to learn, and you'll remember this training for the rest of your life.

# Getting Started: Weeks 1 and 2

Like the Air Force (see Chapter 15), the Navy has only one location for enlisted basic training. The Navy turns civilians into Sailors at the Great Lakes Naval Training Center, which is located on the western shore of Lake Michigan, halfway between Chicago and Milwaukee.

Navy basic training is unique in that much of it is accomplished indoors. There's indoor drill, an indoor obstacle course, and even an indoor firing range, where new recruits learn how to shoot military weapons. Scheduling everything indoors is not just in deference to the cold Illinois winters, but a testament to the fact that most Sailors live on ships or submarines and spend much of their careers inside them.

More than 54,000 recruits go through Navy basic training each year, spending eight weeks in learning how to be a Navy Sailor.

# The big arrival

When you arrive at the Chicago O'Hare airport, you're required to go directly to the USO office and check in with the military staff member present. The USO office and lounge is located in Terminal 2, main floor, upper-level office spaces. (Office spaces are located above the airline ticket counters.) You can see the USO office from the Chicago Police Booth located just prior to exiting the lobby area. Stairs are located at either door 2B or 2C.

Don't take time sight-seeing. Staff members know what time you're supposed to arrive, and if you're too late, you'll get your first chance to experience a basic training chewing out.

The Navy keeps very close track of their new recruit arrival status. If your flight to Chicago is delayed for any reason, make sure that you call the toll-free number — 1 (877) HELP RTC — to let the Navy know of your changed arrival status.

After checking in at the USO, you'll be told to wait (with several other recruits) for the next available transport to Great Lakes. Pretty soon, a basic training instructor will arrive to greet your group and escort you to the bus. This 45-minute bus ride even comes with a tour guide and a movie! After watching a video about Navy basic training, the basic training instructor will be very happy to answer any questions you may have.

Don't be fooled. This instructor/tour guide will be the nicest basic training instructor you'll meet at Navy basic training, but it's just an act. The instructor will undergo a metamorphosis after the bus goes through the gates of the Great Lakes Navy Training Center, and you'll never see that nice guy or gal again.

Unlike the other services, the Navy allows you (actually, it requires you) to make your first phone call home immediately upon arrival. In fact, calling home will be your very first task upon arrival at the basic training recruit reception center. However, hundreds of other recruits will be trying to call home at the same time, so you'll only have a couple minutes to talk — just long enough to tell them that you arrived safely and that (so far) you're just fine.

## P-Days

Navy basic training is officially 8 weeks long, but it's really closer to 9 weeks because the first week is taken up by *in-processing*, or paperwork. You'll spend much of the first week in classrooms, filling out forms to feed to the massive Navy personnel computer systems.

## Do you have what it takes for the 900 Division?

On the first day of processing, you're asked if you have any experience (or interest) in drill, musical instruments, or singing. This isn't just a random question of your interests. If so, you may be assigned to a 900 Division. These special recruits get to do pretty much everything the other recruits in basic training get to do during their 9 weeks, but they also practice to put on shows at events, such as parades and recruit graduation ceremonies.

However, the Navy, like the Devil, hates idle hands, so in between in-processing appointments, your instructors will ensure that you know that you are in Navy basic training, so (from your perspective), basic training has already started.

### First haircuts and smurfs

After the first day's paperwork is completed, you'll be issued Navy sweat suits (known locally as Smurfs), which you'll wear until your first uniform issue a few days down the road.

The Smurf suit is a dead give-away that you're brand new. Wearing your Smurfs into the galley (chow hall) during lunch and dinner will be an experience. You'll be looked at by the older recruits like you just stepped out of the sewer. (Actually, you can see the pity in many of the oldies eyes, who remember their Smurf days). A Smurf is at the bottom of the food chain.

At this point, you'll be told to box up all of your civilian clothing and will have the choice of shipping them back home (at your expense) or donating them to charity.

You'll be strongly encouraged to send your civilian clothing home instead of donating the items to charity. It's not a good idea to resist this suggestion — or any suggestion — during basic training.

Once you get your uniform, you'll find that your status among other recruits is judged by the length of your hair. The longer you've been in basic, the longer your hair will be, and the higher your status. Those fresh from the initial hair cut are only one peg above a Smurf.

Ladies, Navy basic is the only military basic training I know of where female recruits must also have their hair cut. In Navy basic training, however, your hair is cut so that its length does not exceed the bottom of the collar. After you graduate from basic training, you can grow your hair long again, but will be required to wear it up when in uniform.

## *Meeting your RDC*

The real fun begins when you're assigned to a Recruit Division and get to meet your instructor. In the Air Force (Chapter 15), instructors are called MTIs (Military Training Instructors). In the Army (Chapter 14), instructors are called Drill Sergeants. In the Navy, the instructors are called RDCs (Recruit Division Commanders).

As with the Army, addressing an RDC as *sir* or *ma'am* warrants the death penalty. It's vital that you address a Petty Officer as "Petty Officer so-and-so," and a Chief as "Chief so-and-so."

As with MTIs and Drill Sergeants, Navy RDCs are hard of hearing, and you'll have to yell at them in order to be heard. Never, ever forget, this, especially when it comes to Navy Chiefs. Navy Chiefs wait with eager anticipation for new recruits to address them as sir or ma'am. This is normally followed by a tyrannical display, intending to throw recruits into a total disarray of confusion, while demonstrating that it is really Navy Chiefs who are in charge of the Navy (and new recruits).

## *Getting your new ship*

If you've joined the Navy because of your love of the sea, you'll be excited to discover that your new accommodations will be on board a ship. This will be immediately followed by disappointment when you learn it's only a pretend ship.

You'll be assigned to a division, consisting of about 80 men and women. The divisions are housed in gigantic 1,000-person dormitories, which are called ships in Navy basic training. While men and women train together, they obviously don't room together. (Sorry, kids!)

It wouldn't be military basic training if you were allowed to maintain your living quarters like you did at home. During Navy basic training, your ship (barracks) must be kept spotless at all times, and the RDCs will inspect them daily to make sure that you're not slacking off.

While this responsibility is a great source of stress and frustration during the beginning of basic training, by the time you move into week 3, the habit of cleaning up your living area will become automatic — you won't even think about it anymore.

## Navy stress cards

Did you hear the story of how the Navy was issuing *stress cards* so that recruits could call time-out if they felt that boot camp was getting too stressful? I get e-mail questions about Navy stress cards at least once per week. Forget it.

The Navy threw away the stress cards several years ago. At the same time, they toughened up basic training. It's now more stressful than it ever was.

# Standing watch

In the Air Force, standing watch is called dorm guard (see Chapter 15). In the Army, it's called fire guard (see Chapter 14). In the Navy, it's called standing watches. Regardless, it's all the same.

*Standing watch* means that you get to spend significant amounts of time (which could otherwise be used for sleeping) guarding the barracks (excuse me, ship) to make sure that someone doesn't steal it. You get to entertain yourself by listening to people snore or talk in their sleep. You also catch people sleeping at attention, back straight, hands at their sides, *money tight* (hands in position of attention, with stiff hands covering the pockets), feet at a 45-degree angle. They never believe you when you tell them in the morning.

In addition to the standing watch, if you're unlucky enough to attend Navy basic training during the winter months, you can look forward to *snow watch,* in which you will be woken up in the middle of the night to shovel snow if it gets too deep.

# Recruit Petty Officers

After observing the recruits for a few days, the RDCs will select *recruit leaders,* known as Recruit Petty Officers (RPO) in various areas of responsibility. How these student leaders are selected is entirely up to whatever process the specific RDC wants to use. The RDC may select you as an RPO because you're tall, or because you're short, or because you have green eyes, or because you have blue eyes, or because you're older than most recruits there, or because you're younger than most recruits there, or because you volunteered, or because you didn't volunteer, or because you like gravy on your mashed potatoes. In actuality, the RDC will probably select those recruits who, during the first few days, showed that they were on the ball.

Recruit Petty Officers have authority over other recruits in the division within the scope of the duties to which they're assigned. Orders issued by Recruit Petty Officers, acting within their authority, have the full weight of those orders issued by an RDC. Recruit Petty Officers are responsible to RDCs for the proper execution of any orders they receive.

Recruit Petty Officers are charged with preserving good order, discipline, and security within their respective division. Any violation of good order, discipline, and security will be reported by the Recruit Petty Officer to the chain of command for disposition.

In order to distinguish recruits placed in a position of responsibility, Recruit Petty Officers wear a distinctive collar device.

The Navy basic training RPO positions are

- **Recruit Chief Petty Officer (RCPO):** The RCPO is the Chief Honcho among recruits. The RCPO is the primary recruit assistant to RDCs.

- **Recruit Leading Petty Officer (RLPO):** The RLPO is the second Honcho (among recruits) in charge. The Recruit Leading Petty Officer is responsible to the Recruit Chief Petty Officer and RDCs.

- **Recruit Master-at-Arms (RMAA):** The Recruit Master-at-Arms is responsible for configuration and cleanliness of division spaces and the procurement, proper storage, and use of all cleaning gear required by the division.

- **Port and Starboard Watch Section Leaders (PWSL/SWSL):** The Port/Starboard Watch Section Leaders are the senior Recruit Petty Officers for respective watch sections.

- **Recruit Yeoman (YN):** The Recruit YN is responsible to RDCs for performing general clerical duties in the division and assisting RDCs with preparation and maintenance of divisional reports, records, class attendance rosters, and mail pick-up and distribution.

- **Recruit Medical Yeoman (MYN):** The MYN is responsible for assisting the RDCs in preparing and maintaining recruit medical documentation, and coordinating appointments with the Medical Liaison.

- **Recruit Dental Yeoman (DYN):** The DYN is responsible for assisting the RDCs in preparing and maintaining recruit dental documentation and coordinating appointments with the Dental Liaison.

- **Recruit Section Leaders (SL):** Section Leaders are responsible to the respective Watch Section Leader for supervising and assisting the recruits in respective sections.

- **Division Laundry Petty Officer (LPO):** The LPO is responsible to the Recruit Master-at-Arms for executing proper laundry handling procedures and for maintaining the cash box and division expense log.

✔ **Recruit Education Petty Officer (EPO):** The EPO is responsible for assisting RDCs in administering and mustering night study and mandatory night study classes.

✔ **Recruit Athletic Petty Officer (APO):** The Recruit Athletic Petty Officer is responsible for assisting RDCs with Physical Readiness Training.

✔ **Recruit Religious Petty Officers (RPO):** There will be at least a Catholic and Protestant RPO appointed for each division. If a division has three or more recruits of the same faith, a religious petty officer will be appointed to represent that faith. RPOs are responsible for ensuring that all recruits who desire to pray are afforded such an opportunity just prior to lights out.

✔ **Recruit Mail Petty Officers (MPO):** The MPO is responsible for pick-up and delivery of all personal mail.

✔ **Recruit Damage Control Petty Officer (DCPO):** The DCPO is responsible to the Recruit Master-at-Arms for correcting any fire hazards and maintaining division fire extinguishers, including proper location and working order.

# Back to school: Classroom training

Classroom training begins immediately in Navy basic training, and continues almost daily until you graduate. During the first couple of weeks of Navy basic training, you'll attend classes on the following topics:

✔ Grooming standards and uniform wear

✔ Military law and the Uniform Code of Military Justice (UCMJ)

✔ Standards of conduct

✔ Core values

✔ Equal opportunity and discrimination

✔ Naval history

✔ Fundamentals of drill

✔ Navy rank and rate

✔ Rape awareness

✔ Professionalism

✔ Navy chain of command

Your first written test will be at the end of week 2. This is a multiple choice test, and you must achieve a minimum score of 70 percent in order to pass and continue on with basic training. If you fail the test, you'll get one chance for a retest. If you fail the retest, you'll be required to redo the first portion of Navy basic training.

## Swimming qualifications

It doesn't make much sense to spend your career on sea-going ships if you can't swim, and the Navy agrees with that philosophy. In order to graduate from Navy basic training, you must pass a third class swim qualification. The swim qualification test occurs during the first official week of Navy basic training in order to allow time to teach you how to swim if you fail the test.

A third class swim test is a test to determine whether a person can stay afloat and survive without the use of a life preserver in open water long enough to be rescued in a man-overboard situation.

In order to pass the third class swim qualification test, you must be able to

- Deep water jump (jump off a diving board into a deep water swimming pool)
- 50-yard swim (using any stroke)
- Prone float for five minutes
- Demonstrate inflating your trousers or coveralls in order to use them as a flotation device

The third class swim test requirements are the minimum requirements to graduate from Navy basic training. Many Navy jobs have more stringent requirements.

## Gaining confidence on the confidence course

If you pass the first written test (see the section "Back to school: Classroom training"), you get to celebrate with your first visit to the confidence course. If you're in any kind of shape at all, you'll enjoy this part of Navy basic training. To my knowledge, this is the only indoor confidence course in the military.

The Navy basic training confidence course is designed to simulate obstacles you may have to encounter during a shipboard emergency. You don OBAs

(Oxygen Breathing Apparatus, standard equipment for shipboard fire-fighting) carry sandbags, toss life rings, and climb through a *scuttle* (a small circular door) with full sea-bags.

As with the Army and Air Force courses (see Chapters 14 and 15), the confidence course is not an individual event. It's a team effort. Recruits complete the course in groups of four. The object is to cross the finish line as a team, not as individuals.

# Weeks 3 Through 8

Once you get through the first two weeks of Navy basic training, you're almost guaranteed to graduate, as long as you try your best and don't slack off.

By week 4, you're starting to get it, which shows in the attitude of your RDCs. You'll notice that they're not yelling as much and seem more interested in teaching, rather than discipline. Of course, if you make a big bone-head move, you'll discover that they haven't forgotten how to yell at you.

## More time in the classroom

A significant amount of classroom training goes on during this phase of Navy basic training. During week 3, you attend classes about Naval history, laws of armed conflict, money management, shipboard communications, and basic seamanship. You also receive extensive training concerning the types of Navy ships and aircraft and their purposes and capabilities.

Hopefully, you're paying attention in class because you'll face the second written test at the end of week 3. As with other Navy basic training written tests, this test is multiple-guess, and you need to score a 70 percent or better to pass and move on. If you fail this test, you can expect to be recycled to an earlier portion of basic training for some additional study time.

### Navy ships

Not counting submarines and experimental ships, the Navy has many types of Naval ships, each one designed for a specific purpose. You'll want to pay particular attention during these classes because chances are high that your first assignment following basic training and Navy job school will be for sea duty, and you'll be stationed on one of these ships for a majority of your first term of service.

The following list describes different types of Navy ships:

- **Aircraft carriers:** The aircraft carrier continues to be the centerpiece of the forces necessary for forward presence. Whenever a crisis occurs, the first question is always, "Where are the carriers?" Carriers support and operate aircraft that are capable of engaging in attacks on airborne, afloat, submerged, and ashore targets that threaten free use of the sea. They also engage in sustained operations in support of other forces. Aircraft carriers are deployed worldwide in support of U.S. interests and commitments. They can respond to global crises in ways ranging from peacetime presence to full-scale war. Together with their on-board air wings, the carriers have vital roles across the full spectrum of conflict. Aircraft carriers are designated as CV or CVN, the difference being that CVNs are nuclear-powered and CVs are conventionally powered. For example, the *U.S.S Nimitz* is officially designated as CVN 68.

  More than 5,000 sailors are stationed aboard each aircraft carrier, so it's almost like being assigned to a small city (except this one moves).

- **Ammunition ships:** You can't fight a war without bullets, and if you run out of bullets, you want to be able to get more without pausing to let the enemy regroup. That's where the Navy ammunition ships come in. Ammunition ships deliver munitions to warships. Ammunition ships keep the fleet supplied with ammunition and ordnance, independently or with other combat logistic ships. Ammunition is delivered by slings on ship-to-ship cables and by helicopters. Ammunition ships are designated as AE, or T-AE. The T indicates that the ship is part of the Military Sealift Command and is crewed almost entirely by civilians.

- **Amphibious assault ships:** Primary landing ships, resembling small aircraft carriers, these ships are designed to put troops on hostile shores. Modern U.S. Navy amphibious assault ships are called upon to perform as primary landing ships for assault operations of Marine expeditionary units. These ships use a kind of hovercraft known as a Landing Craft Air Cushion (LCAC), conventional landing craft, and helicopters to move Marine assault forces ashore. In a secondary role, using AV-8B Harrier aircraft and anti-submarine warfare helicopters, these ships perform sea control and limited power projection missions.

  Amphibious assault ships are designated as LHA, or LHD. The crew usually includes 104 officers, 1,004 enlisted members, and a detachment of 1,894 Marines, but can vary a great deal

- **Amphibious command ships:** Designated as LCC, amphibious command ships provide command and control for fleet commanders. Commissioned in 1970, these are the only ships to be designed initially for an amphibious command ship role. Earlier amphibious command ships lacked sufficient speed to keep up with a 20-knot amphibious force. The crew consists of 52 officers, 790 enlisted members.

- **Amphibious transport dock:** Designated as LPDs, amphibious transport docks are used as troop transports for amphibious operations. The amphibious transports are used to transport and land Marines, their equipment, and their supplies by embarked landing craft or amphibious vehicles augmented by helicopters in amphibious assault. The crew consists of 24 officers, 396 enlisted members, and the ship carries a detachment consisting of 900 Marines.

✔ **Command ships:** Designated as AGF, command ships serve as the flagships for the Commander, Third Fleet, and Commander, Sixth Fleet. Command ships provide communications and accommodations for fleet commanders and staff. Ships are equipped with air and surface radars, helicopter, chaff launchers, and an electronic warfare suite. The ship's crew includes 516 sailors, plus 120 flag staff officers.

✔ **Cruisers:** Navy cruisers are designated as CG. Cruisers are large combat vessels with multiple target response capability. Modern U.S. Navy guided missile cruisers perform primarily in a battle-force role. These ships are multimission surface combatants capable of supporting carrier battle groups, amphibious forces, or of operating independently and as flagships of surface action groups. The crew consists of 24 officers, 340 enlisted members.

✔ **Destroyers:** These ships, designated as DDG, help safeguard larger ships in a fleet or battle group. Destroyers and guided missile destroyers operate in support of carrier battle groups, surface action groups, amphibious groups, and replenishment groups. Destroyers primarily perform anti-submarine warfare duty while guided missile destroyers are multimission surface combatants. The ship's crew includes 23 officers and 300 enlisted members.

✔ **Dock landing ship:** This class of ships is designated as LSD. Dock landing ships support amphibious operations, including landings via air cushion landing craft, conventional landing craft, and helicopters, onto hostile shores. The crew includes 22 officers and 397 enlisted members. The ship also carries a Marine detachment of 402 Marines, with a surge capability of 102 additional Marines.

✔ **Fast combat support ships:** These ships, designated as AOE, or "T-AOE," are high-speed vessels, designed as oiler, ammunition, and supply ships. The fast combat support ship (AOE) is the Navy's largest combat logistics ship. The AOE has the speed and armament to keep up with the carrier battle groups. It rapidly replenishes Navy task forces and can carry more than 177,000 barrels of oil, 2,150 tons of ammunition, 500 tons of dry stores, and 250 tons of refrigerated stores. The ship has a crew consisting of 40 officers and 627 enlisted members.

✔ **Frigates:** Designated as FFG, frigates fulfill a protection of shipping mission as anti-submarine warfare combatants for amphibious expeditionary forces, underway replenishment groups and merchant convoys. The crew includes 13 officers and 287 enlisted members.

✔ **Underway replenishment oilers:** Thirteen underway replenishment oilers (designated as T-AO), are operated by Military Sealift Command and provide underway replenishment of fuel to U.S. Navy ships at sea and jet fuel for aircraft assigned to aircraft carriers. Three of the newest MSC underway replenishment oilers have double hulls. These vessels are unique in that a majority of the crew are civilian contractors (82). 21 of the crewmembers are active duty Navy.

✔ **Air cushioned landing craft:** Designated as LCAC, these are air-cushioned crafts for transporting (ship to shore and across the beach) personnel, weapons, equipment, and cargo of the assault elements of the Marine Air-Ground Task Force. The air cushion landing craft is a high-speed, over-the-beach fully amphibious landing craft capable of carrying a 60 to 75-ton payload. It's used to transport weapons systems, equipment, cargo, and personnel from ship to shore and across the beach.

The advantages of air-cushion landing craft are numerous. They can carry heavy payloads, such as an M-1 tank, at high speeds. Their payload and speed mean more forces reach the shore in a shorter time, with shorter intervals between trips. The air cushion allows this vehicle to reach more than 70 percent of the world's coastline, while conventional landing craft can land at only 15 percent of the coasts. The craft requires a crew of only five Navy sailors.

✔ **Mark V special operations craft:** The Mark V is used to carry Special Operations Forces (SOF), primarily SEAL combat swimmers, into and out of operations where the threat to these forces is considered to be low to medium. They also support limited coastal patrol and interruption of enemy activities. MARK Vs are organized into detachments comprised of two boats, crews, and a deployment support package mounted on cargo transporters. The detachment can be delivered in-theater rapidly by two C-5 aircraft, by a well or flight-deck equipped surface ship, and, if appropriate, under their own power. These craft have no permanently assigned crew and are operated by SOF (SEAL) personnel.

✔ **Coastal mine hunters:** Designated as MHC, these ships are designed to locate and clear mines from vital waterways. These ships use sonar and video systems, cable cutters, and a mine-detonating device that can be released and detonated by remote control. They're also capable of conventional sweeping measures. The ships' hulls are made of glass-reinforced plastic (GRP) fiberglass. They're the first large mine counter-measures ships built in the United States in nearly 27 years. The crew includes 5 officers and 46 enlisted members.

✔ **Mine countermeasures ships:** These ships are designated as MCM. In the early 1980s, the U.S. Navy began development of a new mine counter-measures (MCM) force, which included two new classes of ships and minesweeping helicopters. The vital importance of a state-of-the-art mine countermeasures force was strongly underscored in the Persian Gulf during the eight years of the Iran-Iraq war, and in Operations Desert Shield and Desert Storm in 1990 and 1991 when the Avenger (MCM 1) and Guardian (MCM 5) ships conducted MCM operations. These ships carry a crew of 8 officers and 76 enlisted members.

✔ **Coastal patrol boats:** Designated as PC, the primary mission of these ships is coastal patrol and interdiction surveillance. These ships also provide full mission support for Navy SEALs and other special operations forces. The ships carry 4 officers, 24 enlisted personnel, and 8 Special Forces personnel (SEALs).

✔ **Rescue and salvage ships:** These ships are designated as ARS. Rescue and salvage ships render assistance to disabled ships and provide towing, salvage, diving, firefighting, and heavy-lift capabilities. The mission of the rescue and salvage ships is four-fold: To debeach stranded vessels, heavy lift capability from ocean depths, towing of other vessels, and manned diving operations. For rescue missions, these ships are equipped with fire monitors forward and amidships that can deliver either firefighting foam or sea water. The salvage holds of these ships are outfitted with portable equipment to provide assistance to other vessels in dewatering, patching, supply of electrical power, and other essential service required to return a disabled ship to an operating condition. These ships carry a crew of 6 officers and 94 enlisted members.

✔ **Submarine tenders:** Designated as AS, submarine tenders furnish maintenance and logistic support for nuclear attack submarines. Submarine tenders are the largest of the active auxiliaries. Their crews are made up mostly technicians and repair personnel. These ships carry a crew of 97 officers and 1,266 enlisted members.

## Navy aircraft

The U.S. Navy has almost as many aircraft as the U.S. Air Force. The primary difference is that almost all Navy aircraft are designed to be able to take off and land on ships, known as aircraft carriers. The types of naval aircraft include

✔ **Cargo aircraft:** Cargo aircraft are primarily designed to carry equipment, supplies, and personnel. Navy cargo aircraft include the C-2A Greyhound, C-9 Skytrain, C-12F Huron, and the C-130 Hercules.

✔ **Communications and surveillance aircraft:** These aircraft provide survivable, reliable, and endurable airborne command, control, and communications between the National Command Authority (NCA) and U.S. strategic and nonstrategic forces. Navy communications and surveillance aircraft include the E-2C Hawkeye, E-6A Mercury, and EA-6B Prowler aircraft.

✔ **Electronic Warfare aircraft:** These sophisticated aircraft perform a variety of important missions, most famously the jamming of enemy radars. The EA-6B Prowler is being replaced by the EA-18 Growler.

✔ **Fighter aircraft:** Fighter aircraft are fast-moving combat aircraft which are used for air defense (shooting down enemy aircraft) and for light ground attacks. The Navy currently has only two kinds of fighter aircraft — the F/A-18 Hornet and the F/A-18 E/F Super Hornet.

✔ **Patrol aircraft:** The Navy currently uses only one type of aircraft for this mission: the P-3C Orion. The P-3C is a land-based aircraft. (It can't land on aircraft carriers.) The P-3 will eventually be replaced by a newer version, the P-8 Poseidon, which is based on the Boeing 737 airliner.

✔ **Trainer aircraft:** These aircraft are used by the Navy for flight training, including instruction of how to take off and land on an aircraft carrier. They include the T-2C Buckeye, T-34C Turbomentor, and the T-45A Goshawk.

## *Basic line handling skills*

Assuming that you pass the second written test, you can put on your gloves and dust off your knot-making techniques, as you'll get to practice basic line-handling skills. After all, the Navy can't have new recruits tying a slip-knot and allowing that aircraft carrier to drift away from the dock!

Sailors use hundreds of different types of knots, but in Navy basic training, you'll be required to use only the three basic types of sea-going knots:

✔ The **square knot** is also known as the *reef knot.* Sailors have used this knot for centuries for reefing and tying things aboard ship because it's very secure. Figure 16-1 shows how to properly tie a square knot.

**Tying a Square Knot**

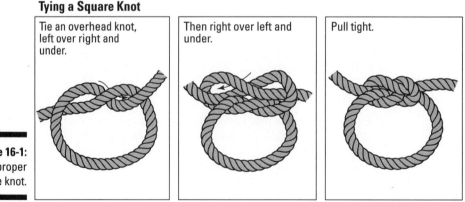

Tie an overhead knot, left over right and under.

Then right over left and under.

Pull tight.

**Figure 16-1:**
A proper
square knot.

✔ The **clove hitch knot** is the second type of Navy knot you'll learn in Navy basic training. The clove hitch is an adjustable knot that's great for temporary uses such as mooring a small craft. Figure 16-2 shows how to tie it.

**Tying a Clove Hitch**

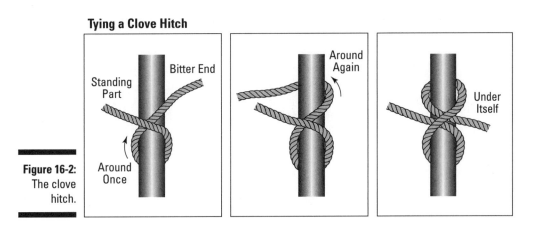

**Figure 16-2:**
The clove hitch.

> ✔ The **bowline** is used to form a fixed loop at the end of a rope. Its chief virtue is that it's extremely easy to tie and untie. This is the third knot you'll learn how to tie in Navy basic training. Figure 16-3 shows you how.

**Tying a Bowline** (or the story of The Nervous Rabbit. There is a rabbit hole under a tree, the rabbit jumps out of the hole, runs around the tree, and jumps back into the hole. The End.)

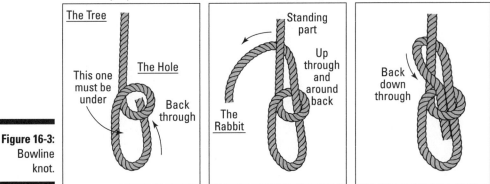

**Figure 16-3:**
Bowline knot.

## Bluejacket's Manual

You can find out everything you need to know about Navy shipboard skills in The *Bluejacket's Manual*. The first edition of this Navy manual was published in 1902, and it has been continually republished periodically since then. While you'll be issued a copy of this 600-page manual in Navy basic training, you can get a head start on required sea-faring knowledge by getting your hands on a copy for advanced study. You can purchase the manual at many book stores, including online at Amazon.com.

*Making a line* ready for use is when you tie two pieces of rope together. The process requires three steps

1. **Coil down.**

   Lay the line in circles, roughly on top of itself. Do not keep the line in a perfect circle.

2. **Flemish down.**

   Starting with one end, spiral the line tightly.

3. **Fake down.**

   Lay the line out in approximately 10-foot lengths. When you get to the end, make a loop and overlap it. Continue this until all line is faked.

In Navy basic training, you're required to memorize these steps. Don't worry, though. You'll get so much practice that memorizing the steps won't be a problem.

# Week 4: First aid, attitude adjustments, and more

During weeks 3 and 4, you'll spend a lot of time in the classroom learning the fundamentals of first aid. For a time, you'll begin to think that someone changed your Navy job contract, and you're now in training to become a Navy doctor or nurse.

During this time, your hands-on first-aid training includes lessons about

- Basic life support
- Bleeding
- Shock
- Soft tissue injuries
- Bones, joints, and muscles
- Environmental injuries
- Chemical, biological, and radiological casualties
- Poisoning
- Medical injuries
- Rescue and transportation

In addition, sometime during week 4, you'll begin to think that someone must have snuck in, stole your RDC, and left an imposter in his place. The new one seems to be much, much nicer than the old one and seems to be more interested in helping you learn rather than seeing how much abuse you can take.

The truth is that if you've made it this far, you're beginning to get it, and there's no longer much reason for yelling and screaming to get your attention. However, if you screw up significantly, you'll find that it only takes a microsecond to bring back the old RDC.

### Initial physical training test

During the week 4 of Navy basic training, you'll also undergo the first fitness test. While there is no official pass/fail for this test, your RDCs will be judging whether or not they think you will have problems passing the final fitness test conducted during the week 7.

If you have problems meeting (or coming close) to the basic training fitness standards (see Chapter 2), you can expect individual fitness attention from your RDC for the remainder of basic training. Individual attention is never a good thing.

### Uniform pickup and graduation photos

By the end of week 4, everyone is pretty sure that you're going to graduate and fairly sure that you'll graduate on time, without having to be recycled for additional training.

At the end of this week, you'll pick up your dress uniforms from the tailor (hopefully, they fit now), and you'll pose for graduation photos. These photos will be available for sale to family and friends during your basic training graduation ceremony.

## Visiting the firing range

Before the elimination of service week (see sidebar), Navy basic training weapons firing consisted of a computerized simulation. Now that service week is no more, there's time to actually let new recruits fire real, live weapons. A visit to the firing range takes place around week 5.

The Navy is unique in that recruits do not fire the standard M-16 rifle during basic training. This is primarily because a long-range rifle is of limited use when it comes to protecting a ship.

## No more service week

The fifth week of Navy Boot Camp used to be *service week.* This was the week that recruits helped to keep Great Lakes clean, most especially in the kitchen (except, in the Navy, the kitchen is known as a *galley).* The galley at Great Lakes takes a lot of cleaning up. In 2003, the galley served 9.45 million meals, consisting of 146,000 pounds of ground beef, 447,000 loaves of bread, 261,000 gallons of milk, and 223,000 pounds of chicken.

However, in October 2003, the Navy eliminated service week. All of this cleaning up is now done by civilian contractors. The recommendation to eliminate service week was made by the Navy Training Board of Advisors. This group of Training School Commanders and Command Master Chiefs from the Fleet meets periodically to review Navy Training.

The elimination of service week has created more than 30 additional hours that can be used for recruit training and administrative tasks.

Instead, Navy recruits fire 45 rounds with the M-9, 9mm pistol, and 5 rounds using the Mossberg shotgun. Chapter 4 has complete information about Navy basic training weapons firing.

## *Week 6's fun: Visiting the confidence chamber and more time in the classroom*

During week 6, you get to visit (drum roll) the gas chamber! (No . . . not the kind they have in prisons. This one only makes you cough and puke.) And actually, the Navy prefers to call its gas chamber the *confidence chamber.*

Eat light on gas chamber day.

Here's how it works:

1. **You and about 100 other recruits line up in multiple rows in the confidence chamber and don your gas mask.**

   You have 30 seconds to don your gas mask while the petty officer is lighting the tear gas tablet.

2. **When it's your row's turn, a petty officer instructs you to take off your mask and remove the filter cartridge, throwing it in a trash can, while stating your full name and social security number.**

   Interesting side note: This is one of the only times in boot camp that you'll hear everyone's first name — if you can care about such matters with a lung-full of tear gas.

3. **When everyone in the row is done with Step 2, you'll be permitted to leave.**

   Once you get outside and finally stop gagging, crying and puking yourself, you get to watch the rows behind you come out and cry, gag, and puke.

If you do get snot or puke, you're not allowed to let it hit the deck (floor). You must either catch it with your hand and wipe it on your shirt or just puke down the inside of your shirt. If you dirty the deck, you don't leave until it's cleaned up.

During week 6, you also spend more time in the classroom, learning more Navy subjects that all sailors must have proficient knowledge of. Classroom training during this week includes

- ✔ Navy uniform wear
- ✔ Grooming standards
- ✔ Dependent care requirements
- ✔ Terrorism threats

# The End Is in Sight: Closing Weeks

You take the final written test at the end of week 7. If you pass this test and the final physical fitness test, which immediately follows, the chances are about 99 percent that you will graduate from Navy basic training on time.

As with all Navy basic training written tests, this one is multiple choice, and covers everything you've learned since the last test. You must score a 70 percent or better to pass and graduate.

If you make it through the final written test and the fitness test, you get to practice your firefighting skills in an actual ship-board fire-fighting exercise. While it's not a ship, the fire is very real. This exercise isn't graded, but you'll get feedback from your instructors concerning what you could have done better. Most recruits find this exercise to be a lot of fun, mostly because there's no pass/fail.

Figure 16-4 shows a recruit having fun while pretending to save the ship from a fire.

**Figure 16-4:**
Navy basic
training
firefighting
drill.

Week 7 winds up with Battle Stations. *Battle Stations* is the culminating event of Navy basic training. It's designed to wrap everything you've learned about swimming survival, teamwork, firefighting, damage control, and more into one massive 12 hour hands-on exercise. (You can find out more about Battle Stations in Chapter 19.)

Don't waste time worrying about Battle Stations. Without exception, every single graduate I've met has told me that Battle Stations was the most fun they had in boot camp. Many have said it's the most fun they've had in their entire lives!

# Chapter 17

# Marine Corps Basic Training

. . . . . . . . . . . . . . . . . . . . . . . . . . . . . . . . . . . . . . . . . . . . . . . .

. . . . . . . . . . . . . . . . . . . . . . . . . . . . . . . . . . . . . . . . . . . . . . . .

Two locations turn men and women into Marines: the Recruit Training Depot at Parris Island, South Carolina, and the Recruit Training Depot at San Diego, California. Where you go depends largely upon where you enlist. Those who enlist west of the Mississippi will likely go through boot camp in San Diego, while those in the East will attend at Parris Island. Only one boot camp turns women into Marines — Parris Island.

Other than geographical differences, such as the lack of sand fleas and better outdoor exercise weather for Hollywood Marines, the training is virtually identical at both locations.

Without doubt, Marine boot camp is more challenging — both physically and mentally — than the basic training programs of any of the other military services. Not only are the physical requirements much higher, but recruits are required to learn and memorize a startling amount of information. More than 70 training days are scheduled in a period a little longer than 12 weeks — but don't let that number fool you. Lots of training occurs on nontraining days, such as the time in Reception, the time spent in forming, and on Sundays and holidays. It has been said time and time again by former Marines that Marine Corps recruit training was the most difficult thing they ever had to do in their entire lives.

## Checking In at Recruit Receiving

Marine Corps basic is officially 12 weeks of training, plus 1 week of processing. However, the training and discipline start as soon as you step off the bus at Recruit Receiving.

You spend the first few days of your recruit training experience at Recruit Receiving, Here, you receive your first haircut and initial gear issue, which includes items like uniforms, toiletries, and letter-writing supplies.

Unlike the other services, which have a packing list of things you should bring with you to basic, the Marines prefer that you show up with just the clothes on your back and your enlistment paperwork. The Marines take care of supplying everything else.

Here's what to expect at Recruit Receiving:

- **First haircut (males):** If you're male, you'll get all your hair cut off, almost immediately. In Marine Corps basic training, you don't wait around for a day or two before this initiation ceremony — it happens almost immediately upon arrival. Unlike Navy basic training (see Chapter 16), female Marines don't have to have their hair cut, but if they choose not to, they must wear their hair off their collar at all times and make sure that it doesn't interfere with the wearing of military headgear. Even if you're a female, I highly recommend getting your hair cut.

- **Medical/dental screening:** While in Receiving, you'll also undergo a complete medical and dental screening. The medical screening isn't as intense as the one you underwent at MEPS for enlistment and focuses primarily on whether you're medically capable of participating in rigorous Marine Corps basic training activities. The dental exam is used to develop a dental treatment plan, which won't begin until after you graduate from basic training.

- **Drug test:** As with the other branches, you will undergo a urinalysis test to check for illegal drug use. As with the other branches, if you test positive for illegal drugs, you'll be immediately discharged. Getting a second chance (waiver) later is almost impossible.

It takes about two weeks for the results of the drug test to come back. If you test positive, you'll be immediately discharged, without graduation, after going through the toughest part of Marine Corps basic training.

- **Initial strength test (IST):** Even though you had to pass this test at MEPS before shipping out, you'll have to pass it again. If you fail the IST, you'll be placed in a special physical fitness platoon, where you'll do nothing but exercise all day, until you can pass the IST and begin the regular basic training. (See Chapter 8 for the IST requirements for both males and females.)

## *Wearing your new specs*

You can't wear contact lenses during basic training (for safety concerns). You also can't wear your civilian glasses after you've been issued your official government-issue glasses, which will happen around Day 2.

GI glasses aren't pretty to look at. In fact, most people call them *BC glasses,* or birth control glasses, on the basis that nobody has ever been known to "get lucky" while wearing them.

During your first couple of days of basic training, you'll undergo a complete eye examination. If you require glasses to have 20/20 vision, you'll be issued BC glasses. (It takes a couple of days after the examination to get them.) BC glasses have thick, hard-plastic frames, with thick, hard-plastic lenses (very hard to break). Think of the movie, "Revenge of the Nerds."

If you don't really need glasses to see, you won't be required to wear them. After you graduate from basic training, you can wear your civilian glasses again, as long as they conform to military dress and appearance regulations. Generally, that means their color must be conservative (no green, glow-in-the-dark frames), no designs or decorations on the frames, and no tinted lenses when indoors or outdoors when in military formation (when lined up for marching). Of course, these rules apply only when wearing a military uniform. In civilian clothes (after basic training) you can pretty much wear whatever kind of glasses you want.

## Doing everything by the numbers

While in Receiving, you'll be introduced to how Marine recruits do everything in Marine Corps basic training — *by the numbers.* When I say by the numbers, I mean recruits are taught how to do things strictly by the Marine Corps' order of operations.

Even something as simple as taking a shower is done by the numbers:

1. **Line up.**

2. **March to shower head.**

3. **Pull the ring and wet your head**

4. **Soap your head and face thoroughly.**

5. **Rinse.**

6. **Soap your left arm.**

    You get the idea!

## Getting out of Receiving

You'll spend between three to five days in Receiving. While in Receiving, you're taught by several different drill instructors. During this time, you'll think you're already in official basic training. Drill instructors will be yelling at you, and you'll do some drill, some marching, wear uniforms, eat, drink, shower, and um . . . other things by the numbers, get chewed out some more, learn to make your bunk (I mean "rack"), and so on.

# Getting Acclimated to Your First Few Days of Real Basic Training

When you're done processing with Recruit Receiving, you'll be marched to a new barracks, where you'll be introduced to your permanent drill instructor. If you think the temporary drill instructors in Receiving were tough, you ain't seen nothing yet.

By this time, you're eager to start the real Marine Corps basic training, but no such luck. Even though, you may feel like you've already been in Marine Corps basic training and you think you've mastered the basics of basic, you must first go through a few days of forming.

## Forming

*Forming* is the three to five-day period when you (and your fellow recruits) are taken to their training companies and you discover who your drill instructors are for the first time. (You've probably already met them during Receiving.) You can expect to have two to four drill instructors assigned to your platoon.

During forming, you'll be put through a crash course — call it Intro to Basic. You'll perfect your knowledge of how to wear your uniform properly and how to properly secure your weapon when not carrying it, among other things. Forming is designed to allow you to adjust to the recruit training way of life before the first actual training day.

## Mastering a new language

As soon as you arrive at basic training, you'll be expected to learn a brand-new vocabulary (no mistakes allowed):

- You don't go upstairs; you go *topside*.
- You don't go downstairs; you go *down below*.
- Your bunk becomes a *rack*.
- The latrine (or bathroom) is a *head*.

- The floor is a *deck*.
- The walls are *bulkheads*.
- The windows are *portholes*.
- The ceiling is an *overhead*.
- You face *forward*. Behind you is *aft*.
- Facing forward, left is *port*, and right is *starboard*.

*Never* call the DI's office an office. It is, and always will be, the *DI House*. While I use the acronym DI in this chapter, *never, ever* call your drill instructor a DI Your drill instructor is referred to as "Drill Instructor *[Rank][Name]*."

Third-person language is also a cardinal rule. It's not me, or I; it's *this recruit*. It's not them, or us; it's *these recruits* or *those recruits*. Never say the word, *you* to your drill instructor. The proper phrase would be "Sir, this recruit does not understand the drill instructor's request, sir."

The Marine Corps is under the Department of the Navy, so Navy terminology is used and should be understood completely.

## Visiting the quarter-deck

Drill instructors aren't supposed to use profanity (sometimes they slip), nor are they allowed to physically touch a recruit (other than for safety reasons, such as on the weapon's range). So, how do they maintain discipline? In the other services, it may be by having you do push-ups or possibly some running. In the Marine Corps, though, you get quarter-decked.

---

## Where the boys are — male/female separation

Unlike the other military branches, men and women don't do basic training together in the Marine Corps. In fact, no women are at Marine Corps basic training in San Diego. All female Marines go through basic training at Parris Island.

However, if you're a male completing basic training at Parris Island, being at the same basic location with members of the opposite sex is the closest you will get to them during basic. At Parris Island, women have separate instructors (female, of course), attend separate female-only classes, and eat separately at the chow hall. If you go through basic training at Parris Island and are very, very lucky, you might get to see a female in the distance. If you attend basic training in San Diego, the only chance of seeing a female is someone's mother or sister during basic training graduation.

Your three drill instructors work as an effective team. The senior DI gives most of the commands and orders. The Second Hat, or *Heavy A,* singles out those who seem to be having problems understanding simple shouted English and administers noteworthy tongue-lashings. To keep things interesting, the Third Hat administers the physical discipline, known officially as IPT (Incentive Physical Training), unofficially known as *quarter-decking.*

The *pit* and the *quarter-deck* are the designated areas for IPT exercise — one is inside, and one is outside. IPT consists of prescribed exercises (a maximum of five minutes outside in the pit, no maximum time inside on the quarter-deck). If you're quarter-decked, you can expect these exercises:

- Bends and thrusts
- Leg lifts
- Side lunges
- Mountain climbing
- Running in place
- Side straddle hops
- Push-ups

Your DI encourages you to do all these exercises as fast as you can. DIs use a combination of individual and group IPTs to keep the platoon on their toes. You should also expect to do *up-downs,* where you'll simply sit down and stand up as quick and as long as the DI wishes.

The quarter deck is a place where the D.I. will become creative in dishing out intense physical training. During the forming portion of week 1, you and your platoon won't be able to do anything right, and you'll be quarter-decked often. Some jobs can expect to be quarter-decked more than usual. For example, because of their relative high visibility, the jobs of platoon leaders, squad leaders, and administrative assistants to the Senior DI can expect more than their fair share of quarter-decking.

Expect to make frequent trips to the quarter deck. The key to limiting your stay is to put forth as much effort as humanly possible. The DIs want to see a recruit give 110 percent even if he isn't physically able to perform the exercises well. Do *not* use strategy, such as pacing yourself. This will only ensure that the DI becomes more creative and extends your time on the quarter deck. A 10-minute trip on the quarter deck seems like a lifetime, and once finished, it will appear as if you just got out of a swimming pool.

# Catching your zzzs and a little free time

Most nights, you'll get a full eight hours of uninterrupted sleep. However, the Marine Corps Recruit Training Regulation allows the Basic Training Commanding General to reduce this requirement to seven hours.

The eight-hour requirement doesn't apply when you're required to perform guard duty, fire/security watch, or mess duty or when the company is engaged in scheduled night events. Under such circumstances, the hours of sleep may be reduced to a minimum of six hours. When such a deviation is authorized, the eight-hour sleep regimen must be restored as soon as possible after the event/circumstances no longer exist. During the Crucible Event, (the final graduation exercise), you normally receive four hours of sleep per night. (For more on this event, see the section "The Crucible: The Mother of All Events," later in this chapter.)

In addition to eight hours of sleep, you'll get some free time each day. The purpose of free time is to allow recruits to read or write letters, watch instructional television (ITV), and take care of other personal needs. (Mail is passed out each day by the DIs prior to free time.) During this free time, the recruits receive no training, and the drill instructors conduct no instruction.

## Recruit Bill of Rights

If you think you don't have any rights in Marine Corps basic training, you're mistaken. The Marine Corps Recruit Training Regulation lists the following *recruit rights:*

✓ Eight hours of uninterrupted sleep, except under certain conditions (see the section "Catching your zzzs and a little free time" for details).

✓ One hour of free time daily, unless removed for punishment, and during processing, forming, weapons and field/combat training, and the Crucible Event.

✓ Twenty minutes to consume each meal.

✓ Attend sick call.

✓ Attend scheduled religious services.

✓ Request mast (meeting with the commanding officer) via the chain-of-command.

✓ Make and receive emergency phone calls.

✓ Receive mail on the day it is received by the parent company except for Sundays, holidays, and during the Crucible Event.

✓ Send mail without fear of censorship.

✓ Make head (bathroom) calls.

✓ Use medication prescribed by a certified military medical officer.

## Grenades and other things that go bang

During your time on the firing ranges, you won't just be shooting your rifle. A few hours will be dedicated to tossing live grenades at simulated targets. Remember, you pull the pin and then throw the grenade, not the pin. You may also use smoke simulators and grenade simulators, which make a loud noise without actually blowing up.

Free time is intended to be a relief period from close, constant association for both recruits and DIs. The Marine Corps Recruit Training Regulation requires the DIs to give you one hour of uninterrupted free time each evening, beginning on the first training day, while in garrison (not out in the field), Monday through Saturday, and four hours on Sundays and holidays while in garrison. Company commanders may authorize two hours of free time on Saturdays (but don't expect it!).

Company commanders may suspend free time for recruits as a result of punishment imposed by administrative or legal proceedings.

## *Receiving your rifle*

Without doubt, Marines fire their M-16 rifle more during basic training than any of the other branches (combined) do during their respective basic training programs. This is consistent with the fact that all Marines consider themselves riflemen first, and whatever Marine Corps job they hold, second.

Like the Army and the Air Force, you'll be issued an M-16 rifle almost immediately in Marine Corps basic training, and you're expected to take care of it, clean it, and take it with you everywhere you go.

The biggest sin in Marine Corps basic training is leaving your rifle unattended. Even though you aren't issued any ammunition, this is a real military rifle, worth hundreds of dollars on the black market. Leaving your rifle unattended, even for a second, is sure to earn you some extended time on the quarter-deck.

About the time that you're issued your first M-16 rifle, you'll be required to memorize the Marine Corps rifle creed. *My Rifle* was written by Major General William H. Rupertus (USMC, Ret.) following the attack on Pearl Harbor, which resulted in the U.S.'s entrance into World War II:

*"This is my rifle. There are many like it, but this one is mine.*

*My rifle is my best friend. It is my life. I must master it as I must master my life.*

*My rifle, without me, is useless. Without my rifle, I am useless. I must fire my rifle true. I must shoot straighter than my enemy who is trying to kill me. I must shoot him before he shoots me. I will . . . .*

*My rifle and myself know that what counts in this war is not the rounds we fire, the noise of our burst, nor the smoke we make. We know that it is the hits that count. We will hit . . . .*

*My rifle is human, even as I, because it is my life. Thus, I will learn it as a brother. I will learn its weaknesses, its strength, its parts, its accessories, its sights and its barrel. I will ever guard it against the ravages of weather and damage as I will ever guard my legs, my arms, my eyes and my heart against damage. I will keep my rifle clean and ready. We will become part of each other. We will . . . .*

*Before God, I swear this creed. My rifle and myself are the defenders of my country. We are the masters of our enemy. We are the saviors of my life.*

*So be it, until victory is America's and there is no enemy, but peace!"*

During week 5, you'll visit the firing range several times and finally get a chance to shoot the darned M-16 you've been carrying everywhere.

Assuming that the instructors are confident and you don't blow your own foot off, you'll qualify with the weapon at the range (see Chapter 4) during the sixth week of basic training.

During week 7, you'll get to shoot your M-16 even more during *field firing*. Field firing more closely represents the type of firing you would do in a combat zone, with pop-up targets and other mild surprises. Shoot all the bad guys you want, but don't shoot the little-girl-with-the-school-books target that is likely to pop up. For more information about weapons training, see Chapter 4.

# Hitting the Books: Classroom Training

Even though there doesn't seem to be enough hours in the day, a surprising amount of classroom learning is accomplished during the first few weeks of Marine Corps basic training. You'll attend classes about

- **Marine Corps Core Values:** You can find out more about these important values later in this section.

✔ **Field first aid:** You'll attend classroom training and participate in practical exercises to treat common field and battle injuries.

✔ **Defensive driving:** No, this class isn't about driving a Jeep or tank in a combat zone. It's about driving home from work or driving while on leave (vacation). A few years ago, the Marines noticed that they were losing too many young troops to simple road accidents, so they added this eight-hour course to basic training.

✔ **Marine Corps rank and insignia:** For more on this topic, see Chapter 5.

✔ **The Code of Conduct:** See the information later in this section.

✔ **The Uniform Code of Military Justice (UCMJ) and military law:** See Chapter 7 and Appendix A.

Generation after generation of American men and women have given special meaning to the title United States Marine. These same men and women live by a set of enduring core values, which form the bedrock of their character. The core values give Marines strength and regulate their behavior; they bond the Marine Corps into a total force that can meet any challenge.

## The Marines' Hymn

*The Marines' Hymn,* the official song of the U.S. Marine Corps, is the oldest official song in the U.S. Military. While the words date from the 19th century, the author of the song itself is unknown. The *Marines' Hymn* is typically sung at the position of attention as a gesture of respect. Before you graduate from Marine Corps basic training, you'll have memorized the entire song. It'll make life easier if you can memorize the song, or at least the first verse, before you depart for basic training.

*From the Halls of Montezuma,*
*To the shores of Tripoli;*
*We fight our country's battles*
*In the air, on land, and sea;*
*First to fight for right and freedom*
*And to keep our honor clean;*

*We are proud to claim the title*
*Of United States Marine.*

*Our flag's unfurled to every breeze*
*From dawn to setting sun;*
*We have fought in every clime and place*
*Where we could take a gun;*
*In the snow of far-off Northern lands*
*And in sunny tropic scenes;*
*You will find us always on the job*
*The United States Marines.*

*Here's health to you and to our Corps*
*Which we are proud to serve;*
*In many a strife we've fought for life*
*And never lost our nerve;*
*If the Army and the Navy*
*Ever look on Heaven's scenes;*
*They will find the streets are guarded*
*By United States Marines.*

Core values will be one of your first, in-the-classroom training courses during Marine Corps basic training. You must memorize the following:

- **Honor:** Honor guides Marines to exemplify the ultimate in ethical and moral behavior; to never lie, cheat, or steal; to abide by an uncompromising code of integrity; to respect human dignity; and to respect others. The qualities of maturity, dedication, trust, and dependability commit Marines to act responsibly; to be accountable for their actions; to fulfill their obligations; and to hold others accountable for their actions.

- **Courage:** Courage is the mental, moral, and physical strength ingrained in Marines. Courage carries them through the challenges of combat and helps them overcome fear. Courage is the inner strength that enables a Marine to do what is right, to adhere to a higher standard of personal conduct, and to make tough decisions under stress and pressure.

- **Commitment:** Commitment is the spirit of determination and dedication found in Marines. Commitment leads to the highest order of discipline for individuals and units. Commitment is the ingredient that enables 24-hours-a-day dedication to Corps and country. Commitment inspires the unrelenting determination to achieve a standard of excellence in every endeavor.

# Getting Physical in the Marine Corps

During Marine Corps basic training, you'll PT almost every day. If your platoon has been doing well and your drill instructors like you, they may give you a Sunday or two off from PT, but time off is not something I would count on.

In addition to daily PT and marching (with full packs) for miles and miles, you'll get to run the confidence course (obstacle course) twice, and practice close-combat skills with pugil sticks at least three times.

A word here about competition: Marine platoons compete against each other in almost every aspect of training, from drills to inspections to pugil sticks to PT to academics. This is no small matter — the competition is stiff and the DIs (and recruits!) take victories and defeats very seriously. A competitive spirit will take you a long way in Marine Corps basic training.

## Training your body: PT time!

Almost every single day of Marine Corps basic training, you'll experience Physical Training (PT). PT normally consists of six limbering exercises, followed by these daily dozen:

- ✔ Side-straddle hops
- ✔ Bends and thrusts
- ✔ Rowing exercise
- ✔ Side benders
- ✔ Leg lifts
- ✔ Toe touches
- ✔ Mountain climbing
- ✔ Trunk twisters
- ✔ Push-ups
- ✔ Bend and reach
- ✔ Body twists
- ✔ Squat benders

You'll do up to 15 reps each and up to 3 sets of each. These exercises are in addition to your required runs and long-distance marches.

Recruit training uses a progressive physical training program, which builds you up to Marine Corps standards. You also experience *table PT,* a period of training in which a drill instructor leads several platoons through a series of demanding exercises while he stands on a table. You'll also run, either individually or as a platoon or squad, working your way up to the 3-mile graduation standard (see Chapter 8). In many cases, your typical run will be 3 to 5 miles.

## Preparing for combat with the infamous pugil sticks

*Pugil sticks* are heavily padded poles you spar with to simulate rifle and bayonet combat. These weapons are an effective and safe way for you to develop the intensity, confidence, and combat techniques of a Marine. You learn how to outmaneuver and overpower an opponent.

For many recruits, pugil sticks training is the most intense physical combat they have ever experienced. Many recruits are somewhat apprehensive about this phase of training, but then find out how much fun it really is. It's almost impossible to get hurt. You're protected by a football helmet and mask, rubber neck roll, and crotch cup (for men).

Only two kinds of blows are permitted: the slash and the horizontal butt stroke, both to the well-protected head and neck. A clean shot ends the bout. The secret is aggression — this is not a defensive sport.

Being a little bit apprehensive isn't a bad thing. The primary purpose of pugil stick drills is to teach you to act, despite your fear. Overcoming your fear and reacting appropriately to contact is a crucial step in transforming a civilian into a warrior.

You'll get a chance to work with pugil sticks a minimum of three times in Marine Corps basic training. Each session is designed to achieve a specific purpose:

- ✔ **Week 2:** You learn the safety precautions and rules of fighting.
- ✔ **Week 3:** In this session, you fight on wooden bridges 2.5 feet above the ground.
- ✔ **Week 4:** You compete with pugil sticks in simulated trenches and confined spaces.

## Heading out for a little walk

Are you ready for a little hike, just to get the kinks out? You'll get your chance at the beginning of week 5 with a short 3-mile hike (with packs) and then again two days later with a 5-mile hike (again, with full packs).

These first two hikes are just an introduction. In Marine Corps boot camp, you'll hike approximately 120 miles in your 13 weeks of basic training. Why do you think they call it boot camp?

The key to doing well on forced marches is to keep the platoon tight and in step with each other. The platoon will average a pace of 3 to 4 mph, so be sure to not fall behind. This will ensure the wrath of every D.I. with in sight.

Funny thing about these Marine Corps basic training hikes. You'll march with your platoon, but the entire basic training company participates in the hike. Your primary job during the hike is to yell louder than any other platoon.

If your platoon doesn't yell louder than the other platoons in the company, your drill instructor to be irritated with you — never a good thing.

Be sure to keep your canteens full during these scheduled hikes. You'll need the water, especially in the summer. You may think a 3, 5, or even 10-mile hike is nothing, but try it in 95 or 100 degree heat while carrying a 30 to 50-pound backpack and screaming at the top of your lungs the whole way. Exhausting.

## The confidence course

Unlike the other services, which give you only one shot at the confidence course, you'll get three shots at it during Marine Corps basic training — first during week 2, again in week 4, and a final try during week 10. See Chapter 14 for more information about the confidence course.

- ✔ **Week 2:** The first time you run the course, it'll be an individual effort, and you'll complete the course wearing just your uniform. If the weather is hot, your instructor may even allow you to remove your uniform shirt.

- ✔ **Week 4:** The second time you go through the course, it will be a group effort (four-man teams), and you'll wear your combat helmet and *flack vest,* which is almost like a bulletproof vest but with a bust designed to repel shrapnel *(flack)* instead of bullets. You'll also carry your M-16 rifle through the course.

- ✔ **Week 10:** Your last attempt through the course will also be a group effort, but you'll complete the course while wearing a gas mask.

The Confidence Course consists of 11 obstacles, designed so that each obstacle is more physically challenging than the last. You should anticipate having to jump, climb, and belly-crawl over and under logs, nets, water, ladders, poles, tall platforms, and ropes for this intense course. The obstacles are

- ✔ Dirty name
- ✔ Run, Jump, and Swing
- ✔ The Inclining Wall
- ✔ The Confidence Climb
- ✔ Monkey Bridge
- ✔ The Tough One
- ✔ Reverse Climb
- ✔ Slide for Life
- ✔ The Hand Walk
- ✔ The Arm Stretcher
- ✔ The Sky Scraper

Although these names sound daunting, the course is designed so that the average platoon can run it in 45 minutes. Like pugil sticks (see the section earlier in the chapter), the confidence course is a great morale builder, as most of the recruits discover that they can negotiate the obstacles with ease (after a little practice and "encouragement" from ever-vigilant drill instructors).

While the Marine Corps basic training confidence course is similar to the Army and Air Force confidence courses, three of the obstacles deserve special mention.

- The **Confidence Climb** is like a vertical railroad track into the sky. Logs spaced apart connect two poles and ascend about 30 feet. You must climb to the top, straddle over the top log, and descend the other side.

- The **Tough One** is the toughest obstacle for recruits to conquer, according to most Marine Corps basic training graduates. You must climb up a rope and maneuver around three logs that act as barriers as you climb. Once through the logs, you walk about 20 feet over wooden beams to two A-shaped structures. You then must climb to the top, swing onto a rope, and inch down to the ground.

- In the **Slide for Life,** three cables stretch off a tower, over a swimming pool, and onto the ground. You start by inching along a cable like a caterpillar. After you traverse a portion of the cable, a drill instructor orders you to hang by your hands and face the end of the pool. From there, you kick your legs up to catch the cable and work your way to the end. It's not unusual for recruits to lose their grip and fall into the pool with a chilling splash. Interestingly, falling into the water happens more during the summer months.

## Wax on, wax off: The Marine Corps martial arts program

The Marine Corps has its own martial art, called MCMAP, and you get a taste of it in Marine Corps basic training. The Marine Corps martial arts system was invented in 2002 and replaces all other close-combat-related systems preceding its introduction.

Belts (rank) in the Marine Corps Martial Arts program are

- **Tan belt:** The tan belt is the first belt following the white belt (beginner) and is awarded after completing classes (27.5 hours) during basic training. This belt signifies the basic understanding of the mental, physical, and character disciplines. The tan belt represents an intermediate understanding of the basic disciplines.

You must pass your Tan belt test in order to graduate from boot camp. Teaching Gray belt or any other higher belts doesn't take place within recruit training.

✔ **Gray belt:** This level is attained after 39 additional hours of training. It signifies an intermediate understanding of the basic disciplines. The Marine must complete the Leading Marines course from the Marine Corps Institute, and most instructors will require that a report be completed on the Marine Raiders.

✔ **Green belt:** The green belt is the third belt, requiring 44 additional hours of training. This belt signifies understanding of the intermediate fundamentals of the different disciplines. The green belt is the first level in which you can become an instructor. As an instructor, you're allowed to teach tan and grey belt techniques and have the power to award the appropriate belt. The prerequisites for this belt include a recommendation from your supervisor, and to be an instructor requires you to be a Corporal or higher.

✔ **Brown belt:** This fourth belt level requires 56.5 hours of training. It introduces you to the advanced fundamentals of each discipline. In addition, as with green belts, you may be certified as MAIs (Martial Arts Instructor) and teach tan through green techniques. To receive this belt, you need the recommendation of your supervisor, a rank of Corporal or higher (although some Lance Corporals may be awarded the brown belt with a waiver), and appropriate Professional Military Education (PME) completed for rank (such as Corporal's Course).

✔ **1st degree black belt:** Black belt is the highest belt color and requires 62.5 hours of supervised training. It signifies knowledge of the advanced fundamentals of the different disciplines. A 1st degree black belt instructor may teach fundamentals from tan to brown belt and award the appropriate belt. In addition, a black belt can become an instructor-trainer, which authorizes them to teach and award all belts, as well as teach and certify instructors. Prerequisites include recommendation of your military supervisor, rank of sergeant or above, and appropriate level of PME completed (such as Sergeant's Course).

✔ **2nd degree black belt:** This belt requires experience as a 1st degree black belt and the rank of sergeant or above.

✔ **3rd degree black belt:** The 3rd degree black belt requires experience as a 2nd degree black belt and the rank of Staff Sergeant or above.

✔ **4th degree black belt:** This belt requires experience as a 3rd degree black belt and the rank of Gunnery Sergeant for enlisted and major or higher for officers.

✔ **5th degree black belt:** This belt requires experience as a 4th degree black belt and the rank of Master Sergeant or First Sergeant (1stSgt) for enlisted and Major or higher for officers.

✔ **6th degree black belt:** This belt requires experience as a 5th degree black belt and the rank of Master Gunnery Sergeant/Sergeant Major for enlisted and lieutenant colonel or higher for officers.

Don't expect to become a black belt in basic, however. That status takes several years.

Because the belts are worn with the Marine Corps Combat Utility Uniform, the complete range of belt colors, such as red, yellow, or purple, are excluded as a practical consideration. After a Marine obtains his gray belt, he can attend an additional training course (such as those at the two Schools of Infantry) to become a martial arts instructor.

## Rappelling

During week 11, you'll learn rappelling, a controlled slide down a rope that prepares you for deployment from helicopters, for navigating difficult terrain, and for gaining access to buildings during raids. From the rappel tower, recruits learn the proper way to brake, regulate speed, and land safely.

Rappelling teaches you technique as well as confidence and courage in a supervised environment.

# Looking Forward to the Highlights of Weeks 4 and 5

Marine Corps basic training isn't conducted entirely in the classroom. You'll have several chances to show your stuff while outside in the fresh air. Of course, training isn't all outside. You also undergo a written test and a barracks inspection.

## Week 4: Individual drill evaluation

The highlight of week 4 is the individual drill evaluation. Your platoon will be evaluated, graded, and compared to the other platoons. The losing platoons are labeled as the worst drilling platoons and receive the wrath of their respective DIs.

You'll be evaluated on a series of drill movements without arms (without weapons), followed by a series of drill movements with arms (with weapons). Make sure that you pay close attention to the following areas when your drill instructor is teaching you drill:

Drill evaluation without arms:

- Position of attention
- Rest
- Halt
- Eyes right/left
- Hand salute
- Facing movements
- Quick time
- Double time
- Mark time
- Half step
- Back step
- Side step
- Face to the left (right) in marching
- Change step
- Face to the rear when marching
- Marching at rest

Drill evaluation with arms:

- Position of order arms
- Position of trail arms
- Port arms from order arms
- Order arms from point arms
- Right shoulder arms from order arms
- Order arms from right shoulder arms
- Left shoulder arms from order arms
- Order arms from left shoulder arms
- Present arms from order arms

- ✔ Order arms from present arms
- ✔ Inspection arms
- ✔ Port arms from inspection arms
- ✔ Sling arms
- ✔ Unsling arms
- ✔ Adjust sling
- ✔ Right shoulder arms from port arms
- ✔ Left shoulder arms from port arms
- ✔ Port arms from left shoulder arms
- ✔ Left shoulder arms from right shoulder arms
- ✔ Right shoulder arms from left shoulder arms
- ✔ Rifle salutes
- ✔ Fix and unfix bayonets
- ✔ Inspection arms from sling arms

# Week 5: Combat water survival and your first written test

The biggest event of week 5 is combat water survival. All Marines must pass basic combat water survival skills in order to graduate from boot camp. Those who don't pass will receive extensive remedial training until they do.

Training in combat water survival develops your confidence in the water. All recruits must pass the minimum requirement level of Combat Water Survival-4 (CWS-4), which requires you to perform a variety of water survival and swimming techniques. If you meet the CWS-4 requirements, you can then be upgraded to a higher level, which is a requirement for certain Marine Corps jobs. All recruits train in the camouflage utility uniform, but those upgrading may be required to train in full combat gear, which includes a rifle, helmet, flack jacket, and pack.

Week 5 also features your first written test. Like all Marine Corps basic training written tests, it will be multiple choice, and you must score a 70 percent or better to pass. The test will encompass all the classroom subjects you've learned in basic training during the first five weeks. (For more on classroom training, see the section "Hitting the Books: Classroom Training," earlier in this chapter.)

# Series Officer Inspection

The series officer inspection will be the first time you and your barracks will be inspected by someone other than your drill instructor. During this inspection, everything is fair game — how you clean the barracks, how you wear your uniform, military knowledge (yes, your drill instructor will ask you questions), the condition of your rifle, and so on.

Unless you want to experience your drill instructor's bad side, it's best not to embarrass him in front of the big bosses.

# The Crucible: The Mother of All Events

Almost all the services now have a cumulating event that puts everything you've learned during basic training to the test. But, the Marine Corps was the first branch to accomplish this when they implemented the Crucible in 1996.

The Crucible is the ultimate test every recruit must go through to become a Marine. It will test you physically, mentally, and morally and is the defining moment in recruit training. The Crucible is no walk in the park, unless your idea of a walk in the park takes place over 54 hours and includes food and sleep deprivation (only 4 hours of sleep per night)and approximately 40 miles of marching. The entire Crucible event pits teams of recruits against a barrage of day and night events requiring every recruit on a team to work together solving problems, overcoming obstacles, and helping each other along.

You can order a DVD outlining the Crucible for $24.95 at www.usmc1.us/ usmc_crucible.html.

# Day 1

On the first morning of the Crucible, you awake at 2 a.m. (0200) After a quick breakfast of MREs (Meal, Ready to Eat), you take part in a 6-mile hike to the Crucible site. Upon arrival at the site, you complete three back-to-back events that last until 6:30 p.m. (1830). The first event is called the *Battle of Hue City,* a one-hour event in which the teams resupply water, ammunition, and MREs through a course that consists of trenches, wire fences, and walls.

After the Battle of Hue City, teams negotiate four warrior stations:

- **Pfc Jenkins Pinnacle:** Teams cross two horizontal cable-supported logs.

- **Pfc Garcia's Engagement:** Individuals demonstrate their knowledge of hand-to-hand combat skills and then participate in a warrior case study of Pfc. Garcia.

- **Lehew's Challenge:** Teams of two climb over an eight-foot high horizontal log.

- **Corbin's Convoy:** Teams react to a simulated improvised explosive device (IED) while on patrol.

No time for sleep yet. After a quick meal of MREs, you participate in the *Leadership Reaction Course,* which is a three-hour event in which you and your team perform six reaction course problems, which test your ability to work as a team to solve problems. Some of the problems include

- Using three wooden boards to cross a number of stumps without touching the ground

- Negotiating a water hole using the same wooden board concept to get from point A to point B

- Transporting a large container over a wall using the limited resources available

After you complete the events, the teams of two face off in a pugil stick bout. After pugil stick fighting, you're split into teams, and your team will participate in one of the four following events:

- **ENoonan's Casualty Evacuation:** Your team will recover a downed pilot and another recruit "shot" by a sniper and transport them over a mile of wooded terrain.

- **Enhanced Obstacle Course:** You'll carry a dummy casualty on a stretcher and ammunition cans from one end of a standard Marine Corps obstacle course to the other, going over all obstacles.

- **Marine Corps Martial Arts Program (MCMAP) Strikes Station:** Recruits are required to demonstrate and conduct five-minute MCMAP strikes.

- **Core Values Station:** Recruits sit inside a hut and receive information on a particular core value from their drill instructor.

It's now about 8 or 9 p.m. of the first day. What's a better way to wrap up the day than with a 5-mile night hike with a time limit of three hours?

Finally, around midnight, it's time to hit the rack for the night.

# Day 2

The second day begins at 4 a.m. After chowing down on some more yummy MREs, you participate in the *Battle of Fallujah,* a one-hour event in which teams resupply water, ammunition, and MREs through the Combat Assault Course.

Following the completion of the Battle of Fallujah, recruits negotiate a bayonet assault course and the following warrior stations:

- **Perez's Passage:** Teams cross a "contaminated area" by swinging on ropes from safe spot to safe spot.

- **Kraft's Struggle:** Teams climb a 10-foot wall and climb down the opposite side by a knotted rope.

- **John Quick Trail (Navigation Station):** Basic map reading and grid coordinate plotting will be reviewed and evaluated.

- **Core Values Station:** Recruits sit inside a hut and receive information on a particular core value from their drill instructor.

After your drill instructor talks to you about core values, you get a chance to try out some more yummy MREs. Following lunch, you take a run through the Combat Enhanced Obstacle Course. Teams have two hours to complete these four events of a modified confidence course:

- **The Sky Scraper:** The team retrieves a "wounded" dummy from the top of an 18-foot tower.

- **Stairway to Heaven:** Team members move two ammunition cans over the top of a 36-foot ladder obstacle.

- **Two-Line Bridge:** Team members cross two 52-foot long ropes with their hands and feet suspended 2 feet and 10 feet off the ground as they carry ammunition cans and water resupply cans.

- **The Weaver:** Team members climb over and under 24 logs, 42 feet in length, ascending to 14 feet as they carry ammunition and water resupply cans.

In addition to the Enhanced Confidence Course, teams go through a Combat Endurance Course, in which teams conduct a simulated patrol, negotiate the obstacles, and report the number and types of obstacles to intelligence sources.

No time for a nap, yet. It's now time for event 6 — *Battle of Khe Sanh.* Teams of four fire two magazines of five rounds each from simulated building structures at unknown distance targets in a time limit of 70 seconds. The number of targets hit and amount of unused ammunition are then recorded. Following this event, team members participate in a 250-meter casualty evacuation where members remove simulated casualties from a simulated danger area consisting of artillery simulators.

Tired of MREs yet? Too bad. You get a hour for supper, followed by the *Night Infiltration Course,* in which teams resupply water, ammunition, and MREs at night in a simulated combat environment. The teams take their ammunition cans, water cans, and simulated MREs through the Combat Assault Course with the added obstacle of darkness.

At midnight, you can hit the rack (subject to one-hour guard duty).

# Day 3

The bad news is that day 3 starts earlier than day 2, at 3 a.m. The good news is that all the events are over. After a final breakfast of MREs, you'll take a leisurely stroll (march) back to basic training. Don't worry; it's only 9 miles.

# Eagle, Globe, and Anchor ceremony

Even though basic training isn't over yet, when you successfully complete the Crucible, you're no longer considered to be a basic trainee. You're now a full-blooded Marine, and you'll note that your drill instructors will start to treat you as such.

Upon return to the base, new Marines receive an Eagle, Globe, and Anchor pin from their drill instructor marking their transition from a recruit to a Marine.

I hope you're hungry after all of those MREs. Following the Eagle, Globe, and Anchor presentation, the new Marines are treated to a breakfast fit for only true warriors. It consists of all-you-can-eat steak, eggs, and potatoes. This breakfast is definitely the best meal you'll have in Marine Corps basic training.

In addition, now that everyone's pretty sure that you've got what it takes to become a Marine, after a good night's sleep, you'll report for your initial dress uniform issue. Don't be too excited yet; you have to turn the uniform in right away so that the tailors can make sure that it fits you properly.

Your dress uniform will be returned to you (all fitted and cleaned) prior to graduation.

## Brother, can you spare some blood?

You may think that you've sweated enough blood during the Crucible, but the Marines want some more. During week 10, you'll be given an opportunity to report to the base medical clinic and donate some blood.

Donating blood is a tradition in the Marine Corps, and, while not mandatory, your drill instructor will strongly encourage you to participate.

Even though you're now considered to be a Marine, it's still not a smart idea to ignore any suggestion from your drill instructor. Plus, cookies and such are usually available for those who are donating blood, and cookies are hard to come by in basic training.

# Meeting the Core Graduation Requirements

You study a lot of material during Marine Corps basic training. How can anyone learn that much in such a short period of time? The good news is that you don't have to excel in every subject to graduate. However, in order to graduate from Marine Corps basic training, you must meet the following minimum qualifications:

- ✔ Pass the physical fitness test and be within prescribed weight standards
- ✔ Qualify for Combat Water Survival at level 4 or higher
- ✔ Qualify with the service rifle
- ✔ Pass the battalion commander's inspection (see the upcoming "Final inspections" section)
- ✔ Pass the written tests (see the next section)
- ✔ Complete the Crucible

If you fail in any of these areas, you're subject to be *recycled* (sent backwards in time to another platoon) or may possibly be discharged.

## Passing the final tests

You'll take the final written test during week 11. Like all basic training written tests, this one will be multiple choice, and you must score a 70 percent or better to pass.

The test will cover all subjects you've studied from weeks 7 to 11. If you fail the test, you'll be given one more chance for a retest, a day or two later. If you fail the retest, you can expect to be recycled, to repeat some, or all, of Marine Corps basic training.

You'll also undergo the final physical fitness test during week 11. You must also pass this test in order to graduate from Marine Corps basic training. You can see the Marine Corps basic training fitness graduation standards in Chapter 8.

## Final inspections

You may think you've had enough inspections by now, but you have two more big ones left before you can graduate. Because you'll be inspected by your drill instructor's bosses, you can expect your DI to be on your case about your appearance and the appearance of the barracks during the last two weeks of basic training.

During week 11, you and your barracks will be inspected by the Company Commander. During the final week of Marine Corps basic training (week 12), the Battalion Commander has the honors.

Passing the Battalion Commander's inspection is a core graduation requirement, so if you screw that up, you can expect to spend some extra time in basic training.

# Chapter 18

# Coast Guard Basic Training

· · · · · · · · · · · · · · · · · · · · · · · · · · · · · · · · · · · · · · · · · · · · · · · · · · · · · · · · · · · · · · · · · · · · · ·

## In This Chapter

▶ Getting there is half the fun

▶ Meeting your new Company Commander

▶ Spending time in the classroom

▶ Enjoying a little free time

· · · · · · · · · · · · · · · · · · · · · · · · · · · · · · · · · · · · · · · · · · · · · · · · · · · · · · · · · · · · · · · · · · · · · ·

Many people don't think of the Coast Guard as a military service, but it is. Even though the Coast Guard is organized under the Department of Homeland Security rather than the Department of Defense, its members wear uniforms, receive the same pay as other military members, have ranks, and are subject to the Uniform Code of Military Justice. Most importantly, federal law defines the Coast Guard as a military branch.

What's more, new Coasties go through basic training, just like new folks in any other branch.

## Arriving at the Airport

You begin your adventures with the United States Coast Guard by arriving at the Philadelphia International Airport. After you arrive, you're required to retrieve your bags and then report immediately to the USO, which is located in Terminal D. If your flight is delayed and the USO folks have gone home, they'll leave directions for you on the USO door.

It's a good idea to call your family from the USO after you arrive. Any future phone calls you make while in boot camp will be at the discretion of your Company Commander (CC).

You then take a bus ride from the airport to the Recruit Processing Center on Cape May. Enjoy the bus ride to Cape May. It's the last bit of freedom you'll have for the next eight weeks.

In the Coast Guard, the fun starts immediately when the bus arrives at Cape May. As soon as the doors to the bus open, you're greeted by that unique military animal that wears a Smokey-the-Bear hat, and the basic training discipline begins immediately.

# Launching into Your First Few Days

When the bus stops and the doors open, you'll likely hear a variation of the following speech (screamed, of course — It's rumored that Company Commanders have forgotten how to speak in a normal tone of voice).

> *"Welcome to Cape May. The first thing you're going do is shut up, sit up. and take your hats off . . . and GET YOUR STINKIN' LEGS OUTTA THE AISLE. Keep your eyes in the boat; don't look at me. You're going do what I say, when I say it, and how I say to do it. You've got ten seconds to get off this bus, and you've just wasted three!"*

The good news is that you'll keep this particular Company Commander only for about three days — long enough for the forming process. The bad news is that these three days does not count toward your total seven weeks, and that the Company Commander you will meet for your actual training will be ten times worse.

Drill practice starts almost immediately when you get off the bus. You'll be instructed to line up on one of the several yellow triangles. The Company Commander will then provide several minutes of instruction and practice with basic facing movements (left face, right face, about face, and so on — see Chapter 9).

Immediately following the drill instruction, the CC will give you instructions about what to do in the event of a fire drill. Pay close attention to this briefing, and don't be surprised if a practice surprise fire drill occurs around 5 the next morning.

These first three days of Coast Guard basic training are known as *forming*. During this time, your temporary CC will get you used to Coast Guard basic training life, and you'll spend countless hours *in-processing,* which is basically the process of getting the paperwork done to make you an official member of the U.S. Coast Guard.

During forming, you'll establish your military pay records (very important if you want to get paid), be issued a military ID card, fill out the forms for your family members to be issued an ID card, pee in the bottle to make sure that you haven't used any illegal drugs, and get your teeth checked out by a dentist, who will establish a dental care plan (for after basic training). Females will also be given a pregnancy test.

Virtually every task you're ordered to do during forming is timed — five seconds to write a name on a tag, ten seconds to find paperwork, and so on. And a Company Commander provides cadence, like a countdown.

If you make a mistake, you'll be yelled at. It's that simple — mistake equals yelling. It's all part of the process to add stress to the training, to break down the civilian in order to build a self-disciplined member of the Coast Guard.

During the first few minutes of forming, you'll be issued a book known as *The Helmsman*, and anytime you're not actively doing something, the CCs will expect your nose to be in the book. *The Helmsman* is your Coast Guard basic training guidebook. It includes all (or at least most) of the information you're expected to learn during Coast Guard basic training.

If you want to read the book before basic training, you can get a copy of *The Helmsman* online at `http://usmilitary.about.com/od/cgjoin/qt/helmsman.htm`.

Get plenty of sleep in your last couple of days as a civilian. No matter what time you arrive at Cape May, your first day will not end until about 0030 (12:30 a.m.). Once you "hit the racks" on that first night, you won't have much time for sleep. A CC will be screaming and yelling at you at 0530 (5:30 a.m.). Company Commanders have one very useful purpose in life — they make excellent alarm clocks. There's no way to shut them off and go back to sleep.

# *Jumping in: The Real Basic Begins*

Your official basic training begins on the Friday afternoon after arrival. This is when you meet your permanent CCs, who will take you to your new squad bay (barracks).

In Coast Guard basic training, company commanders come in two flavors: killers and cupcakes. Which type you draw is a matter of pure chance. The killers make basic tough. The cupcakes allow you to skate through basic training.

Of the two, you'll want to hope you get a killer. You may hate them (especially at the beginning of basic), but you'll learn a lot more.

Your meeting with your permanent CC is somewhat of a ceremony. Your new CC will march smartly to the front of the room and be administered an oath, in which she swears that she will train you to become the best United States Coastguardsmen possible. The Coast Guard is the only branch that has such a ceremony.

## Time for some drill practice

The little bit of drill you learned while in forming won't please your new CC. In his opinion, your entire unit will move like sick goats, and he will waste no time in beginning to teach you how to move properly. In fact, before you get a chance to march over to your brand-new squad bay, your new CC will spend the first two hours teaching you how to march properly. To help properly motivate you, you'll be introduced to the concept of Incentive training (IT).

*Incentive training* simply means exercise as punishment. Any time you mess up, your CC will order you to do some IT, in the form of push-ups, crunches, squats, or flutter kicks. You'll get a chance to do IT a lot during your first six weeks of Coast Guard basic training.

## Fire drill practice

A custom during Coast Guard basic training for the CCs is to conduct lots and lots of fire drill events on the first Sunday after arrival. These drills occur probably to strengthen your response time to emergencies, as search and rescue is a primary mission of the U.S. Coast Guard, so even the cupcake instructors seem to abide by this tradition. All those drills don't sound too bad, until you realize that your squad bay is probably up three or four flights of ladders (steps).

# Studying Up! Classroom Training

You'll start your Coast Guard basic training classes immediately after you move to your permanent unit. You may find the Coast Guard basic training classroom rules to be slightly different from what you may have experienced in high school:

- If asked a question by an instructor, always respond, even if it's with "I don't know the answer, sir."
- When you ask a question, always raise your hand and wait to be called on.
- Never raise your hand with a pen or pencil in it.
- Never scratch or touch your face in class. If coughing, turn your head and cough into your sleeve.
- Never fall asleep in class. If you feel tired, stand in the back of the classroom.

- ✔ Keep your heels together at all times when seated.
- ✔ Keep your pen or pencil on your desk at all times, except when actually writing.

Company commanders are stationed in the back of the classrooms to ensure that you obey these rules. If they catch you breaking a rule, you can expect a long session of IT, immediately following the class.

In addition to following these rules, you have to memorize a staggering amount of information in just a few days.

## Core values

One of your very first classroom lessons will be about Coast Guard core values. Each of the military services has *core values,* an accepted method of behavior and conduct designed to assist you in almost any situation. The Coast Guard core values are honor, respect, and devotion to duty, defined as follows:

- ✔ **Honor:** *Absolute integrity is our standard. A Coast Guard member demonstrates honor in all things: never lying, cheating, or stealing. We do the right thing because it is the right thing — all the time.*
- ✔ **Respect:** *We value the dignity of people: whether a stranded boater, an immigrant, or a fellow Coast Guard member, we treat each other with fairness and respect.*
- ✔ **Devotion to duty:** *A Coast Guard member is dedicated to five maritime security roles: Maritime Safety (Search and Rescue), Maritime Security, Protection of Natural Resources, Maritime Mobility (Waterways Transportation), and National Defense. We are loyal and accountable to the public trust. We welcome the responsibility.*

## The Coast Guard language

Each of the military branches has their own foreign language, designed so that civilians don't understand what they're talking about, and the Coast Guard is no different. Almost immediately, you're required to learn the Coast Guard language. Here are a few of the most common terms:

- ✔ **Room:** Compartment
- ✔ **Bathroom:** Head
- ✔ **Floor:** Deck

- ✔ **Upstairs:** Topside
- ✔ **Stairs:** Ladder
- ✔ **Wall:** Bulkhead
- ✔ **Mop:** Swab
- ✔ **Downstairs:** Below
- ✔ **Bed:** Rack
- ✔ **Ceiling:** Overhead
- ✔ **Flag:** Colors
- ✔ **Rumor:** Scuttlebutt
- ✔ **Stop:** Belay or avast
- ✔ **I understand and will comply:** Aye aye, sir/ma'am
- ✔ **An area for official and ceremonial functions:** Quarterdeck

## Phonetic alphabet

A phonetic alphabet is a list of words used to identify letters in a message transmitted by radio or telephone. Spoken words from an approved list are substituted for letters. For example, my name, "Powers," would be "Papa, Oscar, Whiskey, Echo, Romeo, Sierra" when spelled in the phonetic alphabet. This practice helps to prevent confusion between similar sounding letters, such as "m" and "n", and to clarify communications that may be garbled during transmission.

In Coast Guard basic training, you're required to memorize the phonetic alphabet, and you'll use it on the radio during field exercises.

A: Alpha
B: Bravo
C: Charlie
D: Delta
E: Echo
F: Foxtrot
G: Golf
H: Hotel
I: India
J: Juliett
K: Kilo
L: Lima
M: Mike
N: November
O: Oscar
P: Papa

Q: Quebec
R: Romeo
S: Sierra
T: Tango
U: Uniform
V: Victor
W: Whiskey
X: Xray
Y: Yankee
Z: Zulu

## The guardian ethos

The Guardian ethos may be seen as an unofficial contract with the Coast Guard members and the nation. It serves to define the essence of the Coast Guard.

You'll attend a class about the Coast Guard guardian ethos. While you're not actually required to memorize the ethos, the final test you have to take may have questions about it.

> *I am America's Maritime Guardian.*
> *I serve the citizens of the United States.*
> *I will protect them.*
> *I will defend them.*
> *I will save them.*
> *I am their Shield.*
> *For them I am Semper Paratus.*
> *I live the Coast Guard Core Values.*
> *I am a Guardian.*
> *We are the United States Coast Guard.*

*Semper Paratus* is Latin for "always ready."

# Getting into a Routine: Weeks 2 and 3

The initial fitness test is conducted at the end of week 2. While you're not required to achieve graduation PT standards at this point, if your CC feels that you may be in danger of not meeting graduation standards by final test time, he will assign you to *Physical Fitness Enhancement,* in which you get to awaken one hour earlier than everyone else each day to attend a special fitness session.

Several other events also take place during this time period.

# Required knowledge

Also by the end of week 2, you're required to memorize the basic training *required knowledge*. It's not that you'll have a written test on these subjects at this time, but any CC, at any time, may question you about one of these core study subjects (and trust me, they will). If you fail one of their impromptu quizzes, you can expect some extra time doing incentive training. (See the section "The Real Basic Begins," earlier in this chapter.)

Required knowledge consists of

- General orders (see Chapter 9)
- Coast Guard terminology (see "The earlier section "Coast Guard Language")
- Phonetic alphabet (see the earlier section by this name)
- The position of attention (see Chapter 9)
- Military salute (see Chapter9)
- Addressing Coast Guard personnel (see Chapter 6)
- Military time (see Chapter 6)

# Getting a piece

At the end of Week 2 or the beginning of Week 3, you'll be issued your piece. Don't get too excited. In Coast Guard basic training, a piece is an M-1 rifle.

To make sure that you don't shoot your own foot off or take out your frustrations on your CC, the barrel of this rifle has been filled with lead (not the kind of lead you shoot).

From that day forward, you'll carry your rifle with you at all times, and you'll be introduced to a new type of incentive training, called *piece incentive training,* or PIT. This type of training is much harder.

Piece IT are exercises that take advantage of the 10 pounds of extra weight and heft of the rifle. They include up/down-out/ins, front sweeps, squats, and of course, push-ups.

# Filling out your dream sheet

The Coast Guard is unique in that few nonprior service enlistees are allowed to choose a Coast Guard job at the time of enlistment. Instead, when you graduate from basic training, you're sent directly to a Coast Guard base and are assigned as an *undesignated seaman,* doing various jobs and odd duties.

You remain an undesignated seaman for at least two or three years, checking out the various Coast Guard jobs. Then, if you agree to re-enlist for another term, you can *strike* (apply) for a specific Coast Guard rating (job), if there is a need for that job. If accepted and upon re-enlistment, you are then sent to that job's A school (job school).

This system has its advantages. In the other branches, which allow recruits to select a job right from the get-go, many recruits find that the job they chose was not exactly what they thought it was and spend the rest of their time in the service disappointed. The Coast Guard system allows new recruits to scope things out and see what the various jobs really entail before making a decision.

Although you don't get to select a job this early in your Coast Guard career, during week 2 you do get to fill out your *dream sheet,* listing, in order, the Coast Guard bases where you'd like to be stationed following basic training.

Your choices are preferences only. There is no guarantee you'll get the location you want. The Coast Guard assigns you based on their greatest need. If that happens to coincide with one of your choices, great. If not, welcome to the military.

# Weeks 4, 5, and 6

During week 4, you get a chance to feel like a real military member by visiting the shooting range.

Coast Guard basic training is different from all the other military branches in that

✔ You fire a pistol on the firing range instead of a rifle. The Coast Guard pistol of choice is a Sig Sauer P229 DAK .40 caliber pistol.

✔ You're only required to fire the weapon. You don't have to obtain a certain score to graduate from basic training.

While you're not required to qualify with the pistol in basic training, many Coast Guard jobs and/or duty assignments require you to qualify with the pistol.

For more on weapons training, see Chapter 4.

## Receiving your orders

Shortly after you visit the firing range, you'll receive orders for your first assignment following basic training.

Most CCs like to make this occasion somewhat of a ceremony. Some will take the recruits to the nearby beach in the middle of the night to present the orders, while others will arrange a visit to one of the Coast Guard ships that are in port at the time. Other CCs may read the orders during mealtime in the galley (chow hall).

Receiving your orders without ceremony is a strong indication that your CC is not pleased with your progress and may not expect you to graduate on time.

After you receive your orders, your CC will give you some time to call your new unit so that you can coordinate your travel plans.

## Playing with pugil sticks

During week 5, you get a chance to work out your frustrations with a pugil stick fight. *Pugil sticks* are heavily padded poles you spar with to simulate rifle and bayonet combat. The Coast Guard added this program to its basic training curriculum a few years ago.

One interesting point is that the Coast Guard is the only branch that pits males versus females in pugil stick bouts. CCs pair you up based on your size and weight, not your sex.

## Building confidence with the confidence course

After several years without one, the Coast Guard re-instituted its obstacle course in 2008. It's really not much of a course (compared to the other branches). The Coast Guard confidence course has about seven obstacles, and it takes only 33 minutes or so to run through it.

You can see the Coast Guard confidence course in action online at `http://coastguardnews.com/video-coast-guard-training-center-cape-may-obstacle-course/2008/11/26`.

For more on the confidence course, see Chapter 13.

## Getting a little time off

During week 6, assuming that your grades and performance are up to snuff, your CC will grant you a day of on-base liberty. *Liberty* is the Coast Guard word for time off.

During liberty, you're free to go anywhere on the base. You can visit the base movie theater and watch a movie, visit any of the eateries on base, or visit the Coast Guard Exchange (CGXX), which is sort of like a Walmart for military members. At the CGX, you can purchase retail items and supplies. Many recruits use some of their liberty time to call home.

On-base liberty is a privilege, not a right. Being denied your liberty is a warning sign that you're not performing up to expectations, and there is a very good chance that the CC is considering having you reverted.

## Showing off your marching skills

On Sunday, the day after your on-base liberty, you get a chance to show off your newly acquired marching skills in front of your CC's boss, known as the Section Commander (SC).

By now you may think that you're pretty good at marching. After all, you've done an awful lot of it during the past few weeks, but the SC is a stickler for detail. The Section Commander will evaluate your marching skills, both individually and as a company. This drill evaluation is pass/fail, and you can either fail as an individual, or your entire company can fail (in which case, your CC will not be a happy fellow.)

# Winding Down: Week 7

When week 7 begins, you'll think that someone kidnapped your company commander and replaced him/her with a kinder, gentler brand. This is because you're starting to get it, and your CC is fairly sure that those who are left are going to graduate on time. He no longer feels the need to yell and scream in order to motivate you.

At the end of week 7, usually on Friday, you take your final written test. This test is a combination of open-book (the *Helmsman*) and closed-book, multiple choice.

Like other basic training written tests, you must score a 70 percent or above to pass. The test is challenging, but don't worry overly about it. Historically, the first-time passing rate is over 90 percent.

If you fail the final test and your CC recommends it, you're allowed one chance to retest, while all your basic training buddies are enjoying time away from base. If you fail the retest, you can expect to be reverted.

If you pass your final written test, and you're not in trouble with your CC, you'll be awarded on off-base pass on Saturday. You may think the time away is a reward for good performance, but it's actually designed as a final test to see whether you can honorably represent the Coast Guard while among civilians, in public. If you misbehave or get into trouble while off base by disobeying any rules put in place by your CC, your chances of getting reverted to almost day one are close to 100 percent.

The off-base liberty period is a test. Scattered throughout the community will be basic training staff, wearing civilian clothes. Their job is to watch you and ensure that you act professionally in public. Don't walk around town with your hands in your pockets (a big "no-no"), lean on walls in uniform, or prance around like a drunken sailor (sorry, Navy — just an expression).

Some recruits elect to get a hotel room for the day, ordering delivery pizza, napping, and watching TV. While you can't spend the night (you have to be back on base in the evening), it can be a big morale booster just to get out of sight and hearing of CCs and other recruits for a day.

---

## Time for a cocktail?

Coast Guard basic training is the only military boot camp that allows recruits to consume alcohol during off-base liberty (assuming, of course, that you're of legal age).

However, you are *not* allowed to get intoxicated — not even a little bit. Even if you're behaving yourself, stumbling around drunk is a guaranteed trip back in time to the beginning days of basic training.

In addition to the off-base liberty monitors walking around the town, CCs are stationed at the base gate to look for intoxicated recruits returning from liberty.

# *Monitoring Your Behavior with Performance Trackers*

Ask any graduate of Coast Guard basic training what a "performance tracker" is, and he will wince. *Performance trackers* are small forms that you carry with you in your uniform breast pocket at all times while in basic training. You're required to carry two of them.

If anyone in authority (CCs, instructors, staff members, and so on) sees you doing anything wrong, at any time, they'll request you give them a performance tracker, which is then filled out with what you did wrong and returned to your CC.

You'll certainly have some performance trackers pulled while in basic training. The key is not to have too many pulled. If you have more than five or so pulled per week, you're in danger of being reverted.

# *Getting Reverted*

With the exception of getting kicked out, which rarely happens, getting *reverted* is the worst punishment that can happen to you in Coast Guard basic training. Quite simply, being reverted means you're returned to an earlier day of training. Getting reverted used to give you a chance to relearn required information, or Coast Guard values.

While you can be reverted for almost any reason, the most common reasons for getting reverted are

- Sleeping during class
- Being late for watch
- Not knowing the required knowledge
- Storing dirty laundry
- Writing letters in class
- Reading mail on your rack (bed) or on the toilet
- Getting caught telling a lie

- Disobeying an order from the CC
- Getting drunk on liberty
- Wearing an unserviceable (wrinkled) uniform
- Forgetting to shave (males)

# Worshipping During Divine Hours

*Divine hours* occur every Sunday from 8 a.m. to 1 p.m., and recruits can attend church services. (Protestant and Catholic are offered.) If you're of another religious denomination, inform your Company Commanders, and you may be able to arrange to observe your religious practices off base. Recruits are also allowed during divine hours to read and write letters to home, maintain uniforms, study, and tend to other tasks.

In Coast Guard basic training, you can attend Protestant and Catholic services on base. Services for other faiths are available at off base locations.

You're not allowed to sleep, take showers, or call home during divine hours. That's why this time is called divine hours, and not free time.

# Making It to the Final Week

If you make it to week 8, you've pretty much got it made. If you haven't been reverted by this time, you're chances are very, very good that you'll graduate on time.

The premier event during the final week will occur on Thursday morning, the day before your official graduation, with a practice parade and graduation ceremony. (For more on graduation, see Chapter 19.)

Immediately following graduation, you'll be treated to a special lunch in the galley, consisting of pizza or stacked sandwiches. For the first time ever, you'll be allowed to talk, joke, and laugh with your basic training buddies during a galley meal. This signifies your acceptance from the ranks of beginner to a trusted, accepted Coastie.

# Part V
# Wrapping Up Basic Training

The 5th Wave                    By Rich Tennant

©RICHTENNANT

SPOT

"My husband named the dog. Of course, he's in
the military and I don't have the heart to tell
the kids it's an acronym for Special Patrol
Over The Hill Tactician."

## In this part . . .

*W*hile marching and getting yelled at may not be your idea of a lot of fun, it'll be over in no time. Once basic training is complete, you first must show off your new military skills in front of your family and friends during a graduation parade. Hopefully, you've done well enough in basic training to earn one or more of the several available basic training awards.

# Chapter 19

# Graduation Week

. . . . . . . . . . . . . . . . . . . . . . . . . . . . . . . . . . . . . . . . . . . . . . . . .

## In This Chapter

▶ Preparing for graduation

▶ Entertaining your family

▶ Leaving basic training behind you

. . . . . . . . . . . . . . . . . . . . . . . . . . . . . . . . . . . . . . . . . . . . . . . . .

**N**o matter how tough you found basic training, you'll probably graduate. More than 90 percent of all new recruits do make it through basic training. The vast majority of those who fail do so for reasons beyond their (or their instructors') control, such as for previously unknown medical conditions.

The reason you won't fail is not because it's easy but because your drill instructors (or whatever they are called by the individual services) won't let you fail! They'll drive you to success.

Even though your chances of graduation are almost certain, graduation day is an experience you'll never forget. Graduation signifies the completion of one of the hardest challenges you'll ever face in your life.

Additionally, graduation is the first chance you'll have to see your family and friends since you departed on your epic U.S Military adventure. Plus, you'll look grand showing off your pretty new military uniform.

## Army Graduation Events

Army basic combat training occurs at five different locations. While graduation events are similar, specific graduation activities can vary from one location to another. Fortunately, a couple of weeks before you graduate, you'll send your loved ones a graduation invitation that lists the exact dates and times of your specific graduation events.

## First up: Family Day

All Army basic training graduation schedules include an event called Family Day. Family Day is usually the day before the official graduation parade. The event gives your friends and family a chance to tour your basic training facilities and meet with your training instructors. Family Day is also the first opportunity your loved ones will have to meet up with you since your departure several weeks prior.

Family Day usually begins in an auditorium where your loved ones will meet with combat training leaders and receive a briefing about all you've been going through during the past several weeks. Generally, the briefing is followed by a tour of the basic training facilities where your loved ones can ask questions and observe demonstrations of some skills you learned while in basic training.

Some Army basic training locations grant an *on-post pass* (which means you can have leisure time off-duty with your family but can't leave the base), while others host an official graduation dinner where you can dine with your loved ones and catch up on old times. Either way, while you're able to spend some time with your family, you will be under a strict curfew as to when you must be back in your barracks room. (After all, the next day is a very big day for you.)

Some basic training locations host a fun event for family members. This event may include recruit-performed skits, videos, and drill demonstrations.

If your Family Day events happen to include a formal or buffet dinner, it's customary (but not mandatory) for the recruits to pay for the meals for their guests.

## The main event: Graduation day

The graduation ceremony almost always consists of an official military parade, complete with marching, marching bands, and dress uniforms. Usually the parade is conducted on the post parade grounds, but during inclement weather, it may be conducted at an indoor location, such as the post gym. Tell your family to bring their cameras, as they'll want photos of this impressive event.

Graduation parade ceremonies are usually scheduled for the late morning and last about an hour.

If your Army job training (also known as Advanced Individual Training, or AIT) is located at a different post, you won't get much time after graduation to spend with your family. Instead, you'll be spending the rest of your graduation day out-processing to go to your training base. In most cases, your transportation is scheduled for the same afternoon or evening as your graduation parade. If your AIT is located at your basic training base, it's simply a matter of changing barracks rooms, so you may be able to score a pass to spend additional time with your friends and family.

If your AIT is located at a different Army post, you may be able to get permission for your family to drive you.

## Where your family can stay

Because the graduation events last at least a couple days, your family members should be prepared to get a room. Your spouse and children will be authorized to stay in on-post *billeting* (which is kind of like a military hotel) for between $4 and $20 per night. If your friends or other family members are current or retired military members, they can stay on-post as well. All others (nonmilitary and guests) are allowed to stay in on-post billeting if space is available. You can make reservations for any Army lodging facility by calling 1-877-711-TEAM.

If your friends or family aren't authorized to stay in an Army lodging facility or there are no vacancies, several commercial hotels are near each Army basic training base.

Make reservations at least three weeks in advance, as they book up fast during graduation events.

# Air Force Graduation Events

A couple of weeks before you graduate from Air Force basic training, you'll receive two invitations to your graduation that you can send to friends or loved ones. If you have more than two people planning to attend, don't worry about it. You don't need to have an invitation to attend the festivities. They do, however, make a great souvenir of your special day.

If your friends and family aren't active duty or retired military members and they elect to drive to your graduation, they'll have to stop at the Pass & ID section, located at the Lackland AFB Valley Hi or Luke Street gates, where they'll receive a pass to drive their vehicle on base for the duration of the graduation events. In order to obtain a vehicle pass, they must show the vehicle registration (or rental agreement), a valid driver's license, and proof of insurance.

## The first day: Reception and the Airman's Run

Air Force basic training graduation events always begin on a Thursday. On Thursday morning, your loved ones will attend an hour-long briefing at the Reception Center, where they find out the schedule of events, view a presentation of what you've been going through for the past eight weeks, and learn the rules you're subject to at all times.

Air Force regulations prohibit all public displays of affection while in uniform. However, you're given a break during basic training graduation. Your loved ones will be briefed on the *five-second rule* — in other words, no kissing allowed and no hugs that last longer than five seconds. However, nothing in the rules prohibit multiple five-second hugs, and you'll see a lot of that.

Visitors need to know their loved one's squadron number and what flight he is in when they sign in at the Reception Center. Not only is this information used to notify them that you've arrived safely, but you'll need the information in order to catch a glimpse of them when the squadron runs by the visitors at the end of the three-mile Airman's Run, following your morning briefing. Trust me, the basic trainee will look very different from the last time you saw him. If your family and friends don't know exactly where to look for you, they won't see you as they run by the crowd.

Unfortunately, visitors don't get to greet their basic trainee at this point. You'll run right by your family and friends and continue back to your dormitory to prepare for the afternoon events. Let your loved ones know that they may want to use the next few hours to get something to eat or return to the reception center to buy a few souvenirs.

Your family will be told what time to return to the Reception Center, later on Thursday afternoon. Depending on the time of the year, the next event will either be a retreat ceremony or a ceremony in which you receive your Airman's Coin (see Chapter 15). Of the two, I think the Retreat Ceremony is more impressive. The ceremony involves the lowering and casing of the U.S. Flag, at the end of the official duty day.

Following the ceremony, you'll be dismissed to spend the rest of the day (on base) with your friends and family. During this time, you and your loved ones are allowed to do pretty much anything you want (except drink alcohol), on base.

Here's some advice: Ask your visitors to stop off somewhere and get some good old-fashioned junk food. Your body will be craving it by this time. When I attended my twin daughters' graduation, I stopped and got some KFC, candy bars, sushi, Big Macs, sodas, and chips. They invited a couple of flight-mates who didn't have anyone coming to their graduation events, and we went to one of the base parks for a picnic! I was kind of hoping to save a little KFC for my own dinner (I bought a large bucket), but those four recruits ate everything that wasn't tied down! When they returned to the dormitory later that evening, they bragged about it, and all the other recruits were jealous. Remember, during the past eight weeks, you've been completely junk-food deprived, so a bucket of KFC is almost like winning the lottery.

## Graduation day

The next day is your official basic training graduation ceremony, in the form of an official parade. Your family will be instructed to meet at the Reception Center, where they'll be able to ride a bus to the parade grounds. You, on the other hand, will be marching with your flight to the parade grounds (about 2 miles).

There are no words to adequately describe a properly executed military parade ceremony. Although marching in military formation may be old hat to you by this time, I can guarantee that there will be tears in your loved one's eyes as your flight passes in review.

Immediately following the graduation parade (about one hour), you'll be dismissed to meet up again with your loved ones.

Hundreds of graduating recruits will be trying to locate one of thousands of guests at this time. It's a good idea to have a plan prearranged with your guests. When my daughters graduated, I told them to stay in their spot on the parade grounds, and I would walk out from the stands and meet them there. It worked just fine.

Following the graduation parade, about two hours are set aside for your loved ones to visit your dormitory, see how you've been living, and meet your TIs. You can either ride back with your loved ones on one of the busses, or you can walk the 2 miles back to the dorm area with them.

Tell your folks to take lots of photos, as this is probably the first time they've ever seen you make your own bed!

After your visitors have had a chance to talk with your TIs and view your dormitory, you'll be released for a day of off-base liberty. During this day, you can visit any of the attractions located in beautiful San Antonio, Texas.

You can find plenty to do in San Antonio:

- The River Walk
- Six Flags Fiesta Texas
- The Alamo
- San Antonio Zoo
- Splashtown
- Market Square
- The North Star Mall

Or, if your visitors have a hotel room, you may just want to hang around there for the day, watch TV, and fill up with junk food.

Even if you're of legal age, you are not allowed to consume alcohol during your off-base liberty.

If you achieve the War Hawk physical fitness standards (see Chapter 8) or the Distinguished Graduate award (see Chapter 20), you'll get an extra day on the town. If you don't receive an award, your Sunday will consist of an on-base pass. Either way, it's more time with your friends, family, and loved ones. In either case, make sure that you're back in your dormitory room by the established curfew time. Failing to return by curfew on Saturday or Sunday is the primary reason that graduating recruits get set back in Air Force basic training.

# Navy Graduation Events

Navy basic training graduation includes a formal military ceremony known as *Pass-In Review* (PIR), which is essentially a very impressive parade that neither you nor your guests will ever forget. During your first week at Naval Station Great Lakes, your unit will send home a letter giving your loved ones important information about your graduation, such as your division's graduation date, and your list of four people you have chosen to attend your graduation ceremony. Due to heightened and modified security at the naval station, your guests need to prepare well ahead of time for their trip to Illinois for your graduation, by following the guidelines in the invitation, and making sure that they have proper identification and travel arrangements.

Before the final week of Navy basic training, you'll submit names of up to four guests to security to attend your Pass-In-Review. This list does not include any guest under the age of 12 because they can attend without being on the access list. Anyone over age 12 and not on the access list will not be able to attend your graduation. Your guests should be notified that their belongings are subject to search by security, and no luggage is permitted until after the graduation ceremony. Your loved ones also need to know that outside video and photography are not permitted onboard the Recruit Training Command, but friends and family are permitted to take plenty of pictures while inside the drill hall during your graduation ceremony.

Please remember to inform your guests that photography with cameras, video, and cellphones is prohibited outside of the drill hall and may result in their confiscation!

## Graduation day

Navy basic training graduation events are fairly well standardized. The schedule for Friday is usually as follows:

- 6:30 a.m.: Recruit Training Command Gate 8 is open to your visitors.

- 7 a.m.: The drill hall where the ceremony takes place opens to visitors.

- 8:45 a.m.: Guests must be seated in the drill hall.

- 9 a.m.: The graduation ceremony begins.

- 9:20 a.m.: Recruits arrive at the drill hall.

- 10:30 a.m.: The ceremony concludes with liberty call.

- 9 p.m.: Liberty expires for graduates.

*Liberty call* is free time. In basic training, your graduation liberty call can be on base or off base, but no more than 50 miles from the base.

Keep in mind that if you're attending an A school (job training) in Great Lakes, you may be held up checking into your new command immediately following your graduation, which can take a few hours before you can be released for liberty with your loved ones. If you're attending an A school elsewhere, you're usually allowed to take liberty right away and don't travel to your A school until Saturday. Those who are ordered to travel to their next base on Saturday aren't authorized to be escorted by family members. At best, family members may meet you at the airport for a last farewell, depending on the mode of transportation the Navy has chosen for you.

If you're still waiting for orders to an A school after graduation (which often happens), you'll be relocated to what is called Ship 5. Ship 5 is a separate ship (barracks) that you'll find more accommodating than the one you inhabited during basic training. Each berthing compartment includes a lounge area with couches and chairs, a television with DVD player, board games, and racks of books and magazines. (Note: Ship 5 is also used for those recruits who have been removed from Recruit Training for medical or legal reasons or for failing to meet Navy standards. Most will be waiting for their discharge from the Navy.)

Also keep in mind that your guests won't be allowed on base after the graduation festivities have ended. If they want to meet up with you after you've graduated, they will have to do so at the main gate.

## Things to do on liberty

You'll be briefed on what you're allowed to do (and not allowed to do) during your liberty. If you're late to liberty expiration, you probably won't be allowed to see your loved ones on Saturday. That's why it's recommended that you're dropped off at Buckley Road and Illinois Street at least half an hour before your 9 p.m. curfew. You're not allowed to travel more than 50 miles away from the base (but the good thing is that downtown Chicago is 35 miles away). You're not allowed to drive a vehicle during liberty or use tobacco or alcohol. You must remain in your uniform at all times in public, and you're not authorized to bring civilian items, such as food, clothes, or electronic devices, back to the base with you upon return.

While on liberty, you're free to explore the beautiful Great Lakes and the great city of Chicago. You can do many things in the area on your free time:

- ✔ Six Flags Great America
- ✔ Gurnee Mills shopping mall
- ✔ Chicago White Sox
- ✔ Chicago Cubs
- ✔ Chicago Bears
- ✔ Shedd Aquarium
- ✔ Field Museum
- ✔ Navy Pier boat ride

Regardless of what you may choose to do with your friends and family, make sure that you're back on base by 9 p.m.

# *Marine Corps Graduation Events*

Marine Corps basic training graduation ceremonies are held weekly at the two basic training locations: Parris Island and San Diego. You'll send your loved ones information about your graduation, such as the date, time, and vehicle registration information, during your ninth week of basic training.

Anyone is allowed to attend recruit graduation and Family Day, and there is no limit to the amount of people able to attend. While the actual times for Family Day activities may vary between the two basic training locations, the graduation events are very similar.

Registration on the base begins bright and early at 6:30 a.m. Friends, family, and supporters are able to tour the facilities, get a java refill or eat breakfast, shop for a souvenir, and go to the museum. The first glimpse your guests will see of you is early in the morning during the 4-mile motivational run. Your platoon will run the 4 miles on base with all the guests on the sidelines cheering you on. After the run, loved ones are usually directed to meet with basic training command to watch a basic training movie and/or be briefed about your intense recruit training. After this briefing, your guests will be directed to assemble on the bleachers at the Parade Deck where they will see you pass and review. This briefing is followed by a five-hour on-base *liberty* (free time), where your loved ones will have the opportunity to hear all those horror stories about the transition you've made from a plain civilian to a lean, mean, fighting machine.

On-base liberty times vary between seasons and bases. However, I highly advise that you report to your barracks on time. If you're one second late, it will most likely result in your graduation being pushed back to the following week!

The Marine Corps basic training graduation ceremony starts with the Morning Colors Ceremony, a traditional flag-raising display that includes presentations by the color guard and the Marine Corps band who will play the National Anthem and the Marine Corps Hymn. The graduation itself follows shortly in the morning and lasts about an hour. After you've been officially appointed as one of "the Few, the Proud, a United States Marine," it's off the base for you for a ten-day leave (vacation) before you proceed on to the School of Infantry (see Chapter 3).

# Coast Guard Graduation Events

The United States Coast Guard Training Center in Cape May, N.J., is the Nation's only Coast Guard Recruit Training Center. Unlike the other services, the Coast Guard keeps your graduation events short and sweet. Basically, it's graduate and get outta Dodge as an official Maritime Guardian.

As long as no holiday or special event occurs, you'll have your graduation ceremony on a Friday, followed by five "luxurious" days on leave (vacation) to do whatever it is you want before you report to your first permanent duty station.

Your guests are first invited to breakfast at the Harborview Club at 8:30 a.m. when the training center opens to guests. Breakfast is served until 10 a.m. for a small fee, and reservations are not required. Immediately following breakfast, a Parent's Brief is held at the Ida Lewis Auditorium, where your guests will watch a short video about recruit training and receive information about the morning's activities.

Your graduation starts promptly at 11 a.m. and is over within the hour. Graduation will be the first time your loved ones will get to see you since the beginning of boot camp. Graduation is held outdoors near the ocean during the warmer months and in the gymnasium in the winter. Your guests are able to take pictures, and a commercially produced video of the ceremony will be available for purchase the same day.

If you have a friend or loved one who is active duty military, you can request that he present your graduation certificate, as long as he wears his uniform to your basic training graduation ceremony.

Before departing on your leave, you must return to your barracks and gather up all your gear, which may be a good time for you to show your guests around the training center. The training center closes to graduation guests promptly at 1 p.m.

Cape May is a small island, and your experience there may be more enjoyable with a nice walk or bike ride than using a car. Many people rent bicycles and coast up and down the promenade or Sunset Boulevard. You can take advantage of many nature-themed activities, such as visiting the Cape May County Park and Zoo or the Historic Cold Spring Village. Visitors can even enjoy the amusement and water parks of Wildwood or Atlantic City. Either way, you and your family are sure to enjoy this town if you decide to hang around during your leave.

# Chapter 20

# Getting Your Just Rewards

● ● ● ● ● ● ● ● ● ● ● ● ● ● ● ● ● ● ● ● ● ● ● ● ● ● ● ● ● ● ● ● ● ● ● ● ● ● ● ● ● ● ● ●

## In This Chapter

▶ Earning a medal just for being there

▶ Pushing for a push-up award

▶ Earning honor among honor grads

▶ Setting your marks on a marksmanship award

● ● ● ● ● ● ● ● ● ● ● ● ● ● ● ● ● ● ● ● ● ● ● ● ● ● ● ● ● ● ● ● ● ● ● ● ● ● ● ● ● ● ● ●

*I*f you do a good job at military basic training, you may just earn your very first military award. Some basic training awards, such as decorations, will remain with you for the rest of your military career, while others don't really mean a thing past the basic training walls.

Depending on the branch, there are many different types of basic training awards and many different ways to earn them.

## Army Basic Combat Training Awards

During Army basic combat training, recruits are eligible to earn one or more awards that are designed to motivate recruits toward high levels of performance. Awards can be broken into one of three categories:

✔ Decorations (medals and ribbons)

✔ Physical fitness

✔ Other

You can earn only a few military awards (ribbons and/or medals) while in Army basic training. Ribbons or medals are worn when wearing one of the Army dress uniforms; they're not worn when wearing the camouflaged ACU (Army Combat Uniform).

In addition to ribbons/medals and PT awards, you can earn a badge for shooting well or even a promotion for outstanding performance in Army basic training.

# National Defense Service Medal (NDSM)

The National Defense Service Medal (NDSM) is often called the BX medal because it's awarded to anyone who serves during a time of conflict. Note that you do not have to serve in an actual combat zone to earn the medal; you just have to serve in the U.S. Military during a period of time when the United States is in engaged in combat operations somewhere in the world.

The National Defense Service medal itself is a bronze medallion 1¼ inches in diameter. Shown on the front of the medal beneath the words NATIONAL DEFENSE is an eagle with inverted wings perched on a sword and palm branch. Displayed on the center of the reverse side is a shield taken from the Coat of Arms of the United States. An open wreath made up of oak leaves appears the right side of the Coat of Arms, with laurel leaves on the left side.

The National Defense Service Medal is awarded for honorable active service as a member of the Armed Forces for any period between

- ✔ June 27, 1950, to July 27, 1954 (for service during the Korean War)
- ✔ January 1, 1961, to August 14, 1974 (for service during the Vietnam War)
- ✔ August 2, 1990, to November 30, 1995 (for service during the Gulf War)
- ✔ September 11, 2001, to a date to be announced (for service during the War on Terrorism)

The eagle shown on the medal symbolizes the American bald eagle and stands for the United States. The sword symbolizes armed strength, and the palm signifies victory. The shield stands for the authority under which the medal is given and earned. The oak embodies strength and courage while the laurel signifies honor and achievement.

The National Defense Service medal's ribbon (see Figure 20-1) is 1⅜ inches wide and has 11 stripes.

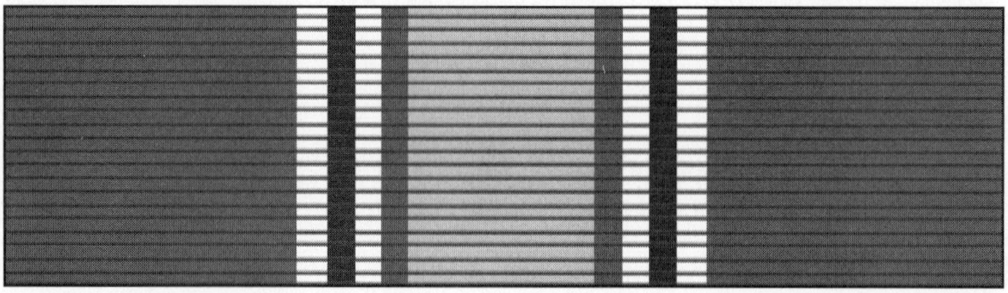

**Figure 20-1:**
The
National
Defense
Service
Medal.

# Army Service Ribbon

Enlisted personnel are awarded the Army Service Ribbon after successful completion of their initial Military Occupational Specialty (MOS) producing course. That means you get this award if you attend Army OSUT (one station unit training that combines basic training and job training in one course). Those officers or enlisted service members that are assigned to a specialty, special skill identifier, or MOS based upon civilian or other service acquired skills are awarded the Army Service Ribbon after completion of four months of honorable, active service.

The Army Service Ribbon is multi-colored with bars of red, orange, yellow, green, and blue to symbolize the complete range of military specialties in which officers and enlisted soldiers may go into upon conclusion of their initial training.

# Army PT awards

The Army awards a badge for exceptional performance on the Army PT test. This badge is often called the PT Stud award, but its official name is The Army Physical Fitness Badge.

The badge is a dark blue disk with a yellow human silhouette in the middle with arms stretched out in front of an American flag surrounded by the words Physical Fitness Excellence. The badge is authorized to be worn on the Army PT uniform only.

The badge is awarded to soldiers who obtain a minimum total score of 270, with a minimum score of 90 on each event of the Army Physical Fitness Test (APFT), which you must pass in order to graduate from Army basic training (see Chapter 8).

The PT Badge may be worn only if you scored 270 or above on your *last* PT test. When you take the semi-annual test again, if you score less than 270, you must stop wearing the badge.

# Marksmanship badge

If you graduate from Army basic training, you've earned the Army Marksmanship Badge. That's because you must earn a badge on the firing range in order to graduate from Army basic training (see Chapter 14).

A recruit can earn three types of badges: Expert, Sharpshooter, or Marksman (see Chapter 4). Suspended on the badge are bars that indicate the weapons you're specifically qualified for. You are only authorized to show three component bars on the badge at one time. This badge is obtained after successful completion of your weapons qualification course.

Each badge has its own distinctive design:

- ✔ **Expert:** A white metal (silver, nickel and rhodium), 1.17 inches in height, a cross patee with the representation of a target placed on the center thereof and enclosed by a wreath.

- ✔ **Sharpshooter:** A white metal (silver, nickel, and rhodium), 1 inch in height, a cross patee with the representation of a target placed on the center thereof.

- ✔ **Marksman:** A white metal (silver, nickel, and rhodium), 1 inch in height, a cross patee.

The good news is that you must successfully be able to toss a grenade without blowing up your drill sergeant in order to graduate from Army basic training, so you'll get an additional weapons bar to hang from your badge.

## Basic training promotions

If you do exceptionally well in basic training and your drill sergeant likes you a whole lot, you can receive a promotion (up to E-4) in Army basic training. Promotions beyond the rank of E-3 during basic training are rare, but it has been known to happen. The Army doesn't have an official Honor Graduate award in basic training, electing instead to hand out promotions to outstanding achievers.

# Air Force Basic Training Awards

Without a doubt, the Air Force gives more awards for exceptional performance during basic training than any other branch. Not only can you win the standard medals, decorations, and certificates, but you can even earn an extra day on the town.

## American Defense Service Medal

This award is often called the BX ribbon because you get it for simply being on active duty in the military. For complete information about this award, see "Army basic combat training awards," earlier in this chapter.

# Air Force Training Ribbon

Here's another BX ribbon because you get it for simply graduating Air Force basic training. The ribbon has a wide center stripe of red, flanked on either side by a wide stripe of dark blue and a narrow yellow stripe edged by a narrow dark blue stripe (see Figure 20-2).

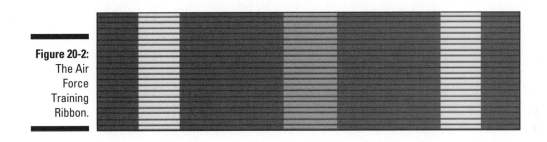

**Figure 20-2:** The Air Force Training Ribbon.

# Basic Military Training Honor Graduate

The Air Force Basic Military Training Honor Graduate ribbon is awarded to recruits who are selected as either an honor graduate or distinguished graduate in Air Force basic training. The honor graduate is the recruit with the highest combined scores on all academic tests and practical exams (such as marching, marksmanship, and so on). Distinguished graduates are those who score within the top 10 percent of the training flight.

You must also meet the Thunderbolt physical fitness award standard (see "Air Force PT awards," later in this chapter) in order to be selected as an honor graduate or distinguished graduate.

The ribbon has a wide center stripe of ultramarine blue flanked with equal stripes of yellow, Brittany blue, and white on either side (see Figure 20-3).

**Figure 20-3:** The Air Force Basic Training Honor Graduate ribbon.

## Small Arms Expert Marksmanship Ribbon

The Small Arms Expert Marksmanship Ribbon is awarded to those who score expert when firing the M-16 rifle or the M-9 pistol (see Chapter 4). If you qualify as an expert with both weapons, you get a bronze service star which is worn in the middle of the ribbon.

The ribbon has a very wide center stripe of laurel green, flanked on either side by a thin yellow stripe, with a wide light blue stripe at the edges.

## Air Force PT awards

There are two Air Force basic training physical fitness awards:

- ✔ The Thunderbolt Standard
- ✔ The War Hawk Standard

Chapter 8 has complete information about how well you must perform in order to meet these standards.

If you achieve the Thunderbolt Standard, you'll be awarded with a special T-shirt and a certificate, suitable for framing. If you achieve the highest standard (War Hawk), you get the certificate, T-shirt, and an extra day on the town following gradation!

## Other Air Force basic training awards

You can also earn two final awards during your stint at Lackland:

- ✔ **Airman's coin:** You receive your individual Airman's coin (see Chapter 15) after you successfully complete the crucible, the Air Force basic training cumulating event. The Airman's coin signifies that you are a respected and valued member of the United States Air Force.
- ✔ **Honor flight:** If your flight exhibits outstanding performance in the areas of teamwork and dedication during your stay, your team may be designated as the honor flight. The honor flight is basically the top-rated flight in your basic training squadron chosen by Air Force basic training Group leadership.

While it's not mandatory, it's not uncommon for the TI to give all members of the honor flight an extra day on the town following Air Force basic training graduation.

# Navy Basic Training Awards

The Navy doesn't give very many awards for individual performance during basic training, preferring instead to give group awards for outstanding performance of the entire basic training division. However, like all the services, you'll get one medal just for graduating basic training.

You can earn three Navy medals while in basic training:

- ✔ **National Defense Service Medal:** Like all the services, graduates of Navy basic training are entitled to wear the National Defense Service Medal. (See "Army Basic Combat Training Awards," earlier in this chapter.)

- ✔ **Navy Expert Rifleman Medal:** This medal replaced the Navy Sharpshooters Medal in 1910. It's awarded to those who qualify as expert with the rifle during basic training (see Chapter 4). An unadorned ribbon signifies Marksman. The same ribbon with a bronze S signifies Sharpshooter. Navy personnel who obtain a first and second Expert qualification wear the ribbon bar with a bronze E. Upon attaining the third and final Expert qualification, a silver E is attached to the ribbon.

- ✔ **Navy Expert Pistol Medal:** This medal replaced the Navy Sharpshooters Medal in 1910. It is awarded to those who meet expert qualifications with the M-9 pistol on the Navy basic training firing range (see Chapter 4). An unadorned ribbon signifies Marksman. The same ribbon with a bronze S signifies Sharpshooter. Navy personnel who obtain a first and second Expert qualification wear the ribbon bar with a bronze E. Upon attaining the third and final Expert qualification, a silver E is attached to the ribbon.

With the exception of honor graduate, all other Navy basic training awards are presented to the group as a whole, rather than the individual. Certain organizations (like the Navy League) provide individual awards that are given during graduation ceremonies.

In addition, during your training, your basic training division will compete for a variety of awards, including awards for overall excellence, military drill, inspections, fitness, and academic achievement. Your division will be awarded flags and streamers that are carried in dress parades and reviews. Streamers are awarded to each winning division for athletic competitions, such as track and field, tug of war, swimming, and volleyball.

Honor recruits are the top 10 percent (academically) of each Navy basic training division. Each honor recruit is awarded a commemorative token from the commanding officer and a certificate of recognition.

# Marine Corps Basic Training Awards

The Marine Corps tends to be less generous with their awards than the other services. There are fewer individual awards because the Marines feel that they are an elite force (because they're trained to be a superior service) and being identified as such is enough. For example, it's normal for Marines to wear their utility uniforms without insignia denoting special training.

You can, however, earn a few awards while at Marine Corps basic training.

As with the other services, all graduates of Marine Corps basic training are awarded the National Defense Service Medal.

While the Army and Air Force award ribbons for successful completion of basic training, the Marine Corps issues the Eagle, Globe, and Anchor emblem to their successful graduates. The seal has an American bald eagle with wings spread, standing on a globe superimposed on an anchor, with a scroll in its beak displaying the Marine Corps motto, Semper Fidelis. The seal is set in a scarlet background encircled by a blue band with gold rope inscribed with the words in gold, Department of the Navy, United States Marine Corps.

Additionally, Marine Corps basic training honor graduates don't get a certificate or plaque, but they usually earn a promotion to the next highest rank (up to E-3).

The Marines prefer to focus more on unit/group competition rather than individual achievements. During basic training, Marine Corps units compete for almost everything, including group competitions for shooting, PT, academics, and drill. Those units that score the worst often are given a nickname, such as the "booger" platoon, while the winners receive trophies for their unit (and generally smiles from their instructor).

Marines do earn individual marksmanship badges indicating their proficiency on the firing range (see Chapter 4).

# Coast Guard Basic Training Awards

The Coast Guard also has a few goodies in store for those who go above and beyond for basic training. These awards include medals for displaying your proficiency with things that go "bang" and the standard medal just for joining.

As with the other services, you can earn a variety of medals and decorations during Coast Guard basic training:

- **The National Defense Service Medal:** Like the other services, the Coast Guard awards the National Defense Service Medal just for joining during a time of war. (See "Army Basic Combat Training Awards," earlier in this chapter.)

- **The Marksmanship Medals:** You can earn a marksmanship medal while at Coast Guard basic training. It is called the Coast Guard Pistol Marksmanship Ribbon.

  The Coast Guard Pistol Marksmanship Ribbon is a plain black color with two thin white stripes on each end for marksman qualification, with a device added to denote a sharpshooter or expert status. The Coast Guard Rifle Marksmanship Ribbon is very similar to the pistol ribbon, except it has four thin white stripes instead of two.

- **Basic Training Honor Graduate Ribbon:** Those Coasties who graduate in the top 3 percent of their class are designated as basic training honor graduates and are entitled to wear the Coast Guard Honor Graduate Ribbon. Recipients are determined by written tests, instructor evaluations, PT scores, and performance in practical exercises. The ribbon is one of the few awards with no accompanying medal. The ribbon is multicolored consisting of white, navy, and red bars, with one yellow bar in the center.

Additionally, the Coast Guard gives award certificates for outstanding performance in the areas of physical fitness, pistol expert, drill, best shipmate, leadership, seamanship, and academics.

# Part VI
# The Part of Tens

The 5th Wave    By Rich Tennant

"That was a nasty patch of turbulence. I'd better go back and reassure the recruits."

# *In this part . . .*

**1**t wouldn't be a For Dummies book without The Parts of Ten. In this part, you discover ten ways to keep your drill instructor from wringing your neck. You also find out ten things you can do in advance to make your military basic training experience much easier. (Anything you can do to make basic training easier is a good thing!)

# Chapter 21

# Ten Ways to Prepare for Basic Training

**M**ilitary basic training is tough — quite possibly, the toughest thing you've ever done in your life. Fortunately, the failure rate is relatively low because the instructors are trained not to let you give up, no matter how much you struggle.

A lot is thrown at you during military basic training. You can make your basic training life much easier by preparing yourself. That way, once basic training actually starts, you can concentrate on the hard stuff.

## Discover How to Address Instructors

Two or three days after basic training starts, properly addressing instructors will become second nature. But you can impress your instructors and save yourself a lot of grief (and push-ups) if you know the accepted customs before you even step on the base.

Just to make it difficult, all the branches have different rules for basic training. For example, in Air Force basic training, all instructors are addressed by sir or ma'am. However, in Army basic training, if you call your instructor sir or ma'am, you're likely to listen to a long tirade from your instructor about how she works for a living, while you're simultaneously performing several push-ups.

The following list gives you a heads-up on how to address each instructor based on the branch you join:

- **Air Force:** Air Force drill instructors are always addressed as sir or ma'am, depending on gender. Additionally, Air Force drill instructors prefer that you create a *sir sandwich* — that is, you say sir or ma'am at both the beginning and end of each sentence, such as "Sir/ma'am, I just came from the chow hall, sir/ma'am."

- **Army:** The correct way to address Army drill instructors is by using the title "Drill Sergeant," as in "Yes, Drill Sergeant" or "No, Drill Sergeant."

  When you speak to an Army drill sergeant, stand at parade rest, look straight ahead, and yell your response. (Drill sergeants are notoriously hard of hearing.)

  When you're in position of *parade rest,* look straight ahead, not directly at your drill sergeant. Whatever you do, don't look your drill sergeant directly in the eye, or he will loudly ask, "Are you eye-balling me, boy?" (There is no good answer to that question.)

- **Coast Guard:** During the first two weeks of Coast Guard basic training, you address your instructors as sir or ma'am, depending on gender. Just to keep you on your toes, the Coast Guard changes the rules a couple of weeks after basic training starts. During week 2 of Coast Guard basic training, you attend a class about Coast Guard rates and ranks. After that class, you're expected to address your instructors by rank and last name, such as "Yes, Petty Officer Jones" or "No, Petty Officer Jones."

  If you forget, and address your instructor by sir or ma'am after the course, don't worry. Your drill instructor will be very happy to (loudly) remind you.

- **Marine Corps:** Like Air Force drill instructors, Marine Corps drill instructors also like to be addressed as sir or ma'am, but you'll note significant differences in speech between Air Force and Marine Corps recruits. When you address drill instructors, third-person language is a cardinal rule during Marine Corps basic training. Never, ever say, "Are you ready?" The correct phrasing is "Is the drill instructor ready?"

  Likewise, when speaking of yourself, don't say, "I'm hungry." Instead, say, "This recruit is hungry, sir." When speaking of other recruits, say, "Those recruits are hungry, ma'am," not "they're hungry."

- **Navy.** Like the Army, addressing a drill instructor with sir or ma'am during Navy basic training warrants the death penalty. The correct way to address a Naval drill instructor is by rank and last name. For example, if your drill instructor is a petty officer with the last name of "Smith," you'd reply, "Yes, Petty Officer Smith" or "No, Petty Officer Smith." If your drill instructor is in the rank of E-7 or higher, you'd address him as "Yes, Chief Smith" or "No, Chief Petty Officer Smith." You can find more information about military rank titles in Chapter 5.

# Memorize Military Ranks

Everyone in the U.S. Military has a rank. Military rank tells others where you stand in the military hierarchy. Individuals who out-rank you can give you orders, and you can give orders to those you out-rank.

Military rank insignia is worn visibly on the uniform on the collar, the upper sleeve, or the center of the chest, depending on the service. You're required to memorize the military ranks of your service before you can graduate basic training, so why not get a head start and memorize them before you leave for basic training? You don't have to memorize the ranks of the other services, if you don't want to, but it wouldn't be a bad idea, as you're certain to come into contact with members of the other branches following basic training graduation.

Chapter 5 includes a handy-dandy rank chart for all the branches.

# Get in Shape

By far, the No. 1 reason for being *set back,* or *recycled,* in basic training — in other words, being returned to an earlier stage of basic — is failure to meet the physical fitness standards. Certainly, failing basic training for this reason is almost impossible (because the instructors will simply keep you there until you can pass), but who wants to spend even one day longer in basic training than absolutely necessary?

Taking time to get into shape prior to arriving at military basic training goes a long way toward putting a smile on your instructor's face and making your basic training life much easier. As a minimum, you should strive toward the goals listed in Table 21-1.

| Table 21-1 | Basic Training Minimum Fitness Requirements | | | |
|------------|--------|----------|---------|----------------|
| *Branch* | *Gender* | *Push-Ups* | *Sit-Ups* | *Run in Minutes* |
| Army | Male | 42 | 52 | 2 miles in 15:54 |
| Army | Female | 19 | 52 | 2 miles in 18:54 |
| Air Force | Male | 45 | 50 | 1 ½ miles in 11:57 |
| Air Force | Female | 27 | 50 | 1 ½ miles in 14:21 |

*(continued)*

### Table 21-1 (continued)

| Branch | Gender | Push-Ups | Sit-Ups | Run in Minutes |
|---|---|---|---|---|
| Navy | Male | 62 | 51 (curl-ups) | 1 ½ miles in 11:00 |
| Navy | Female | 24 | 51 (curl-ups) | 1 ½ miles in 13:30 |
| Marine Corps | Male | 3 | 50 | 3 miles in 28:00 |
| Marine Corps | Female | 15-second flexed arm hang | 50 sit-ups | 3 miles in 31:00 |
| Coast Guard | Male | 29 | 38 | 1 ½ miles in 12:51 |
| Coast Guard | Female | 23 | 32 | 1 ½ miles in 15:26 |

# Get a Haircut

One thing you don't want to do upon arrival at military basic training is to stand out in any way. That means no blue hair, no facial hair, no long hair, and no shaved heads.

Guys, get a regular haircut with the sides and back tapered. The hair on the sides of your head should not touch your ears. Don't overdo it and show up with a crew cut, or your instructor will (loudly) inquire as to whether or not you think you're good enough to impersonate a military member.

Ladies, the Navy is the only branch that requires women to cut their hair for basic training. The standards are such that the length of your hair can't pass below the bottom of your collar, and the bangs (if you have them) can't touch the eyebrows. Women joining the other branches don't have to cut their hair, but keep in mind that your hair must always be neat and styled in such a way that it doesn't touch the bottom of your collar, and your bangs can't touch your eyebrows. If you choose to wear your hair in a ponytail, keep in mind that the ponytail can't extend below the bottom of the collar. Hair pins must be a neutral color or the same color as your hair. Keep in mind, maintaining that standard with long hair while running the obstacle course or performing physical training (PT) is hard to do. You may want to give some thought about showing up with a short, page-boy type style.

Ladies, don't show up at military basic training with a man-style hairdo. (Women aren't allowed to shave their heads.) That style is considered a fad in the military and isn't allowed. In the military, all women's hair styles are required to be feminine.

# Open a Bank Account

Everyone in the military is required to have a bank account because the military uses direct deposit to pay you. If you don't have a bank account, you can't get paid.

If you show up to basic training without a bank account, you're required to open one at the on-base bank or credit union upon arrival at basic.

 Make sure that you have an ATM card and that any family members you financially support also have access to the account.

# Gather Your Important Paperwork

Fortunately, your recruiter and the fine folks at the Military Entrance Processing (MEPS) center will take care of much of your paperwork. They'll gather all your important enlistment paperwork, such as your enlistment contract, into a huge packet for you to take with you.

 If you're married, pack a certified copy of your marriage certificate. If you have kids, bring certified copies of their birth certificates. You need these items to enroll them in the military healthcare system and to send them forms for a military dependent ID card. You also need these documents to start your monthly housing allowance so that your family has the means to pay the rent.

Pack a few pre-addressed, prestamped envelopes with you so that you can write the folks back home. This approach is even better than an address book — all you have to do is stick the letter inside, seal the envelope, and drop it into a mail box.

Put a few wallet-sized photos of your loved ones in your purse or wallet. Don't take more than four or five. These photos will give you something to cherish at the end of those days when it seemed that nothing went right, and you hate all military training instructors.

# Memorize Your Basic Training Chain-of-Command

Chain of command is the first written test you'll take in basic training. You usually take this test within a week or two after arrival. This test is considered a primer to get you in shape for all the memorization work you have to do during basic.

A *chain of command* is nothing more than a list of your bosses, beginning with your training instructor and ending with the President of the United States (who is the commander-in-chief of the U.S. Military).

The chain of command is used to resolve problems. If you have a problem that you can't resolve, you ask your immediate supervisor for help. If she can't resolve it, you speak with her boss, then his boss, and so on through the chain until the problem is resolved.

# Master Military Time

Military members tell time differently than civilians. In the military, you don't meet a friend at the gym at 3 p.m. You meet him at 1500 hours. You don't have supper at 6 p.m. You have it at 1800 hours. If your training instructor tells you to report to his office at 1300 hours, you'd better know what time to be there.

The military uses a 24-hour clock. That means, for example, that 1 a.m. is 0100 hours, and 1 p.m. is 1300 hours. Chapter 6 gets you telling time the military way in no time at all.

# Memorize Your Service's Core Values

All the services have *core values* — standards that their members are expected to live by. In basic training, you're required to memorize the core values for your branch and state those values any time the drill instructor orders you to.

# Know Your Social Security Number

Remember in those old war movies, if the hero was captured, all he was required to tell the enemy was his name, rank, and serial number?

Well, the military gave up on serial numbers several decades ago. Today, the military identifies troops by means of their Social Security number. However, like the old serial numbers, you use your Social Security number in the military for everything. You use it to sign in for chow. You use it to resolve a pay problem. You use it when reporting in for sick call. You include it on pretty much every piece of military paperwork you're required to fill out or sign.

If you're holding up the chow hall line while you dig into your wallet for your Social Security card, not only are you going to make a lot of hungry people mad, but your training instructor is likely to resolve this situation by having you spend the next 12 hours yelling your Social Security number to everyone you see. In other words, memorize your Social Security number.

# Chapter 22

# Ten Ways to Make Your Drill Instructor Happy

## In This Chapter

▶ Realizing that honesty is the best policy

▶ Properly addressing your new boss

▶ Dressing to impress

*A*ctually making a drill instructor happy is probably impossible to do because they seem to be born without that particular emotion. However, if you can practice ten simple rules, you can keep your drill instructor the least unhappy as possible.

Many of these tips are common sense, and others will be second nature after your first few days of military basic training. Doing the right things, the right way right, right from the beginning can go a long way in keeping your drill instructor off your back.

## Always Tell the Truth

Drill instructors hate liars. A simple "I don't know, Drill Sergeant." Is preferable to straight out lying or telling your drill instructor what you think he she may want to hear. If the drill instructor asks you, "Did you take a shower today?" and you didn't, then trust me — the drill instructor already knew the answer before he asked the question.

Drill instructors like to set up little traps to test your honesty and integrity. Don't fall into their traps. I can promise you that the consequences of skipping a shower would be much less than the consequences of getting caught in a lie. Lack of integrity (lying) can actually get you discharged from boot camp.

# Always Use the Proper Method of Address

I understand it may be easy to forget how to properly address your drill instructor during the first couple of stressful days of basic training because you're trying so hard not to mess up or get noticed. *I* understand it, but believe me, your drill instructor won't.

Without doubt, the thing that new recruits get chewed out for the most during the first few days of military basic training is using incorrect terms of address, especially under stressful situations. Just to make it a little more difficult, all the services have different rules about properly addressing your instructors:

- **Army:** Army drill instructors are addressed as Drill Sergeant, as in "Yes, Drill Sergeant," or "No, Drill Sergeant." When speaking to your Army drill sergeant, never, ever use the term sir or ma'am. It's a cardinal sin to address an enlisted member with such a horrific term in the U.S. Army.

- **Air Force:** Unlike the Army, Air Force training instructors like to be addressed with a courtesy sir or ma'am. Be careful not to concoct a sir-sandwich when addressing these animals. Saying something like, "Sir, no sir" or "Ma'am, I have no excuse, ma'am" is a sure way to drive them up the wall.

- **Navy:** Like Army instructors, Navy basic training instructors (lovingly referred to as RDCs) hate being called sir or ma'am. If your instructor is below the pay grade of E-7, the proper term of address is Petty Officer. If they're pay grade E-7, you must refer to them as Chief or Chief Petty Officer. If they're pay grade E-8 (you can tell because they have a star above the anchor on their rank device), you must address them as Senior Chief. If they're pay grade E-9 (two stars above the anchor), you must address them as Master Chief. Chances are they will be an E-7, but to be safe, make sure that you know the difference. For example, if your RDC is in the pay grade of E-6 and his last name is Smith, you would say "Yes, Petty Officer Smith." If she is an E-7 named Jones, you would address her as Chief Jones.

- **Marine Corps:** Like the Air Force, Marine Corps drill instructors want you to address them as sir or ma'am, depending on their gender. However, it's not exactly like the Air Force because the Marines also want you to use third person language, such as "Sir, those recruits are trying to waste the drill instructor's time."

- **Coast Guard:** The Coast Guard is unique in that it changed the rules in the middle of the game. Before you attend your class on Coast Guard ranks, you address your drill sergeants with the horrific sir or ma'am. After you attend the Coast Guard ranks class (around week 2 of basic training), you're expected to address your instructors by their rank and last name.

# Leave Your Drill Sergeant's Stuff Alone

While wandering around the barracks, you may see something that belongs to your drill instructor laying on a desk or footlocker. I can guarantee it's not an accident. The drill instructor is testing to see which of the new recruits can't be trusted to leave someone else's property alone.

As sure as I'm writing this book, some recruit will pick up the drill instructor's "Smokey the Bear" hat and try it on. Big mistake. No, scratch that, extremely huge mistake. Touching anything that belongs to the drill instructor without specific permission to do so warrants the death penalty. (Okay, the drill instructor won't kill you, but you'll wish you were dead.)

# Don't Make Excuses

If you want to get on your drill instructor's bad side, the quickest way is to make an excuse. Even if it's a good excuse, I can guarantee your drill instructor will not think it was good enough. If you were supposed to do something and you failed to do it, or you do something you weren't supposed to do, the correct response is *always* "I have no excuse." I don't care if aliens flew down from space and made you do it (or not do it). That's not an excuse, so therefore you have no excuse.

# Help Out Those Who Need It

Every basic training unit has at least one or two folks who are dumber than dirt and just don't seem to get it. Your instructor is looking for those who make a little extra effort to help those folks along. It's called *teamwork,* and it's a very desirable trait for military members (especially leaders) to possess.

During the first several days of basic training, instructors will be watching for those who possess this trait, and these folks will be the first ones selected for student leadership positions. Becoming a basic training student leader is a distinct advantage to winning a basic training leadership award (see Chapter 20).

# Follow Directions to the Letter

Remember how your high school teachers would encourage you to think for yourself and find innovative ways to get things done? Forget about it. In basic training, instructors do not want to see a better idea. (The time for better ideas will come after basic training.) In basic training, your instructors want you to do as you are told, when you are told, and nothing extra.

Basic training is all about teaching uniformity, and instructors have no time to waste on those who would rather march to the beat of a different drum.

## Avoid Eye Contact

Instructors refer to eye contact as *eyeballing,* as in "Are you eyeballing me, boy?" Making eye contact is a big no-no in basic training. Looking your instructor in the eye is an indication that you consider yourself on equal footing with your instructor, and that won't be true until the day you graduate.

When speaking with your drill instructor, you should always look straight ahead, especially if you're at the position of attention. If your drill instructor happens to be standing directly in front of you, look at his chest. (I know this is inappropriate in certain civilian settings, but this is how we do it in the military.) If your drill instructor happens to be standing directly in front of you, stare straight ahead. Chances are there will be a height difference so that you aren't making eye contact. If you and the drill instructor are of identical height, avert your eyes just enough to avoid his eyes.

Army recruits are permitted to look the drill sergeant in the eye, as long as the recruit is not at the position of attention.

## Be Serious at All Times

You may consider yourself to be the class clown, and maybe even some of your classmates and teachers thought you were funny in high school. I can promise you, your drill instructor will not be amused. Basic training is a serious enterprise, and jokes and laughter aren't appreciated. Even if your instructor tells a joke once in a while, don't try it on your own.

Never smile or laugh in the presence of the DIs. This will ensure a trip to the quarter-deck.

# Remain Absolutely Motionless at Attention

This also catches a lot of new recruits. The drill position of "attention," means to stand absolutely still (see Chapter 9). It doesn't mean you can scratch where it itches, sneeze, or move your aching legs.

One of the purposes of drill is to display the self-discipline of the unit members, and if you're moving around scratching yourself or looking at the pretty girls (or guys) walking by, it's very obvious. At least, I guarantee your drill instructor will see you move and comment (loudly) about it.

# Dress Conservatively Upon Arrival

I know you've heard all that advice about first impressions and all that. But, it really means something during military basic training. Just as you'll be scoping out your new drill instructor when you first meet him, he'll be scoping you out as well. Drill instructors like to assign nicknames to new recruits when they first meet them, and you don't want to go through several weeks of basic training being known as "hippie" because you chose to show up with long, stringy hair.

# Chapter 23

# Ten Ways to Get in Shape for Basic Training

### In This Chapter
▶ Making realistic goals

▶ Applying fitness standards

▶ Weighing in on the prize

▶ Sticking to your plan

*T*he services use aerobic fitness, muscular strength, and body composition to determine your overall fitness. Your overall fitness levels are important to establish your ability to perform physically. You must meet certain minimum physical fitness standards in order to graduate from basic training. The reason most recruits are recycled in basic training is because they don't meet the physical fitness standards. Reasons for failing include injury, lack of preparation, and poor overall fitness. By preparing your body at home for the extreme physical training routines you can expect at basic, your health and readiness benefits will increase. Developing a plan on your own months prior to shipping out will improve your body composition, physical activity, and overall fitness levels. Arriving to basic training prepared is the best way to ensure optimum performance.

If you discover that you don't like being in the military, don't think that you can simply fail the physical fitness training tests and get out. It doesn't work that way. Each year, a few recruits will attempt to fail the standards because they want to get out, only to discover that the instructors will simply keep them there (exercising constantly) to help them get into shape. The instructors are available to help you pass the physical fitness tests, no matter what it takes — and whether you want to or not.

# Write Down Your Goals

You can't determine where to begin if you don't know where you're going. Sit down with a pad and pen and assess the situation. Locate your weakest points with your physical ability and overall health. Do you drink enough water per day? Can you even do a sit-up? What distance can you run and in what time? Are you overweight?

Next, figure out your strong points. For example, you may eat a lot of green, leafy vegetables. You may already be where you want to be with your big, beefy, military-ready muscles. You may a successful runner because you were the captain of the track and field team. Plotting out your weak and strong points can help you narrow in on what you need to focus on for your specific goals.

Another question to ask is how much time do you want to give yourself to achieve these goals. Hopefully, you're thinking well ahead of the game. Changing your lifestyle to accommodate a healthy diet and physical training program is most successful and permanent if it's achieved over a long period of time. Preparing a list of goals six months to a year out from basic training is advised as a minimum, but don't get stressed if the time isn't there. The sooner you make a plan, the sooner you can work toward your goals, and the sooner you will see results.

After you make your list of goals, keep them with you and look over them daily. Keeping your goals in mind will help you check them off the list much easier, and you'll want to succeed!

# Develop a Stretching and Warm-Up Routine

Warming up and stretching your tendons and muscles is extremely important in order to improve technical proficiency and injury resistance. Develop a warm-up routine first and then concentrate on stretching. You should stretch before and after almost every workout.

Warm up to stretch — don't stretch to warm up — because when muscles are cold, they are resistant to lengthening, and you won't get as good of a stretch.

Some experts recommend that you stretch only after (not before) strength training, but it's a good idea to warm up and stretch before and after running and aerobics. It's always recommended to consult with your doctor or your personal trainer to find out what routine may be best for you.

# Familiarize Yourself with Current Military Fitness Standards

Chapter 8 explains each military branch's physical fitness standards. Your recruiter may also be able to point you in the right direction. By familiarizing yourself with the current regulations for military fitness specific to your branch, you can arrive at basic training prepared to basic training.

For example, if you're a 24-year-old male in the Army, you must run 2 miles in 17½ minutes or less. You must also be able to do a certain amount of push-ups and sit-ups (the military way) within 2 minutes in order to pass your physical fitness test and graduate from Army Basic Combat Training. You can look up the information specific to your age, gender and your service of choice in Chapter 8. If you can meet these requirements before you step foot on basic training soil, you're ahead of the game. Now that's preparation!

# Join a Workout Program or Get a Fitness Buddy

No one expects you to be a professional. That's why so many options exist for healthy lifestyle changes, such as programs for eating right and getting in shape. Consider hiring a personal trainer, enrolling in an exercise class, such as aerobics or kick boxing, and working out with a friend (perhaps a friend who plans to join the military as well).

Ask your recruiter or do some research online about the *PT Pyramid.* Using the PT Pyramid method is a great way to start a foundation of fitness needed to pass fitness tests. So, using this exercise routine is sure to get you in shape for basic training.

Having others around will help you finish your workout even when times can get tough and you just want to quit. You're far more likely to stick it out if someone else is pushing you to keep running for 30 more seconds. Plus, having a workout buddy around will give you a spotter in times of need, such as when you're lifting or squatting. You don't have to go at this alone, because it's so much easier and even fun when others are with you rooting you on.

# Practice Good Nutrition

Probably the most important part of getting in shape is a healthy diet. Giving your body the nutrients required for optimum performance is ideal when attempting to improve the way your body functions and when demanding physical increase.

Circulating your body with fresh water each day is extremely necessary. Make sure to drink enough water and stay away from obvious no-no's, such as soda and other sugar-filled beverages. Cut out anything overprocessed, high calorie, grease-filled, fried, white-flour based, and sugary. Focus on a balanced diet.

If you find yourself overweight, don't starve yourself skinny. This is not satisfying or healthy and won't give long-term results. Starving yourself can make you weak and fragile and unable to take the stress basic training causes. Training your metabolism to burn the calories you take in is a lifestyle change that is sure to stick, and you may find it surprising that it seems you eat more food, not less, when you follow a healthy diet.

Don't deprive yourself, though. If you feel the need to satisfy that sweet tooth at your local ice cream spot, remember to have everything (mostly) in moderation. Pick one day a week to treat yourself to that sundae. Hey, with all your hard work of exercising and eating right, it's a sweet treat you've earned.

# Test Yourself

There's no better way to see how prepared you are for the actual physical fitness test in basic training than to run your own practice tests at home. First, you'll need to make your own test. Your test should be as close as possible to your branches physical fitness test because perfecting skills that aren't done the military way can be a waste of time, especially if your basic training instructor has to retrain you to do it his way. Review Chapter 8 in this book to familiarize yourself with the military physical fitness standards and locate the specific standards that apply to your service, gender, and age.

Next, make sure that you're doing push-ups and sit-ups the military way. Some branches also require you to do pull-ups and curl-ups. You need to have the proper form. If you're unfamiliar with the way the military does push-ups, sit-ups, and other exercises, you can ask your recruiter to help you. He should be able to show you the proper form in the recruiting office or take you out for a day of training. Additionally, you can find plenty of military-based videos online that show you how to do certain exercises the military way.

The Marine Corps even has a physical training program that recruits can join while in the Delayed Entry Program, or DEP. In fact, most Marine recruiters will make this program mandatory.

All the branches' physical fitness tests involve running. Whether it be a 1½-mile run in 11 minutes or a 3-mile run in 28 minutes, all the branches will give you a certain distance to run and a certain timeframe to complete the task. You can use your local track (usually four times around equals 1 mile), and time yourself on how long it takes to run the distance required for your branch of choice. Remember to check Chapter 8 for specific time limits, based on your gender and age.

After you have your personal guidelines hashed out, you can run your physical training practice test. It's helpful to have your training buddy there with you to time your run and count your reps. It's also a good idea to do your physical fitness test once per week. If you find yourself needing improvement (not making the cut), keep practicing and training in between tests. If you find yourself passing your test with flying colors, keep your practice test so that you remain sharp on your buttons and ready to ace basic training.

# *Meet the Military's Weight Requirements*

In order to join any branch of the military, your weight must fall within certain strict requirements established by each individual branch. You can find these requirements in chart form at your local recruiter's office and online:

- ✔ **Army:** http://usmilitary.about.com/od/army/a/
  weightcharts.htm

- ✔ **Air Force:** http://usmilitary.about.com/od/airforcejoin/a/
  afmaxweight.htm

- ✔ **Navy:** http://usmilitary.about.com/od/navy/l/blfitmenu.
  htm

- ✔ **Marine Corps:** http://usmilitary.about.com/od/marines/a/
  marweight.htm

- ✔ **Coast Guard:** http://usmilitary.about.com/library/milinfo/
  blcgweight.htm

A few factors determine where an individual should fall on any services' weight requirement chart, but these factors differ by branch:

- ✔ The Army uses sex, age, and height to determine your maximum allowable weight. You also must qualify to the minimum weight standards.

- The Air Force has no minimum standards and uses only height to determine any applicant's maximum weight.

- A Sailor's maximum weight requirement is determined by using sex and height, with no minimum standards.

- If you're planning to join the Marines, your gender and height will decide how much you can weigh (and how little).

- For the Coast Guard, the circumference of your wrist is used to establish your frame type, and your maximum weight requirements are determined by your frame type, height, and gender.

You need to know what the weight limitations are for your body during the enlistment process and before you ship out to basic training. If you fall within the guidelines when you first enlist and then gain too much weight while in the DEP, you may find yourself booted out before you're really in! You must fall within the requirements when you weigh in at MEPS the day before you ship out to basic, or you can't go. At best, you may receive an extension, but you're allowed to stay in the DEP for only one year or less.

The best thing to do is to remain cautious about gaining too much weight and prevent it from happening. Using your exercise routine and practicing your healthy eating habits will help you find success with managing stubborn weight gain.

# Stick to Your Workout Plan

Sticking to your workout plan may sound easy if you're naturally self-motivated, but if you're a natural procrastinator, easily distracted, or just not a big fan of exercising, you may find yourself in trouble with checking your goals off any list you've created.

Keeping yourself motivated is psychologically necessary in order to succeed. If you're feeling like you want to give up or skip a day or two, remember that you'll never regret working out, but you may regret choosing to skip it. Skipping your workout can lead to extreme lack of motivation, and you may develop a poor attitude and a sense of failure. A solution is to do something you like to do that is also exercise, because you'll be more willing to do the activity again if you're having fun. Swimming, playing basketball, riding your bike, and dancing are all examples of exercise that can be fun and rewarding.

For basic training preparation, though, you also have to stick it out with those push-ups and runs, so it's best here to use a workout buddy. Someone telling you to do something and pushing you to do it can prevent laziness, procrastination, and lack of motivation as well.

You may not always have someone there to help you exercise, which is why it's a good idea to develop self-control. Self-control is a behavior that receives a long-term reward when overcoming bad will power. You may want to work out in the mornings rather than some other time throughout the day so that you don't have any time to talk yourself out of it. Try to arrange your day in such a way that it prevents obstacles and excuses from getting in the way of your workout routine.

# Don't Overstress Your Body and Prevent Injuries

Repeating the same motions over and over again, such as in a weekly or daily exercise routine, can cause Repetitive Stress Injuries (RSI). RSI occurs when a muscle, joint, or tendon is overexerted. Overstressing your joints and tendons can restrict movement capability, cause inflammation to the area, and cause pain. Suffering from RSI can really put a damper on your basic training preparation plans!

In order to prevent stress and injury to your body during your physical training, you must prepare your body for each activity you're introducing your body to ahead of time. For example, if you're preparing for a weight-lifting routine, start with 20 reps of the lightest dumbbell. Then, increase the weight during your sets until the actual weight for your workout is achieved. If you plan to do cardio, start with a brisk walk, lead it into a light jog, and then gradually move into the advanced run or sprint you had intended for the workout. Your daily warm-up and stretching routines will really help you to prevent injury and stress as well. Also, you need to make sure that you're equipped with the proper exercise gear, such as running shoes, knee pads, and wrist supports.

Keeping a good posture throughout your day and while exercising is very important. The posture you have while you're sitting at a desk is likely the same posture you'll have during your exercise routine. Ensure that you're practicing good posture in order to prevent back, neck, shoulder, and ankle injuries.

Lastly, make certain that you listen to your body. If you feel tired, maybe it's time to give those joints and tendons a rest. That way, they're not too sore or injured for the next workout. If you feel like your movement is restricted, you have inflammation, or you're experiencing pain, stop your workout and consult your doctor immediately. The last thing you (or your recruiter) wants is for you to become injured right before you ship out to basic training.

Be careful. If you become injured and can't leave for basic training by your ship-out date, you may be discharged and lose your slot.

# Stay Positive

To stay positive, take a step back and evaluate the situation you're in. Look at the big picture and focus. Joining the military is something you want to do, and succeeding in your goals is the ideal outcome. You'll face challenges, and deciding ahead of time to stay positive through the good and the bad will help you maintain that positive attitude.

Remind yourself that you're eating healthy foods, getting plenty of rest, and sticking to your strict exercise program in order to breeze through the tough parts of basic training, and it'll be worth it in the end. Your body will feel and act better, and you'll see positive results. Things may not always work out your way, but keep your eye on the prize with a smile on your face, and you'll find that everything falls into place a little easier.

# Appendix A

# Punitive Articles of the Uniform Code of Military Justice (UCMJ)

*T*he UCMJ consists of 146 articles. Many of these articles consist of information about selecting juries, types of court-martials, gathering evidence, and other information about the military justice system. However, articles 77 through 134 are known as the *punitive articles* because they list behaviors that are considered to be military crimes.

You don't actually have to memorize the punitive articles for military basic training, but you'll be tested on whether or not a particular behavior constitutes a military crime, so I suggest you give this information a detailed look.

**Article 77 — Principals.** This article prohibits aiding and abetting the commission of a crime.

**Article 78 — Accessory after the fact.** This article makes it illegal to give comfort or assistance to someone you know committed an offense.

**Article 79 — Conviction of lesser included offenses.** This article says that you may be found guilty of a lesser included offense, even if you are not found guilty of the actual offense you were charged with. For example, if you were found not guilty of rape, the court-martial could still find you guilty of assault, even if you were not charged with assault.

**Article 80 — Attempts.** This article makes it a crime to attempt to commit an offense, even if the actual offense was not carried out.

**Article 81 — Conspiracy.** Article 81 makes it a criminal act to plan to commit an offense with one or more other people.

**Article 82 — Solicitation.** This article makes it illegal to advise or try to convince another to violate articles 85, 94, or 99 of the UCMJ.

**Article 83 — Fraudulent enlistment, appointment, or separation.** This article makes it illegal to lie on any enlistment paperwork.

**Article 84 — Effecting unlawful enlistment, appointment, or separation.**
This article makes it illegal to help or encourage anyone to lie on enlistment paperwork.

**Article 85 — Desertion.** *Desertion* is defined as unlawfully absenting yourself from the military with the intent to remain away permanently. In time of war, the maximum punishment for this offense is death.

**Article 86 — Absence without leave (AWOL).** AWOL can be anything from being a few minutes late for work (duty) to remaining away for several days, or even several years. The difference between this offense and desertion is that Article 86 does not require the prosecution to prove that you intended to remain away permanently.

**Article 87 — Missing movement.** This is similar to AWOL, in that it makes it a crime to purposely miss any scheduled military transportation.

**Article 88 — Contempt toward officials.** This article makes it illegal to use contemptuous words against the President, the Vice President, Congress, or certain other public officials. While only commissioned officers can be charged under this particular offense, military regulations prohibit this conduct for all military personnel, so enlisted members can be charged under Article 92.

**Article 89 — Disrespect toward a superior commissioned officer.** If you disobey an order given to you by a commissioned officer, you can be charged under this article. The maximum punishment is quite severe: One year in prison followed by a bad conduct discharge.

**Article 90 — Assaulting or willfully disobeying superior commissioned officer.** Assaulting a commissioned officer could get you a dishonorable discharge plus ten years in prison. Disobeying a commissioned officer's order could send you to jail for five years.

**Article 91 — Insubordinate conduct toward warrant officer, noncommissioned officer, or petty officer.** Being insubordinate (disrespectful) toward a warrant officer, NCO, or petty officer can get you sent to jail for nine months. If you hit one, you could spend up to five years in jail.

**Article 92 — Failure to obey order or regulation.** Disobeying a regulation or a lawful order issued by an enlisted person who outranks you is a crime in the military.

**Article 93 — Cruelty and maltreatment.** Military members who mistreat their subordinates can receive a dishonorable discharge and one year in prison. Don't get your hopes up — you may think your basic training instructor is cruel and is mistreating you, but it's not considered a crime, as it's all in the name of training.

**Article 94 — Mutiny and sedition.** If you convince or try to convince others to disobey orders, that's *mutiny*. *Sedition* is encouraging mutiny. The maximum punishment is death.

**Article 95 — Resistance, flight, breach of arrest, and escape.** This article prohibits resisting arrest and escaping from confinement.

**Article 96 — Releasing prisoner without proper authority.** This article prohibits releasing a prisoner who is under your control without permission.

**Article 97 — Unlawful detention.** This article prohibits arresting or detaining someone if you don't have the authority to do so.

**Article 98 — Noncompliance with procedural rules**. This article prohibits interfering with the court martial process.

**Article 99 — Misbehavior before the enemy.** This article prohibits cowardly acts and other inappropriate conduct in view of the enemy.

**Article 100 — Subordinate compelling surrender.** Only a commanding officer can make a decision to surrender the forces. It is a violation of the UCMJ for a subordinate to take this action.

**Article 101 — Improper use of countersign**. This article prohibits giving the countersign to someone who is not authorized to know it. It also prohibits knowingly giving the wrong countersign (although that would be stupid, as it's liable to get you shot).

**Article 102 — Forcing a safeguard.** Tricking or sneaking your way through a guard post is a violation of this article.

**Article 103 — Captured or abandoned property**. This article requires the proper safeguarding of property captured from the enemy.

**Article 104 — Aiding the enemy**. This article prohibits giving aid or comfort to the enemy.

**Article 105 — Misconduct as a prisoner.** If you are a prisoner of war or a prisoner of the military justice system, this article prohibits you from engaging in misconduct.

**Article 106 — Spies.** This article is enforceable only during time of war. It prohibits spying against interests of the United States military.

**Article 106a — Espionage.** This article prohibits spying against the United States. (It doesn't have to be during time of war.) This is one of the few offenses that authorizes the death penalty.

**Article 107 — False official statements.** This article makes it illegal to provide false information on any official military document.

**Article 108 — Military property of the United States — sale, loss, damage, destruction, or wrongful disposition.** Perhaps you've heard of the phrase "damaging government property." This article prohibits that, as well as the illegal sale or disposition of such property.

**Article 109 — Property other than military property of the United States — waste, spoilage, or destruction.** This is the same as article 108, except the property does not have to belong to the military.

**Article 110 — Improper hazarding of vessel.** This article prohibits any action that would endanger military ships.

**Article 111 — Drunken or reckless operation of vehicle, aircraft, or vessel.** This is the equivalent of the civilian DUI" except it includes not only vehicles, but also ships and aircraft.

**Article 112 — Drunk on duty.** It's a military offense to show up for work drunk (or to get drunk while at work).

**Article 112a — Wrongful use, possession, and so on of controlled substances.** Illegal drug use or possession.

**Article 113 — Misbehavior of sentinel or lookout.** Individuals on guard duty must behave properly.

**Article 114 — Dueling.** In the military, you can't challenge someone to a duel.

**Article 115 — Malingering.** *Malingering* means not doing your job or being lazy when it's time to work.

**Article 116 — Riot or breach of peace.** In the military, it's illegal to engage in a riot or cause the general community peace to be disrupted.

**Article 117 — Provoking speeches or gestures.** This article prohibits any speech or gesture that is likely to provoke someone else to violence or extreme anger.

**Article 118 — Murder.** The maximum punishment for murder is death.

**Article 119 — Manslaughter.** This is the same as murder, but you really didn't mean to kill the person. This'll get you 15 years in prison plus a dishonorable discharge.

**Article 120 — Rape and carnal knowledge (for offenses committed before October 1, 2007).** This is another offense where the maximum penalty is death.

**Article 120 — Rape, sexual assault, and other sexual misconduct (for offenses committed on or after October 1, 2007).** After October 1, 2007, the death penalty is authorized only in the case of child rape.

**Article 120a — Stalking.** Stalking someone else is a crime in the military.

**Article 121 — Larceny and wrongful appropriation.** Larceny means to steal something. Wrongful appropriation means to borrow something without permission.

**Article 122 — Robbery.** This means stealing property directly from an individual.

**Article 123 — Forgery.** Forging anything of value or any official document is a crime in the military.

**Article 123a — Making, drawing, or uttering check, draft, or order without sufficient funds.** Bad checks.

**Article 124 — Maiming.** This means injuring another person to the point where they're incapacitated.

**Article 125 — Sodomy.** This article prohibits sex with a child (under 16), or any unnatural sex act with another.

**Article 126 — Arson.** Setting things on fire (unlawfully) is a crime in the military.

**Article 127 — Extortion.** Threatening someone else is a military crime.

**Article 128 — Assault.** Assault can be anything from attacking someone to getting into a fight.

**Article 129 — Burglary.** Interestingly, the theft/break-in must occur at night in order to be charged under 129.

**Article 130 — Housebreaking.** Entering someone else's dwelling without permission (even if you don't steal anything) is an offense under the UCMJ.

**Article 131 — Perjury.** This means lying under oath during any legal proceeding.

**Article 132 — Frauds against the United States.** Defrauding the U.S. Government is a no-no and will get you jail time.

**Article 133 — Conduct unbecoming an officer and gentleman.** This is a general article, designed to prevent commissioned officers from acting like a fool.

**Article 134 — General article.** Article 134 is designed to be used for any criminal activity that is not specifically included in the UCMJ, such as adultery, bigamy, or even assaulting a *public animal* (any animal owned by the government, such as a police dog). It prohibits "conduct prejudicial to good order and discipline" or "conduct of a nature to bring discredit on the armed forces."

# Appendix B

# Military Enlisted History

*L*azerous Long (a fictional character created by Robert A. Heilein) once said, "A generation which ignores history has no past — and no future." The military certainly believes in this philosophy. While in basic training, you'll study the history of your particular military branch, especially as it applies to enlisted personnel.

Usually, the kind folks at Wiley want me to avoid history in my *For Dummies* books, but I convinced them that this appendix is a special case. After all, during military basic training, you'll not only be required to learn about enlisted history for your branch, but you'll take one or more written tests on this subject as well. Wouldn't it be easier (and safer!) to study about it before you head off to basic training, rather than during basic, while performing guard duty?

## Army Enlisted History

The United States Army is as old as our country itself. Known as the *Continental Army,* it was established in 1775 with George Washington as its first commander. Old George had it a bit easier than the Army Chief of Staff today — the Army was quite a bit smaller, consisting of Corps departments known as the Adjutant General's Corps, the Army Corps of Engineers, the Finance Corps, and the Quartermasters Corps. Shortly afterwards, Calvary and Field Artillery units were formed.

The new U.S. Army was sort of a copycat of its British cousins, adopting many of the same ranks, customs, and methods of battle. In fact, its first leaders were former British soldiers. The French and Prussians also got into the act by providing training and resources to this fledgling military force.

After we kicked out the British, the powers-that-be decided the United States had no need for an Army of its own. Instead, they turned most defense responsibilities over to the individual states. They were smart enough however, to retain a small military force consisting of a regiment to guard the Western Frontier and one battery of artillery guarding West Point's arsenal.

When the American Indians started getting froggy (because they rightfully resented being kicked off their land), it became apparent that they were too much for the states to handle individually. To solve this problem, in 1791, the United States created the first trained U.S. standing Army called the *Legion of the United States.*

# The Army in the War of 1812

In 1812, the fledgling United States decided they didn't have enough land and wanted to take over a portion of Western Canada. Britain (who owned this land at the time) strongly disagreed and started burning everything in sight, including our nation's capital. While the United States was unsuccessful in taking over a part of Canada, we were successful enough to again drive the British away from our land.

In the early 1800s, as U.S. settlers moved steadily west, those pesky Indians once again began to display their disagreement. The U.S. Army responded by uprooting them and forcing them to move lock, stock, and barrel to designated lands, called *reservations.*

Not to be left out, Mexico decided to war with the new country over disagreements about who owned most of Texas and part of Southern California. After two years of bloody fighting, the United States got its way, and this land, and the territories that eventually became California, Utah, Colorado, Arizona, Wyoming, and New Mexico, became U.S. property.

Prior to the Civil War, enlisted rank depended very much on ones Army job. As early as 1815, enlisted ranks consisted of sergeant major (who were in charge of the other enlisted personnel), quartermaster sergeants (who were in charge of supplies), principal musicians (who led the musicians), sergeants (who told the combat troops what to do), corporals (who helped the sergeants), musicians (who made music to help men march), artificers (who built things), and privates (who did everything else). A little later, the Army added *enlisted men of ordnance,* which consisted mostly of troops who were responsible for ammunition. In 1833, blacksmiths (who worked with metal), farriers (who shoed the horses), buglers (who blew bugles), and chief buglers (who were in charge of the buglers) were introduced.

Don't you think Army enlistment ranks (see Chapter 5) are a bit simpler today?

# The Army in the Civil War

The Civil War actually began when the South opened fire on the Union-held Fort Sumter in South Carolina. The Confederates initially enjoyed several military victories and had them Yankees on the run during numerous encounters. Eventually, old honest Abe was able to turn it around, with victories in Gettysburg and Vicksburg, leading to the surrender of the Confederates in 1865 at the Appomattox Courthouse.

The Civil War was a particularly bloody war, with 8 percent of white males dying in the battle. This includes 6 percent of that amount in the North, and 18 percent of casualties in the South.

While not busy with historic battles and other mundane factors of war, the U.S. Army took some time during the Civil War to once again modify their enlisted ranks. The new ranks consisted of: sergeant majors; quartermaster sergeants; commissary sergeants; leaders of bands; principal or chief musicians; chief buglers; medical cadets; ordnance sergeants; hospital stewards; regimental hospital stewards; battalion sergeant majors; battalion quarter-master sergeants; battalion hospital stewards; battalion saddler sergeants; battalion commissary sergeants; battalion veterinary sergeants; first sergeants; company quartermaster sergeants; sergeants; corporals; buglers; musicians; farriers and blacksmiths; artificers; saddlers; master wagoners; wagoners; privates; and enlisted men of ordnance.

After the Civil War, the U.S. Army again turned its attention to the Native Americans who amazingly didn't seem to want to move to reservations. At the same time, the United States felt it would be fun to start getting involved in other countries' businesses, resulting in the Spanish-American War and the Philippine-American War.

# The Army in World War 1

In 1917, the United States entered World War I to help out Britain, France, and Russia. Yes, this is the same Britain we were fighting years before. The United States military was successful in raining on the German's parade. After the end of the war in 1918, the Army decided it had too many troops for peace time and began a rapid discharge program.

In 1920, the Army (once again) changed its enlisted ranks, resulting in an enlisted rank structure that is very similar to what is in effect today. The new enlisted ranks were structured as Master Sergeant ( E-7), Technical Sergeant (E-6), First Sergeant (E-5), Staff Sergeant (E-4), Sergeant (E-3), Corporal (E-2), and Private First Class (E-1).

# The Army in World War 11

Letting all those soldiers out at the end of WWI turned out to be a mistake because the Army would need these troops to respond to the Japanese attack on Pearl Harbor, and the U.S.'s resulting entry into World War II in 1941. It turned out that the "war to end all wars" wasn't.

World War II was fought on two primary fronts — Europe and the Pacific. Millions of Army Soldiers got their first taste of combat. In Europe, the goal was to stop Hitler in his tracks and to put an end to Nazi Germany. In the Pacific, the United States wanted to teach Japan a lesson: It's not nice to bomb Hawaii. Victory was gained in Europe when Nazi Germany surrendered and achieved a few months later in Japan when the United States used the first nuclear weapons, resulting in Japan's surrender.

## The Army in Korea and Vietnam

In 1950, on the advice of the Soviet Union, communist North Korea invaded South Korea. The United States thought it should get involved (to stop the evil communists), but lacked United Nation's approval. This lack of support changed when the Soviet Union walked out of a U.N. security council meeting in protest, allowing the United States to get its approval without a Soviet veto.

Most Americans believe that the Vietnam conflict began long after the Korean War. In actuality, they both kind of began around the same time. At the same time that the United States was deploying thousands of soldiers to fight in Korea, it was also deploying soldiers to ward off communist advancement in South Vietnam.

After three years of fighting in Korea, United Nations forces were finally able to force the communist North Koreans back behind the 38th parallel, and a cease fire was announced. It's interesting to note that the Korean War has never officially ended — it's merely under a cease fire.

Without doubt, the conflict in Vietnam was America's least popular war. As I said, U.S. involvement in the country of Vietnam actually began at the same time the United States was fighting a war in Korea. The primary reason for the unpopularity of the Vietnam conflict with the American public is that the United States was forced to reinstitute the policy of drafting male citizens for military service. Thousands of men were drafted and deployed to fight in Vietnam (and surrounding countries). While the U.S. Army was somewhat successful in individual battles, it failed to gain control in the thick jungle terrain dominated by communist forces. After several years of fighting, citizens of the United States grew weary of war, and in 1973, the U.S. Military was forced to withdraw.

In 1958, Congress approved the two new enlisted pay grades of E-8 and E-9 (see the upcoming section "Creation of the super grades"), and the Army established its modified enlistment rank structure to be as follows: Sergeant Major (E-9), Specialist Nine (E-9), First Sergeant (E-8), Master Sergeant (E-8), Specialist Eight (E-8), Platoon Sergeant or Sergeant First Class (E-7), Specialist Seven (E-7), Staff Sergeant (E-6), Specialist Six (E-6), Sergeant (E-5), Specialist Five (E-5), Corporal (E-4), Specialist Four (E-4), and Private First Class.

# The Cold War

Most historians concur that the Cold War was actually going on at the same time as the Korean conflict and the U.S. military action in Vietnam. This is true because the entire concept of the Cold War involved two nuclear capable countries (the Soviet Union and the United States) trying to dominate the other. Ultimately, the United States won this game with the collapse of the Soviet Union (and various subordinate countries) in 1991.

The Cold War began over distrust between two superpowers. While Russia resented the United States for not recognizing it as a legitimate part of the international community, the United States grew anxious over Russia's continuous invasion of Eastern European nations and believed the Russians wanted to dominate the world. Both nations began using scare tactics, which eventually turned into an arms race shortly after the end of WWII.

During the time of the Cold War, the Army was involved in several smaller operations, including the Invasion of Grenada in 1983 and the battle with Panama in 1989.

# The Army spends time in the Gulf

The next significant conflict occurred in 1990, when Iraq invaded the country of Kuwait. Iraq's leader, Saddam Hussein, claimed that Kuwait was illegally slant-drilling under the border — in effect, stealing Iraqi oil. Iraq further justified its actions by stating that Kuwait was historically part of Iraq in the first place. (I guess they read a different history book than the rest of us.)

After a successful invasion, in which thousands of Kuwaiti's were captured or killed, the king of Kuwait yelled for help, and the United States was quick to respond. At first, the United States responded by deploying thousands of Army Soldiers to the neighboring country of Saudi Arabia (the United States had convinced the Saudis that they may be next) and demanding Iraq's complete withdrawal from Kuwait. The buildup of American forces in Saudi Arabia (and surrounding countries) was officially known as *Operation Desert Shield*. When U.S. forces ultimately entered Kuwait with the purpose of kicking Saddam's forces out of the country, the Operation was renamed *Operation Desert Storm*.

The United States was successful, but, like a spoiled child, Sadam's military set fire to hundreds of oil wells on its way out of town. It took the Kuwaiti's many years to extinguish the fires, and millions of gallons of oil burned away.

The Army was able to take a break from combat activities (for the most part) for the remainder of the '90s. During this time, Congress did authorize the

Army to increase significantly in size, which resulted in a temporary relaxation of enlistment standards. Many enlisted were allowed to join without a high school diploma, and the Army began to approve thousands of medical waivers. As a result, the Army was able to meet its new congressionally mandated strength.

## September 11, 2001

Tragedy struck our Nation with the sudden terrorists attacks of September 11, 2001. The United States blamed terrorist leader of Al-Qaeda (Osama Bin Laden) at the time, and intelligence resources claimed Bin Laden was living in Afghanistan. The United States demanded that the Taliban (who were in charge of Afghanistan at the time) hand over Bin Laden, and it refused. The United States replied (essentially), "Hand him over or cease to exist as a government." The Al-Qaeda leaders offered to hand Bin Laden over to the United Nations, but not to the United States. This wasn't good enough for President Bush. On October 7, 2001, President Bush ordered the United States military to attack Afghanistan, with the dual purpose of removing the Taliban from power and capturing Osama Bin Laden. This was known as *Operation Enduring Freedom*. While the first part of the operation was a quick success, it took the United States until 2011 to locate Osama Bin Laden (who had fled to neighboring Pakistan). Bin Laden was killed in a swift attack led by Special Operations Forces.

After the United States removed the Taliban from power in 2003, U.S. attention shifted back to Iraq as Sadam continued to violate one U.N. sanction after another. President Bush demanded that Sadam allow inspectors into the country to search for weapons of mass destruction — or else. Apparently not learning his lesson from last time, Sadam refused. Thus began the second Gulf War, in which the United States and allies invaded Iraq. Eventually, Sadam was captured and executed by an Iraqi court.

The Army's role in the *Global War on Terrorism* started after September 11 and continues today. Many Soldiers have bravely given their lives in support of this cause. Thousands of Army Soldiers are currently deployed to regions around the world with only one purpose — protect the United States from those who would do it harm.

## Creation of the Super Grades

The U.S. military has had warrant officers in its ranks since the late 1700s. In 1958, all military branches got together and petitioned Congress to create two new enlisted pay grades. The services were concerned because many enlistees could be promoted to the pay grade of E-7 after only 12 or 14 years of service. Therefore, nothing would motivate them to excel during the remainder of a 20-plus year career.

Congress was hesitant to spend the money, so the service chiefs told Congress that if it would approve the new enlisted grades, the services would agree to eliminate the warrant officer pay grades. The services planned to use these new *super enlisted* pay grades to do many of the jobs warrant officers were doing anyway.

After consideration, Congress agreed and established the enlisted super grades (E-8 and E-9) in 1958. However, the services were quick to note that while Congress authorized the new enlisted pay grades, it failed to include a provision to eliminate the warrant officer ranks. The Air Force never really wanted to use warrant officers in the first place. While the other branches used warrant officers as highly trained technical specialists, the Air Force primarily used warrant officers to supervise enlisted personnel, and the Air Force felt the new enlisted super grades could do this better. The Air Force was the only branch to keep the promise, and that's why there are no Air Force warrant officers today. The last active duty Air Force warrant officer (CWO4 James H. Long) retired in 1980. The last Air Force Reserve officer (CWO4 Bob Barrow) retired in 1992.

# Air Force Enlisted History

The Air Force is our Nation's youngest military service. Until the passage of The National Security Act of 1947, signed by President Truman on July 26, the Air Force did not exist as a separate entity. The Army was responsible for all air power missions for the U.S. military on land, while the Navy handled all air power over the water.

Army general Billy Mitchell is considered by many to be the father of the United States Air Force. Because he argued so hard for moving air power out of the hands of the Army and creating a separate service, he ultimately received a court-martial for insubordination. After his court-martial in 1925, he elected to separate from the Army, and in honor of his achievements, the new Air Force later named a bomber (the B-25 Mitchell) after him.

## The Air Force becomes official

The new US Air Force was supposed to be an equal part of the national military establishment. It had a Chief of Staff (General Carl Spaatz) and a Secretary of the Air Force (Stuart Symington) serving under the newly organized Department of Defense (which replaced the Department of War). The old US Army Air Force and Army Air Corps ceased to exist and were absorbed into the new organization.

The new Air Force was established mostly by redesignating Army units as Air Force units. The same Soldiers, pilots and aircraft were kept.

For the average enlisted airman, the immediate change was scarcely noticeable. In many areas, the establishment of the Air Force had little impact on the lives of enlisted personnel until months or even years had passed. What were designated as organic service units were taken over as newly designated Air Force units. Units that provided a common service to both the Army and the Air Force were left intact. Until 1950, for example, if an enlisted airman became seriously ill, he was likely treated by Army doctors in an Army hospital.

There was also, at first, no change in appearance. The distinctive blue uniforms of the U.S. Air Force were introduced only after large stocks of Army clothing were used up. Familiar terms slowly gave way to new labels. By 1959, enlisted airmen ate in "dining halls" rather than "mess halls," were eyed warily by "air police" instead of "military police," and bought necessities at the "base exchange" instead of the "post exchange."

At first, the Air Force was too busy to worry about changing the enlisted ranks. However, changes were slowly introduced. In the Army, a Corporal is considered to be a noncommissioned officer. The Air Force began its changes by removing Corporal from its noncommissioned officer status in 1950. Then, in 1952, the Air Force officially changed the names of the lower four ranks: Private to Airman Basic; Private First Class to Airman, Third Class; Corporal to Airman, Second Class; and Sergeant to Airman, First Class. At the same time, the Air Force dumped the Army enlisted insignia and created its own design.

## The Air Force in Berlin

If you're a history buff, you probably recall that the city of Berlin was divided at the end of WWII. Part of the city was controlled by the communist Soviet Union (officially, it was actually controlled by the East Germans), and part of it was controlled by the democratic West. The problem was, the only way to get to Berlin was to drive smack-dab through the middle of East Germany.

In 1948, the Soviet Union got froggy and decided that the West would no longer be allowed to drive through East Germany to reach Berlin. This maneuver effectively cut off the Western government in Berlin from receiving food and supplies.

For their part, the Soviets did not think that resupplying the city by air was even feasible, let alone practical. The Air Force quickly proved the Soviets wrong. For 15 months, the 2.2 million inhabitants of the Western sectors of Berlin were sustained by air power alone as the Air Force flew in 2.33 million tons of supplies on 277,569 flights. The Berlin airlift was arguably air power's single most decisive contribution to the Cold War, and it unquestionably achieved a profound strategic effect.

Enlisted personnel served as cargo managers and loaders (with a major assist from German civilians), air traffic controllers, communications specialists, and weather and navigation specialists. Of all the enlisted functions, perhaps the most critical to the success of the airlift was maintenance. The Soviets' eventual capitulation and dismantling of the surface blockade represented one of the great Western victories of the Cold War — without a bomb having been dropped — and laid the foundation for the NATO (North Atlantic Treaty Organization).

# The Air Force in Korea

Before dawn on Sunday, June 25, 1950, communist North Korea attacked South Korea. Some five years earlier, when Japan surrendered at the end of WWII, the United States proposed that American forces disarm Japanese forces in Korea south of the 38th parallel and Soviet troops perform the same task north of that line. Once the Japanese were disarmed and removed, Korea was to become independent after almost 50 years of rule by Japan, but it didn't work out that way. The two rival countries wound up splitting the entire Korean peninsula.

The Soviet Union supported the Democratic People's Republic of Korea (North Korea), and the United States stood behind the Republic of Korea (South Korea). When South Korea elected their first president in August 1948, the United States terminated the military government and began withdrawing occupation forces. As the decade of the 1940s drew to a close, Korea seemed less important than other areas in the world. In the aftermath of the Berlin blockade, the Truman Administration concentrated on Europe, even though basic national policy called for opposing the spread of communism anywhere in the world.

The first aerial combat between the United States and North Korea took place over Kimpo (South Korea) on June 27, 1950. Enlisted personnel served as gunners aboard the B-26 for the first several months of the conflict and on B-29 aircraft throughout the war. Even though the Air Force and Navy air power went all out on the North Koreans, they continued to advance throughout the South. The two months following the invasion marked an increase in Air Force activity, to include B-29 strikes and the introduction of F-51 aircraft. By mid-September, the North Korean offensive had clearly failed. Fighting the North Koreans to a standstill required the combined efforts of the air, land, and sea forces of several nations. Although the United States Air Force didn't completely win the day, it helped by destroying North Korean tanks, supply routes, and transportation networks. Ultimately, North Korea retreated behind the 38th Parallel (which is where they started from).

# The Air Force in Vietnam

The United States Air Force was heavily involved in the Vietnam War. The Air Force began to bomb North Vietnam in 1964. A year later, the Air Force began Operation Rolling Thunder, which was a massive bombing campaign. The main objectives of this campaign was to destroy the enemies will to fight, while trying to force North Vietnam into peace negotiations. During Operation Rolling Thunder, which lasted from 1965 to 1968, the U.S. Air Force dropped more bombs than it did in all of WWII. Aside from heavily damaging the North Vietnamese economy and infrastructure, Rolling Thunder failed in its political and strategic goals.

The United States Air Force continued to play a significant role during the Vietnam War. Operation Linebacker and Linebacker II demonstrated that air power could be highly effective, possibly even more effective than ground power. (Trust me, those old Army Generals didn't want to hear this.) The Air Force's bombing campaign was instrumental in finalizing the Paris Peace Negotiations for Vietnam.

While many military historians consider the Vietnam conflict to be a failure on the part of the U.S. military, the Air Force wouldn't be what it is today without this experience. During this conflict, the Air Force was able to bring many theoretical concepts to actual life, including the use of air commandos, aerial gunships, and pararescue combat missions. The period resulted in development of workable doctrines, units, and equipment.

The Air Force continued to upgrade their technology and capabilities in the years following the Cold War. The USAF participated in several operations, including Grenada in 1983, Libya in 1986, and Panama in 1989.

# The Air Force in the Gulf

The United States Air Force was instrumental during the first Gulf War. The Air Force's mission during this campaign was named Operation Instant Thunder, and boy, did the Air Force live up to that name. The aerial strike force was made up of about 2,300 combat aircraft, of which approximately 1,800 were USAF aircraft. This force flew over 100,000 sorties (flights), dropping over 88,000 tons of bombs, widely destroying military and civilian structure in the Gulf. The Air Force made great use of their premier stealth fighter-bomber, the F-117 Nighthawk, and the F-4G Wild Weasel. Interestingly, the Air Force was just about to retire the A-10 Thunderbolt, but decided to keep it around for a few more years after its outstanding performance in the bombing campaign. Overall, the Air Force's mission in the Gulf was successful.

# Changes in the Air Force

In 1993, the Air Force significantly changed its rank insignia for enlisted personnel. For senior NCOs, the Air Force basically took one stripe off the bottom and added it to the top. Thus, Master Sergeants (E-7) had five stripes at the bottom of their insignia and one stripe above. Senior Master Sergeants had five stripes at the bottom and two stripes above. Chiefs were given five bottom stripes, with three stripes on top. Stripes for noncommissioned officers (E-5 and above) were adorned with a white star. Those in the rank of E-4 and below (airmen) wore a dark blue star. A few years later, the powers-that-be felt that the term Senior Enlisted Advisor (the top enlisted man in each wing) was too namby-pamby and changed it to Command Chief Master Sergeant. After all, would you be more willing to accept orders from some advisor or the Command CHIEF Master Sergeant?

After the first Gulf War, the Air Force underwent a period of significant downsizing. It seems kind of weird that Congress would decide that the Air Force was too large after it did so well in the Gulf. Occupying the Gulf, though, was mostly a job for the ground forces, so while the Army and Marine Corps was able to increase in size, the Air Force (and the Navy) helped to pay for this by decreasing in size. In fact, between 1980 and 1996, the Air Force lost well over 200,000 airmen. At the same time, the Air Force reorganized, going from 13 to 8 major commands. Gone was the famous Strategic Air Command (SAC), its mission absorbed by the Air Combat and Air Mobility Commands.

Despite downsizing, the Air Force continued to be involved in its share of worldwide military operations. The Air Force maintained its bases in the Persian Gulf and Turkey, providing security against Saddam Hussein's threatening forces. It also engaged in numerous peacekeeping and humanitarian operations throughout the World, in places like Somalia, Rwanda, Haiti, and the Balkans. At the same time, the Air Force continued to maintain substantial forces in South Korea, to deter a possible invasion from the North. The Air Force continues to this day to be a valuable component of NATO, helping to maintain peace and security.

# The Air Force in freedom operations

The Air Force also played a significant role during Operation Enduring Freedom, the invasion of Afghanistan. The Air Force flew hundreds of sorties with B-1, B-2, B-52, F-15E, F-16, and AC-130H/U, RC-135, U-2, E-3, EC-130E/H aircraft, flying more than 325 missions. It also launched hundreds of UAVs (Unmanned Aerial Vehicles) which were used first for reconnaissance (spying) and later to drop actual bombs. From the beginning of Operation Enduring Freedom in October 2001 to September 2002, well over 20,000 bombs and missiles were dropped on the bad guys. In addition to its combat operations, the U.S. Air Force participated in numerous humanitarian missions throughout the area, dropping supplies (medicine, food, and water) to needy civilians. The U.S. military is still engaged in operations in Afghanistan and the surrounding areas today.

The Air Force played a large role in Operation Iraqi Freedom (the second Gulf War) in March to May 2003. The primary purpose of this engagement was to remove Saddam Hussein from power as the leader of Iraq and to institute a democratic government. After only 21 days of combat operations, the United States succeeded in this mission. Combat operations and humanitarian aid missions still go on in Iraq today.

The U.S. military plans to withdraw all combat forces from Iraq by the end of 2011, but recent events (fighting) leave this in question as of the date this book is due to the publisher.

# Navy Enlisted History

If you decide to enlist in the United States Navy, you'll be joining the largest Navy in the entire World. The U.S. Navy has the most (and largest) combat ships in existence today. The Navy has 11 carrier ships (floating airports) and more than 3,700 aircraft. (The U.S. Air Force has about 6,000.) Aside from aircraft carriers, the Navy's fleet consists of approximately 75 submarines, 30 frigates (fuel and supply), 59 destroyers (ships with big guns), 22 cruisers (the normal warship), and around 30 amphibious assault, transport, and docking ships (used in various operations). Over 400,000 sailors are currently on active duty and in the Naval Reserves. All combined, the U.S. Navy is a successful and powerful military force.

## The Old Navy

Did you know that the United States disbanded its Navy for almost a decade, and during this time, there was no such thing as the United States Navy? Therefore, you can divide the history of the U.S. Navy into two separate periods: the first period. The *Old Navy* (1775 to 1785) describes the U.S. Navy in use before the Revolutionary War. It consisted of several sailing ships and made use of the first ever ships coated with iron, also known as ironclad. After the Revolutionary War, the U.S. Congress decided that — among other reasons — the United States could no longer afford to support a Navy, and all the ships were sold. The last Old Navy ship to hit the auction blocks was a frigate, *USS Alliance*. The second period, called the *New Navy,* was established by the Naval Act of 1794. When pirates began to attack American commercial shipping in the Mediterranean, Congress decided that the United States might need a Navy after all.

If you had enlisted in the Old Navy around 1775, picking your guaranteed job (excuse me, *rating*) would have been a relatively simple thing. After all, there were about 14 jobs. Better yet, your pay depended on your Navy rating. You could be a Landsmen, Seamen, Able Seamen, Boatswain's Mate, Quartermaster, Gunner's Mate, Master-at-Arms, Cook, Armorer, Sailmaker's Mate, Cooper, Cockswain, Carpenter's Yeoman, and Yeoman of the Gun Room. Additionally, forget about four-year enlistments and reassignments. You signed up for one cruise, aboard one ship.

## The New Navy

The *New Navy* originally consisted of only six frigates. The *USS Chesapeake, Constitution, President,* and *United States* frigates each had 44 guns, and the USS Congress and Constellation were armed with 36 guns each. Congress somehow found a total of $688,888.28 to build these new ships. As with other Congressional programs, certain cost over-runs occurred, so the six new ships wound up costing approximately $1,776,721.82. But the new United States now had a Navy.

The New Navy came about just in time. Americans were just sticking these new ships into the water when France and Britain began their own little skirmish. At first, the United States decided to stay out of it, but France started to capture U.S. commercial ships. In fact, by 1797, France had captured about 300 American vessels. Congress decided it was time to get this New Navy off the ground. It officially established the Department of the Navy on April 30, 1798, with a total of 14 combat vessels. It didn't take long to turn the tide against France. The fledgling Navy's first major victory was the capture of the French frigate, *L'Insurgente* by the *USS Constellation.* France quickly decided that it had had enough, and by the end of 1800, peace was established with the United States.

Even though war was over with France, Congress learned its lesson and decided it should probably keep a Navy. The President asked Congress to pass legislation authorizing a permanent Navy, and Congress agreed, authorizing a reduced size of 6 active duty ships, 7 reserve ships, 45 officers, and 150 enlisted sailors. The few remaining ships were sold (again), and many enlisted sailors were let go. Excess officers were also discharged and given four months' severance pay. Of course, Congress later changed the law, allowing the Navy to take on more Sailors. In fact, more than 328,000 Sailors and Officers are in the Navy today.

# The Navy in the War of 1812

The next challenge for the U.S. Navy occurred in 1812. Curiously, this conflict is taught in American history classes as the War of 1812. Once again, the bad guy was the British Empire. It owned a large chunk of Canada, and America wanted a piece of it. Additionally, the British were not happy with the way the United States were treating the American Indians. The United States wasn't very happy that Britain continued to draft Americans into their Navy. After all, the United States had itsr own Navy to support. Finally, because of its ongoing war with France, the British attempted to tell the United States who it could and could not trade with.

The U.S. Navy began this war severely outnumbered. In fact, the British had 50 warships for every 1 American warship. Even so, the United States Navy held its own, capturing numerous British warships and privateers. This is not to say the British did not capture several U.S. ships as well. However, by 1815, the United States had turned the tide, and a peace treaty was signed. Both sides had gained a significant amount of territory during the war, but the Treaty of Ghent required both to return the land. As a result of the treaty, Britain and the United States began to get along, and open trading was restored.

# The Navy in a time of peace

The end of the war brought over 30 years of peace. The U.S. Navy finally had a chance to modernize and grow. The problem was (as it is today), money. Congress simply didn't have enough of it. Nearly half of the Navy's promised new ships never made it out of the docks. They remained there, half-built, until the time of ships with sails had passed by. The French and British were adopting the newfangled steamships, which put the United States sailing ships to shame. By the 1840s, the United States got wise and began buying steam-powered vessels of their own.

The Navy enlisted recruiting program had yet to come to its full fruition. Most Navy enlisted Sailors were not born in the United States Those few who were American-born were usually considered undesirables or criminals. In one year, the Navy was able to recruit only about 90 new Sailors. Interestingly, it was illegal (at the time) for black men to join the U.S. Navy, but this law was often violated in order to meet manning goals.

The Navy was suffering from a shortage of qualified officers. This problem became apparent during the *Somers Affair,* which was an alleged mutiny aboard the *USS Somers* in 1842. The Captain, the ships highest ranking officer, significantly mishandled the incident, leading to the unlawful conviction and execution of three crewmembers. While the Army had established its military academy (WestPoint) as early as 1802, the the Navy had no effective way to select and train its officers. Congress authorized the Navy to open its own officer academy in Annapolis, Maryland, in 1851.

So why does the Navy refer to its enlisted ranks as *rates?* In the other branches, your military pay grade is called your *rank.* In the Navy, your pay grade is referred to as your *rate.* This term dates from the old-time sailing days. In those days, your Navy rank (rate) depended on how many ship-board jobs you were qualified (rated) to do. For example, a Sailor qualified to work only when the ship was at port was rated the lowest enlisted status of *Landsmen.* When you were certified to work on a ship at sea, you would be promoted to *Seaman.* Those authorized to work on the sails (up in the masts) while at sea were promoted to the rating of *Able Seaman.* While the names may have changed over the years, the tradition remains the same.

# The Navy in the Civil War

The American Civil War not only divided the country, but divided the U.S. Navy as well. Almost 400 midshipmen, warrant officers, and commissioned officers left the U.S. Navy in order to join the Confederacy. Worried that their ships may be captured, Union forces burned all of their Naval ships at the Norfolk Naval Yard. This plan didn't work out so well, as Southern forces found one of the ships, and salvaged it — reinforcing it with armor and renaming it *CSS Virginia.* The North thought an armored ship was a dandy idea and built one of its own, the *USS Monitor.*

At the beginning of the war, President Lincoln decided to employ the U.S. Navy in order to block supplies from reaching Confederate ports. The Confederacy responded when the *CSS Virginia* successfully defeated the blockade. The very next day, the Union's ironclad, the *USS Monitor,* attacked the *CSS Virginia,* the first engagement of the new ironclad ships. The engagement ended in a draw.

While both sides continued to build ironclad ships, the North's monitor ships turned out to be the more effective vessel, and the South's ironclads couldn't compete.

The South did, however, gain a significant advantage when it introduced the concept of submarine warfare. The South used its submarines and mines (called *torpedoes*) to protect its harbors. The Confederate's torpedoes were responsible for the sinking of the Union monitor, the *USS Tecumseh,* thus birthing the famous phrase," Damn the torpedoes, full speed ahead!"

Ultimately, the North's efforts were rewarded. By effectively blockading the Southern states, they caused the South's economy to fail, which resulted in a severe food and supply shortage. Additionally, the standard of living dropped significantly in the South, contributing to famine and food riots, which ultimately brought an end to Southern resistance by 1865.

# Changes made in the Navy

After the war, Congress once again decided the Navy was too large. It may have been right this time, as the Navy had grown to be the second largest in the world, surpassed only by the British Navy. With over 700 ships, more than 51,000 Sailors were wearing Navy uniforms. No matter how you look at it, that's big. Within 15 years, the Navy scrapped 650 ships and downsized by 45,000 Sailors. While the Navy probably could have used some brand new ships, especially as many of them were damaged during the war, Congress refused to allocate funding for Navy improvements.

Most Americans have no idea that the U.S. Military was involved in a conflict with Korea almost 80 years before the war in Korea that grabbed all the headlines. It's true. In 1871, a small Navy taskforce was deployed to Korea to ask for an apology for the apparent murder of many shipwrecked U.S. sailors. After a short sea battle, the Navy sent in 650 Marines who were successful in capturing Korean forts. The Koreans still refused to apologize, and the Admiral in charge of the mission decided to withdrawal all forces before the beginning of the typhoon season.

The condition of the U.S. Navy continued to decline. When President James Garfield took office in 1881, he commissioned a study which found that out of 140 ships in the Navy's inventory, only about 50 were sea-worthy, and most weren't even combat ships. This offered a unique opportunity to modernize the U.S. Navy. Garfield's Secretary of the Navy, William H. Hunt, established an advisory board with the job of recommending improvements for the debilitated Navy. A contributing factor was the attitude of the U.S. Navy's officers and Sailors who truthfully felt that their inferior ships would not hold up in a time of war.

The panel determined that the U.S. Navy desperately needed an upgrade. President Garfield asked Congress to provide funding for four modern war ships. Congress initially said, "No." President Garfield persisted, and Congress agreed to fund three protected cruisers and a dispatch vessel. This new breed of vessels was quickly dubbed the ABCD ships, as they were named the *USS Atlanta, Boston, Chicago,* and *Dolphin.* Two more protected cruisers, the *USS Charleston* and *Newark,* were added to the fledgling fleet, as well as the first ever U.S. Navy battleships, christened *USS Texas* and *Maine.*

Over the next few years, the Navy continued to modernize and increase in size. By 1890, the U.S. Navy was rated as the fifth largest Navy in the World.

# The Navy in Panama

With an eye on gaining control of the Panama Canal, President Roosevelt convinced the Panamanian rebels to proclaim Independence with the

U.S. Navy's support. With the help of *USS Nashville,* Panama's claim for independence from Columbia was successful. In exchange, the United States gained control of the entire Panama Canal Zone in 1904. Of course, it did cost the United States about 10 million dollars — nothing worth having is ever free. A year later, in order to protect its new interest, the United States built a large naval base in Cuba called Guantanamo Bay. By gaining control of the Panama Canal, the United States was able to considerably decrease the distance of sea travel between the East and West.

In the meantime, the United States was busy perfecting its latest Naval weapon — the submarine. An inventor from New Jersey, John Holland, developed the first officially commissioned submarine in 1890, which (not coincidentally) was named after him. At the same time, the Navy continued its expansion program. President Roosevelt oversaw the development of 16 new battleships dubbed the *Great White Fleet.* Roosevelt sent his new fleet around the World allowing dignitaries to tour the vessels at every stop. This went a long way toward convincing other countries that the United States was a world power to be reckoned with.

The quickly expanding Navy also learned a couple of lessons from this epic voyage:

- ✔ It learned how important the Panama Canal really was.
- ✔ It learned the importance of establishing more fueling stations that were not controlled by the British.

## The Navy in World War 1

At first, the United States intended to stay out of World War I. But then the Germans sank a U.S. commercial tanker and a British cruise ship *(Lusitania)* with many U.S. passengers aboard. The U.S. President responded by asking Congress to provide additional funding for the Navy. Congress agreed and passed the Naval Act of 1916, which allocated $500 million dollars for Navy construction. Specifically, Congress funded the construction of almost 70 submarines, 50 destroyers, 10 scout cruisers, 6 battle-cruisers, and 10 new battleships.

Officially, the United States entered World War I in 1917. The U.S. Navy's participation in this war was somewhat limited. Mostly, it transported troops, escorted convoys, and laid a minefield or two. The U.S. Navy achieved it first World War I victory when it sank the German U-boat, U-58, in 1917.

Interestingly, the Navy holds the distinction of being the first U.S. Military service to allow women to join with a job other than a nurse. During World War I, the Navy allowed women to enlist as Yeoman (administrative aids).

Ironically, while African-Americans were allowed to serve legally for the first time in World War I, they were almost immediately discharged following the conclusion of hostilities around 1919.

The Navy (in terms of number of Sailors) had become the largest Navy in the entire World, with over 500,000 officers and enlisted men and women.

## The Navy and the attack of Pearl Harbor

President Roosevelt proclaimed December 7, 1941, to be "a date which will live in infamy." On this day, the Imperial Japanese Navy launched a devastating surprise attack on the U.S. Naval base located in Pearl Harbor, Hawaii. Japan would soon learn that this attack was a bad move. Japan intended to deter the United States away from interfering with their military actions in the Pacific. Instead, it convinced the United States to declare war with the Empire of Japan. A few days later, Italy and Germany declared war on the United States. World War I, the "war to end all wars" apparently wasn't. World War II had begun.

The Japanese sent two waves from six aircraft carriers to Pearl Harbor. The attacks consisted of over 300 Japanese torpedo planes, fighters, and bombers. The attack on the Navy's Hawaiian installation was devastating, sinking four out of eight battleships and inflicting damage on the remaining four. The Japanese also took out three destroyers, three cruisers, a minelayer, an anti-aircraft training ship, and almost 200 U.S. aircraft. The Japanese attack killed more than 2,400 service members and civilians and wounded almost 1,300.

## The Navy in World War II

So, that explains how World War II began in Japan, but what about the European theater? It turns out, German and Italy immediately took Japan's side, supporting the attack on Pearl Harbor, and declared war on the United States. I guess we should have made sure the Hawaiian Islands didn't get in the way of all of those Japanese bombs.

Drawing the United States into the European conflict turned out to be a mistake on Germany's part. The United States immediately decided to put the Japanese conflict on hold and concentrate American efforts in Europe first.

One of the first priorities of the Navy was to concentrate on destroying the problematic German submarines, which were a serious threat to allied shipping. This phase of the operation (beginning in 1941) is commonly referred to as the *Battle of the Atlantic.* This engagement actually continued throughout the rest of the war.

While neither side appeared to have an advantage for a while, the Allies eventually gained control by destroying the German ships and submarines. The victory was gained at great cost, however. The Allies lost 3,500 merchant ships and almost 200 warships. The Allies destroyed approximately 783 German U-boats.

A significant Navy contribution to the Allied success of World War II was in the extremely important, but often underestimated, area of ground force transportation — that is, making sure Soldiers and Marines got to where they needed to be, when they needed to be there.

Meanwhile, the Navy wasn't ignoring the Japanese threat. The first major campaign by the Allies against the Empire of Japan (remember them?) is known as the *Battle of Guadalcanal* in 1942.

The primary objective of this battle was to prevent Japan from utilizing the Solomon Islands, which the Japanese wanted for supply and communication. Coincidentally, the Americans intended to use these Islands as bases for themselves. For a change, this time the good guys (the Allies) outnumbered the bad guys (the Japanese). The Americans quickly established control of the Islands, including the airfield, Henderson Field, and kicked the Japanese out.

Upset with losing its strategic airfield, the Japanese launched numerous attempts to regain control. In a four-month period, the Japanese attacked the base with almost daily aerial assaults, three major ground offenses, five night-time surface actions, two carrier battles (and a partridge in a pear tree). All the Japanese attempts made to regain the airfield were unsuccessful, and by 1943, the Japanese withdrew all forces from the area.

The U.S. Navy's success in taking over and gaining control of Pacific regions, including the Guadalcanal, was a significant factor that led to Japan's ultimate surrender and subsequently the end of World War II.

## The Navy during the Cold War

After WWII, the U.S. Navy found itself undergoing a drawdown once again. By 1948, the number of Navy vessels in use were reduced to under 300. Fortunately, this drawdown trend was short lived. The Korean conflict, along with Soviet tensions, convinced the U.S. Congress that a strong Navy was vital to the interest of the United States. After modernizing, the U.S. Navy became America's 911 Force, able to respond quickly to hot spots around the world. To hasten response time, Navy fleets were stationed in various geographical locations throughout the World.

The U.S. Navy holds the distinction of being the first military service to make use of nuclear power for purposes other than blowing things up. In 1954, the *USS Nautilus* became the first nuclear-powered submarine. The *USS Enterprise,* commissioned in 1961, was the world's first nuclear-powered aircraft carrier (still in use today). The *USS Nimitz* was the first of the nuclear-powered Nimitz-class carriers, of which there are ten in current use.

Unlike the other branches, the U.S. Navy did not play a major role during the Korean War — not because it wasn't good, but rather because the North Koreans did not have its own navy to speak of. The Navy's war-time role consisted mostly of providing artillery support for U.N. forces.

Like the Korean War, the Navy's involvement in the Vietnam conflict was somewhat limited. Navy aircraft carriers did, however, contribute significantly to American air power in the region. The Navy flew thousands of air strikes against targets throughout the region. Additionally, the Navy established control over the rivers in Vietnam using gunboats. This special breed of Sailors became known as the *Brown Water Navy.*

By 1978, the Navy's fleet had diminished to unacceptable levels due to President Johnson's and Nixon's desire to save money. The Navy's inventory consisted of less than 120 submarines and a little over 200 ships. At the same time, the Soviet Union had concentrated on increasing the size of its Naval forces. In fact, it surpassed the United States Navy in all areas except aircraft carriers. President Reagan launched a program to upgrade the Navy from its present diminished force to almost 600 modern combat vessels.

## The Navy in the Gulf

Actually, the U.S. Navy was militarily involved in the Persian Gulf long before the other branches joined into the Gulf War. Since 1949, the Navy has been continuously patrolling the Gulf region.

It's probably a good thing that the Navy stuck around in the region for so long. If it wasn't for its continued presence, representing the military forces of the United States, it's doubtful that Saudi Arabia would have felt comfortable allowing U.S. ground and air forces to be based in its country following Iraq's invasion of Kuwait.

Not only was the U.S. Navy able to guarantee continued unfettered shipping in the region, despite Saddam's attempts to hinder such, but it was able to discourage Iran from expanding its control throughout the Gulf region.

Unsurprisingly, the U.S. Marine Corps was heavily involved in the fighting in the Persian Gulf. As usual, the Navy was tasked to be its taxi service. What's more, the Marines got most of its supplies via Navy transport. The Army found that it also had to rely upon the Navy to help transport Soldiers and combat supplies to the Persian Gulf battle fields. Once the Navy transported the Marines and Soldiers to the battlefield, it assumed responsibility for keeping these massive forces supplied. In fact, the Navy spent over $7 billion to upgrade its ships just for this purpose.

I don't mean to imply that the Navy's role in the Persian Gulf was nothing more than a taxi and supply service. On the contrary, the Navy saw its share of historic combat operations. The ships of the Navy launched hundreds of Tomahawk II cruise missiles and naval aircraft flew sorties from six carriers in the Persian Gulf and Red Sea.

On the surface, the U.S. Navy's role in the liberation of Kuwait may sound small. But, everything is not as it seems. Not only did Navy fighters supplement the U.S. air forces combat role in the region, but the Navy's control of the seas allowed the coalition forces to deploy unhampered to Saudi Arabia in preparation to launch a counter-offensive into Kuwait.

When Serbia embarked on ethnic cleansing in Kosovo, it was the U.S. Navy (and U.S. Marine Corps) to the rescue. In 1999, the Navy and Marine Corps launched hundreds of sorties on numerous Serbian targets to convince Serbia to give up its attempt at ethnic cleansing. After 78 days of relentless Navy and Marine Corps bombing, the Serbians had had enough.

## September 11, 2001

When the World Trade Center and the Pentagon were attacked in 2001, the U.S. Navy, along with the other services, actively entered President Bush's War on Terror. The U.S. objective was to "wipe al-Qaeda from the face of the Earth." I'm just kidding; the official objectives were to capture al-Qaeda leaders, stop terrorist activities, and ensure the destruction of terrorist training camps in Afghanistan.

On October 7, 2001, the U.S. launched a massive strike including Air Force aircraft and Navy fighter aircraft and missiles. Operation Enduring Freedom had begun.

In 2003, President George W. Bush decided to invade Iraq for a second time. The Iraqi leader, Saddam Hussein had continually violated the cease-fire provisions set at the end of the first Gulf conflict, so finally the U.S. President said, "Enough!" As with the other conflicts in the Gulf, the Navy's role did not make it into the history books. However, the Navy's use of ship-board aircraft and off-shore firepower made it possible for the U.S. ground and air forces to launch a successful invasion with minimal loss to American lives.

As with all the military branches, the Navy continues to be engaged in the *War on Terror* today. The War on Terror is not a fight against any specific group (although al-Qaeda seems to be at the top of the list). Rather, the War on Terror refers to organizations designated as terrorists and regimes that were accused of having a connection to them or providing them with support or were perceived, or presented as posing a threat to the United States and its allies in general.

At the time this book goes to press, the Navy has diminished in size significantly since World War I. However, this statement is somewhat misleading, as it doesn't take into account the vast technological improvements that have occurred since that time. (These days, a little modern Navy goes a long way.) Because of its weapons technology, size, and ability to project force far from American shores, the current U.S. Navy remains a potent asset for the United States.

# Marine Corps Enlisted History

The United States Marine Corps, an amphibious force, has been involved in one way or another in almost every conflict known to the United States.

Around 1775, when the U.S. Navy learned that swabbies fight better at sea than on land (and Soldiers don't really like hanging out on ships), the Continental United States established the *Continental Marines*. If you care to notice, there is no Department of the Marine Corps. There is a Department of the Army, a Department of the Navy, and even a Department of the Air Force, but no Department of the Marine Corps. While the Marines were officially created as a part of the U.S. Navy, in 1798, Congress established the Marine Corps as a separate military service. The Marine Corps is officially organized under the Department of the Navy with the Secretary of the Navy officially in charge of both branches. (There is no such thing as a Secretary of the Marine Corps either.) Even though the Marines are officially a separate entity, they're often referred to as the Infantry of the Navy.

The official mission of the U.S. Marine Corps is to conduct ship-to-ship fighting, provide discipline enforcement and onboard security on ships, and assist and engage in landing forces. (If you ask any Marine what the official mission of the Navy is, he'll tell you its to act as a taxi service for the Marine Corps.)

# Establishing the Marines

In Washington's time, there was no separate U.S. Marine Corps. Colonial Marines were aboard the rebel ships, there to fight on land and on sea, but not to act as Sailors and help sail the ships. In 1775, the Second Continental Congress ordered the Navy to land the first official Marines in Halifax, Nova Scotia to fight the British in order to take out a British Navy base and to capture supplies from the British enemy. On November 10, 1775, Congress officially authorized the Colonial United States to establish the first official U.S. Marine Corps in order to provide ground attack capabilities to the Navy. This date is important — it's the date the Marines use to celebrate its birthday each year. The annual Marine Birthday Ball is a very big deal in the Marine Corps.

Did you know that the first commanding officer of the Marine Corps was actually a bartender? It's true. On November 28, 1775, Samuel Nicholas was offered a commission as a Captain in order to command the Marines' first two battalions. His selection, however, was based, not on the fact that he owned a prominent bar, but because of his established and proven leadership qualities. Many historians believe that the Marines' first recruiting office was located in Nicholas' tavern, but officially, the Marines recognize Tun Tavern in Philadelphia as its first recruiting post.

Congress was hoping that George Washington would help staff the new Marine Corps with some of his Soldiers. Washington was not thrilled about the idea. Instead Washington advised it to raise the personnel by enticing unemployed seamen. Congress agreed, and former seamen made up a substantial portion of the initial Marine Corps. Nicholas also appointed a few more officers. Interestingly, these officers were selected to act primarily as recruiters, rather than combat leaders. The favorite new recruiting spots? You guessed it — bars. These new officers/recruiters were successful in gathering about 1,500 recruits, mostly by targeting the working class looking for better opportunities. At least the fledgling Marine Corps had its priorities in order. In light of limited funding, the new recruits were issued weapons rather than uniforms.

# The Battle of Nassau

The Marine Corps first official combat engagement is known as the *Battle of Nassau.* On March 3, 1776, Commander Hopkins of the Navy directed his entire force of Marines to make its first historical landing at Britain's Fort Montagu in order to take Britain's supplies, delaying a planned surprise attack against Britain's Fort Nassau. As a result, when Hopkins and his men finally made their way to Fort Nassau to obtain Britain's shots, shells, and cannons, the British had been tipped off and fled.

By March 16, 1776, Hopkins' squadron withdrew from the New Providence area and headed back toward Rhode Island. Along the way, the fleet participated in numerous battles with the British enemy. While successful in capturing many British vessels, the fleet encountered only a handful of casualties. Lieutenant John Fitzpatrick is documented as the first Marine to be killed in combat. The crews managed to dock successfully in New England April 8, 1776.

During the month of April 1776, John Martin became the first black American Marine to enlist in the Continental Marine Corps when he officially signed to serve aboard the Continental ship, *Reprisal,* in Philadelphia.

On July 4, 1776, the Declaration of Independence was signed. During this time, additional Marines were recruited to guard and board new frigates and state vessels as they awaited sail.

Finally, in 1777, the Marine Committee approved the first Continental Marine Uniform. The color of choice, you may ask? Green. A green uniform made it easy to distinguish the Marines from the blue attire of the Army and Navy, and the red from the British. The Marines wore a short, green jacket with white trim and a high leather collar. (This clothing is why Marines are often called *leathernecks* today.). These newly spruced up Marines were topped with a round, black hat (for enlisted) and a small, cocked hat (for officers).

The final official operation as Continental Marines was to chaperone a large quantity of silver from Boston to Philadelphia in order to open the Bank of North America.

## The Marines during the War of Independence

During America's War of Independence, the Marines would primarily stick to the Naval conflicts of the war. Marines would sit atop of the upper masts of the ships with a good view to fire upon the enemy. Their primary duties were to engage in ship-to-ship combat operations and to protect their Naval fleet. Amazingly, the Marine Corps lost only 49 men during the entire revolution.

Following the end of the Revolution, there were no more British to fight with due to peace, so the Continental Congress decided to disband the Marines. The last Continental Marine was discharged in September 1783. Overall, there were almost 2,000 enlisted Marines, and over 100 officers.

# Re-establishment of the Marine Corps

After some time had passed, the United States ran into a quarrel with France, known as the *Quasi-War.* Congress then decided it should re-establish its defense in the water. Congress introduced the new United States Navy and Marine Corps by signing the Act to Provide a Naval Armament on March 27, 1794, and the Act for Establishing and Organizing a Marine Corps on May 5, 1798. These acts specified the plans for new frigates, and the number of Marines needed to man them. Led by newly appointed Major William Ward Burrows I, 500 Marines were enlisted to protect and serve aboard the new ships. Officers and noncommissioned officers were appointed to command the privates. Soon thereafter, the Marines were sent off with the Navy to manage raids against the French and Spanish.

With the green, leather-necked uniforms long gone from the colonial times, the new Marines had nothing to wear, so they received a leftover stockpile of blue uniforms with red trim (similar to the dress uniform Marines wear today). Burrows realized they needed an appropriate meeting point and barracks for the Marines as well. President Thomas Jefferson and Burrows (who was then made Lieutenant Colonel Commandant of the Marine Corps) chose a patch of land in Washington, D.C., and hired architect George Hadfield to construct the new barracks. The Marine Barracks and Commandants House is still in use today. Historically, Burrows is also known for founding the United States Marine Band in 1798. The Marine Band has played at every presidential inauguration since being introduced in 1801.

# The First Barbary War

The Marines are famously known for their involvement in the First Barbary War (1801–1805). First Lieutenant Presley O'Bannon and William Eaton chaperoned a group of eight Marines and 300 mercenaries in an attempt to capture Tripoli from the Barbary pirates. Prince Hamet Karamanli from the Ottoman Empire was so impressed with the promising Marines, he gave the Marines a Mameluke sword, inscribed in memory of the Battle of Tripoli Harbor. (This battle is where Marines became known for the tradition of carrying swords.) This battle was also commemorated in the *Marines' Hymn,* which is still the official Marine Corps hymn today.

The *Marines' Hymn* is the official hymn of the United States Marine Corps. It's the oldest official song in the United States military. The Marines' Hymn is typically sung at the position of attention as a gesture of respect. However, the third verse is also used as a toast during formal events, such as the birthday ball and other ceremonies. You'll be required to memorize the words of the Marine Corps hymn during basic training.

**Marines' Hymn**

*From the Halls of Montezuma,*
*To the shores of Tripoli;*
*We fight our country's battles*
*In the air, on land, and sea;*
*First to fight for right and freedom*
*And to keep our honor clean:*
*We are proud to claim the title*
*Of United States Marine.*
*Our flag's unfurled to every breeze*
*From dawn to setting sun;*
*We have fought in every clime and place*
*Where we could take a gun;*
*In the snow of far-off Northern lands*
*And in sunny tropic scenes;*
*You will find us always on the job*
*The United States Marines.*
*Here's health to you and to our Corps*
*Which we are proud to serve;*
*In many a strife we've fought for life*
*And never lost our nerve;*
*If the Army and the Navy*
*Ever look on Heaven's scenes;*
*They will find the streets are guarded*
*By United States Marines.*

# The Marines and the War of 1812

During the War of 1812, the U.S. Marines became known and respected for its ship-to-ship combat actions, and as experienced marksmen. In fact, tradition holds the Marines to be so respected during the battle that the British spared the Marine Barracks at Washington D.C., while it burned everything else in sight. The Marines, overall, were responsible for establishing several Navy and Marine headquarters and for holding the lines during battle. The War of 1812 would produce less than 50 Marine casualties.

After the War of 1812, the Marines became quite unorganized and unproductive, mostly in part due to poor leadership. However, in 1820, Archibald Henderson was sworn in as the official fifth Commandant of the Marine Corps, and things began to turn around for the better. Henderson is known as the longest serving Commandant of the Marine Corps and as the Grand old man of the Marine Corps. During this time, Henderson took advantage of every opportunity to deploy his Marines in expeditionary duties and landing party operations. This was a little different than having the Marines simply guard U.S. ships and Navy bases. The Marines swiftly made its presence known as an amphibious threat all over the world, taking part in conflicts in places like Nicaragua, Buenos Aires, Sumatra, China, Fiji, Peru, West Africa, Key West, the Caribbean, the Gulf of Mexico, and elsewhere. Showing its value to the United States prompted Congress to pass another act in 1834, called the Act for the Better Organization of the United States Marine Corps. The Marines were here to stay.

The Mexican-American War (1846–1848) is a notable period for the Marines. Approximately 200 Marines made their way to Mexico City to battle their Hispanic rivals at Chapultepec Palace (also known as the Halls of Montezuma) and to capture the city. Because the Marines lost so many officers and NCOs, the Marines recognize their memory with blood stripes in today's dress uniform. The Marines were successful in taking over the Palace and went on with other engagements throughout the region.

## The Marines and the Civil War

The Civil War broke out in the United States in 1861 and lasted for about five years. The Union-backed Marines started out with almost 2,000 men, but it quickly divided between the Marine Corps and the newly created Confederate States Marine Corps. The Marines collectively played an insignificant role in the Civil War and were activated for only a small number of land operations throughout the campaign. Its main purposes were to create blockades and perform other ship-board duties.

Corporal John F. Mackie was the first Marine to be awarded the Medal of Honor on July 10, 1863, for his heroic actions during the Civil War.

## Upgrading the Marine Corps

After the Civil War, steam ships were introduced. This development left the Marine marksmen with no masts or rigging to perch upon, as they had grown accustomed, because they were replaced with smokestacks. While nothing major to speak of occurred during the latter part of the 19th century, the Marines were well known for its security and helpful presence in foreign affairs. It was the Marines' duty to protect lives and United States property wherever needed. A phrase made popular by Richard Harding Davis in 1885 states, "The Marines have landed and have the situation well at hand."

Many Marine traditions and customs stem from this era. This is the time when the *Marines' Hymn* was first introduced. The Marine Corps emblem, still in use today, was established; it's a globe with an anchor and the American bald eagle. Always Faithful, in its Latin form, Semper Fidelis became the Marines motto in 1883. A couple years later, the first ever manual for enlisted Marines was produced, entitled, *Marines' Manual: Prepared for the Use of the Enlisted Men of the U.S. Marine Corps.* The Marines also found useful the first landing manual entitled, *The Naval Brigade and Operations Ashore.*

In the early 1900s, the United States Navy surmised it would assign the Marines to take full responsibility for the defense and seizure of advanced naval bases worldwide. The Marines established a permanent base in the Caribbean, equipped with a newly formed expeditionary battalion. Marines also hunkered down in Panama during the Panamanian rebellion, in which Panama gained their Independence from Columbia. Lastly, the Marines formed the Advanced Base School and the Advanced Base Force. While the Marines continued to deploy around the world to protect and serve, it also sharpened its landing skills during many training sessions.

Not only were the Marines becoming experts as an amphibious threat across the globe, but it also began to feel the need to grow some wings. Lieutenant Alfred Austell Cunningham made this request to the Naval Aviation Camp on May 22, 1912. Soon enough, Marines began to train as Marine Aviators. Even so, these aviators felt the desire to detach from the Naval Aviation program, in order to become its own separate entity. In January 1914, the Marine Section of the Navy Flying School was established in Culebra, Puerto Rico, by Lieutenant Bernard L. Smith. This led to the first Marine Aviation Company, which consisted of 10 officers and 40 enlisted Marines. In early 1917, the first Marine Aviation Company was officially commissioned for duty with the Advanced Base Force at the Philadelphia Naval Yard. The Marines had grown wings.

Prior to World War I, the Marines were deployed all over the world. The Marines spent a lot of time in China during various ordeals in order to protect the westerners from threats and even murder. The Marine Corps were also involved in the *Banana Wars.* The Banana Wars were actions from the United States against insurgents and guerrillas who were causing strife in the Caribbean, Central, and South America. While in Cuba, the Marine Corps assisted in establishing and occupying Guantanamo Bay Naval Base. The Marines also spent a great amount of time in Nicaragua in order to prevent a rebellion and construction of the Nicaraguan canal. (The Americans had to have control.) Over 200 Marines would give their lives during these conflicts.

Major Smedley Butler and Gunnery Sergeant Dan Daly are the only two Marines to be twice awarded the Medal of Honor for their heroic actions in Mexico and Haiti in the early 1900s.

# The Marines in World War 1

The veteran Marines were experienced, trained, and well equipped to handle the conflict of World War I. The Marine Corps most notable action throughout the war occurred in 1918 when it fought in the Battle of Belleau Wood. The battle was fought between the United States 2nd Division — which included a brigade of Marines — and the Germans, who were trying to defeat the Allies and gain control of the area of Balleau Wood near Paris, France. The Marines took over the situation, making it clear that it wasn't going to back away, even over-riding a couple Allied orders to retreat. Marine Captain Lloyd W. Williams is known for the famous saying, "Retreat? Hell, we just got here." As the Marines proceeded to advance through the high wheat fields and thick, wooded outskirts, it was bombarded with heavy enemy fire. It was during this time when Gunnery Sergeant Dan Daly uttered the legendary words, "Come on, you sons of bitches, do you want to live forever?" Although the Marines suffered almost 10,000 casualties (and approximately 2,000 deaths), the Marines were successful in expelling the Germans. On June 26, 1918, the report sent out to the officials stated, "Woods now U.S. Marine Corps entirely," which ended the most barbarous and merciless battle the United States would fight in the war.

Overall, the Marines saw exponential growth throughout the war. The 1st Marine Air Squadron was renamed the 1st Marine Aviation Force in July 1918. This squadron provided fighter and bomber support to the Navy's Day Wing of the Northern Bombing Group. The Marines' First Aeronautic Company was also deployed to hunt German U-boats in the Atlantic. A total of eight aviation squadrons dropped more than 14 tons worth of bombs during the war. While the Marines entered World War I with 511 officers and 13,214 enlisted personnel, it left with 2,400 officers and 70,000 men. Of these, 2,461 died for the United States, and almost 10,000 were wounded. A total of eight Marines would earn the Medal of Honor in World War I.

# The Marines in World War II

By the start of World War II, the United States Marines grew to its highest number in history, at 475,000. This expansion included a Parachute Battalion, 20 Defense Battalions, over 130 air squadrons, and 6 divisions. With experience in all areas of battle (land, air, and sea), Marines would participate in almost every conflict in the Pacific War. The Marines were highly successful in its role in World War II, notably due to the secret Navajo code it used for communication. Its top-notch efforts during the war earned it a spot adjacent to the Arlington National Cemetery, where the Marine Corps War Memorial was dedicated in 1954.

Desegregation of the Marine Corps began in 1942, when the United States allowed African-American recruits to join the service. The first African-American to become a U.S. Marine Corps officer was Frederick C. Branch.

Marines were mostly deployed in the Pacific Theater during World War I, although they played a small role in the European Theater, Middle East, and North Africa. The Marines' typical role away from the Pacific was to guard Navy bases and U.S. property. By the end of the war, 19,733 Marines were lost, and almost 70,000 were wounded. Marine Aviators destroyed 2,355 Japanese aircraft, and the Marines lost almost 600 aircraft. In total, 82 recipients received the Medal of Honor.

## A Rocky Road for the Marine Corps

After World War II, the Marine Corps ran into a little trouble with American support. It first encountered a major budget cut and a substantial drawdown. For example, the Marine aviation program had over 100,000 personnel during the war and was reduced to less than 15,000 members by1948. Secretary of Defense Louis A. Johnson was really pushing for a unified military and wanted what was left of the Marine Corps to merge with the Army. The Marines struggled with these political issues for some time, but gained Congressional support when the National Security Act of 1947 became official. This act protected the Marine Corps from any proposed dismantling.

Things were still difficult for the Marines because President Harry S. Truman's known animosity toward the branch. Truman and Johnson then decided to gang up on the Marines. Johnson tried to completely eliminate the Marines aviation program, by giving all the budget to the Navy and Air Force. Even so, Johnson cut the Navy's amphibious ships and most surface fleets. At every meeting, he would propose to cut back and/or terminate the Marine Corps branch entirely. The Chief of Staff then announced there would be no official celebration of the Marine Corps birthday. He also decided he didn't even want the Marine Corps Commandant around him at all. He ordered the Commandant to keep away from all Joint Chief of Staff gatherings and would not let him ride in the military limousines or receive special salutes during military occasions. If the Marines had to stick around, Truman and Johnson were going to make it as miserable as possible.

It wasn't until Secretary of the Navy John L. Sullivan swiftly resigned that things began to change. In 1949, Johnson was investigated as to whether or not he should be charged with malfeasance. While he was ultimately cleared of any wrongdoing, he resigned in 1950, leaving a weakened military behind. The Chief of Staff was then replaced by George Marshall. The Douglas-Manfield Bill was passed a while after Johnson was replaced, and it allowed the Commandant to resume participation in meetings with the Joint Chief of Staff. The Marines were also granted three divisions and air wings, which granted permanent participation in military duties around the globe.

Despite the hardships Marines faced during this time, it managed to develop better technology. Jet aircraft gradually phased out the old propellers in the aviation program. This is the time when the Marine Corps started using helicopters for its amphibious tasks as well. The first Marine helicopter squadron became official in 1947. Helicopters were found useful during the Marines' amphibious landings because they were more detailed at the shore-line than the attack bomber aircraft used before. Transport helicopters were developed to ease the transition between ships and land. The Marines began using the HMX-1, the Sikorsky HO3S-1, and the Piasecki HRP-1 helicopters for amphibious operations.

## The Marines in China and Korea

From 1945 to 1949, approximately 50,000 United States Marines were deployed to Japan and China. Their main duties were controlling major infrastructure points and protecting or evacuating Americans in the areas during the hostile time when the Communist Party of China was winning the Chinese Civil War.

When the Korean War began in 1950, it was "surprisingly" the Marines who showed the most preparation and experience. During the Battle of Inchon, the Marines brought in its HO3S1 helicopters along with other air and ground forces during its swift amphibious landing in order to push back the North Koreans. While this maneuver worked, the Marines were later overwhelmed with a large number of troops from China. Even though the Army retreated, the Marines regrouped and continued to blast the enemy with all it had. The Marines continued in the war in Korea until the North Koreans finally retreated back over the 38th parallel in 1953. When all was over, 4,267 Marines would give their lives in this war, while over 20,000 were injured. The Medal of Honor was awarded to 42 men for their services in the Korean War.

During the war, Marine aviation numbers increased again since Johnsons previous cutbacks. The Marine aviation program now had 4 air wings, 20 aircraft groups, and almost 80 squadrons.

After the Korean War, the United States Marine Corps was deployed to a number of areas across the globe. In 1956, Marines were deployed to Egypt during the Suez Crisis in order to evacuate Americans. In 1958, Marines participated in Operation Blue Bat during a crisis in Lebanon. In the late '50s, Marines went back to Cuba to once again protect Americans from harm during the Revolution. In 1962, the Marine Corps was sent to Thailand to help prevent communists from overthrowing the government. During Operation Power Pack, Marines were deployed to Haiti to evacuate Americans, but decided to stick around to force peace within the area.

# The Marines in Vietnam

The Vietnam War occurred from 1955 to the Fall of Saigon in 1975. The United States Marine Corps was particularly useful during conflict in Vietnam due to its experience with amphibious landings. The Marines operated in South Vietnam in the Northern I Corps region. It constantly fought against the Viet Cong guerillas and the North Vietnamese Army. The Marines withdrew from the area in '71, but would return again at the end of the war to evacuate Saigon. During the war, the Marines would lose 13,091 personnel, and almost 100,000 were wounded. Fifty-seven Marines were awarded the Medal of Honor for their duties in Vietnam.

It was also during this time when many Marines were considered not so patriotic and less than satisfactory. A lot of Marines were court-martialed, and many were even found guilty of nonjudicial crimes. Some U.S. Marines even went AWOL and deserted the Corps or just didn't show up to their assignments here and there. But, the branch took note and began to discharge those not becoming of a Marine, and enlisted those who would show their courage and strength and follow orders. With a fresh outlook, the Marines began to improve morale.

# The Marines remain an active force

In the early '80s, the Marines were continuously sent back and forth to Lebanon to take part in the Lebanon War with the Multinational Force in Lebanon (MNF). It was an incredibly hostile area, which the Marines discovered the hard way. On October 23, 1983, 220 Marines, 18 Sailors, and 3 Soldiers lost their lives when the Marine Barracks was bombed. This incident marked the highest peace-time loss for the Marines in history. As the violence amplified, the Marines were urged to retreat, and finally pressure from the States to return led the Marines back home by February 1984.

From the early 1980s to the early 1990s, the United States Marine Corps was successful in a number of conflicts and operations. In 1983, Marines were involved in Operation Urgent Fury, when it responded to threats in Grenada. It was successful in calming down the island and keeping Soviet-Cubans from forming a military there. In 1989, Marines were deployed to the Philippines for Operation Classic Resolve, where it was assigned to protect the United States Embassy in Manila. In late 1989, Marines were involved in Operation Just Cause during the Invasion of Panama, where it took out military dictator, Manuel Noriega. The most notable activity during this time was in 1990 when Marines were activated for Operation Desert Storm in Kuwait during the Gulf War. Almost 100,000 Marines were sent to the desert to help liberate Kuwait from Saudi Arabia and Saddam Hussein. A total of 23 Marines would give their lives during the first Gulf War.

Operation Desert Storm in Kuwait was the largest Marine Corps operation in history, with approximately 92,990 Marines deployed.

# September 11, 2001

Horrific terrorist attacks occurred on September 11, 2001, in the United States, prompting President George W. Bush to announce a Global War on Terror. The fixed mission of the Global War on Terror is "the defeat of Al-Qaeda, other terrorist groups and any nation that supports or harbors terrorists". Since 2001, the Marine Corps, alongside other military and federal agencies, has engaged in global operations throughout the world in support of that mission.

The first major deployment for the Marines for the War on Terror was in Afghanistan for Operation Enduring Freedom, and Operation Strike of the Sword. After seizing Kandahar International Airport, Marines were free to circulate its battalions and squadrons in the area in hopes of taking out the threat of Taliban forces and the terrorist group, Al-Qaeda. Over 100 Marines have been killed in the war so far.

The Marines are also well known for serving in Operation Iraqi Freedom, in 2003. When the Marine Expeditionary Force invaded Iraq, the unit involved received the Presidential Unit Citation, a prestigious award rarely given. After the initial attack and take-out of Saddam Hussein and his regime, the Marines were sent back to perform guard duty and occupied areas of Iraq in order to protect the safety of civilians and to promote improved security. In 2009, President Barack Obama announced an accelerated withdraw of American combat forces, prompting the Marines to eventually leave the area and hand over its responsibilities to the U.S. Army. Approximately 178 Marines have lost their lives in the War in Iraq, while almost 9,000 were wounded. Only one Marine, Corporal Jason Dunham, received the Medal of Honor. The United States Marine Corps continues to this day to fight the Global War on Terror.

# Coast Guard Enlisted History

The Coast Guard differs from the other military branches in a few ways. First off, the United States Coast Guard is primarily ran by the Department of Homeland Security, while the other military branches are ran by the Department of Defense. While the Army, Navy, Air Force, and Marine Corps are usually training for war or deployed for operations dealing with war and peace, the U.S. Coast Guard is deployed for a multitude of reasons every day. The Coast Guard is known for its adaptability to different responsibilities and emergencies as they may arise. The President of the United States and

Congress are able to transfer operation of the Coast Guard to the Department of the Navy at any given point they feel it necessary that the Coast Guard take part in war operations in both domestic and international waters. The United States Coast Guard, or USCG, is a maritime, military service responsible for an array of missions including law enforcement. The Coast Guard's enduring roles are officially Maritime Safety, Maritime Security, and Maritime Stewardship. The 11 statutory missions as defined by law are divided into homeland security missions and nonhomeland security missions (see Table A-1).

| Table A-1 | Security Missions |
|---|---|
| **Homeland Security Missions** | **Nonhomeland Security Missions** |
| Ports, waterways and coastal security | Marine safety |
| Drug interdiction | Search and rescue |
| Migrant interdiction | Aids to navigation |
| Defense readiness | Living marine resources |
| Other law enforcement | Marine environmental protection |
| | Ice operations |

## The establishment of the Revenue-Marine Cutters

The Coast Guard has actually been around since the late 1700s, but it hasn't always been known as the Coast Guard. Immediately after the Revolutionary War, the Continental Navy disbanded, which left vital American imports at great risk. Import tariffs was the number one source of income for the new America. The United States began to struggle when smuggling of American goods from unsecured waters began to strongly affect the Nations income. On August 4, 1790, the Revenue-Marine service was established by Secretary of the Treasury, Alexander Hamilton, in order to enforce American tariff laws and combat smuggling. The Tariff Act then prompted the construction of 10 cutters (nautical vessels) and 100 revenue officers. For about a decade, the Revenue-Marine was the only American armed service patrolling the waters.

While the Revenue-Marine officers were out and about at sea, they realized they could also help out boaters in distress. Even so, Secretary of the Treasury Louis McLane officially requested the Revenue-Marine cutters to start organizing cruises year-round to assist mariners in need. Congress liked the idea of having a seagoing force available to help distressed sailors added to the mission of protecting the Nations travelling goods. Therefore, in 1837, Congress included lifesaving missions to the to-do list for the maritime service.

# The Cutters engage in battle

The Revenue-Marine service began to take on many responsibilities aside from tariff security. The cutters were involved in the Quasi-War with France, the War of 1812, and the Mexican-American War. Their duties at war were to assist the newly formed Navy with capturing or assisting to capture enemy vessels. They were also given the task of slave trade prevention from Africa to the United States. In fact, the Mariners seized around 500 slave ships between 1795 and 1865. The Mariners also began to enforce environmental protection as early as 1822, when the Cutters were asked to protect government timber from illegal poaching. Even in the Civil War, the Revenue-Marine servicemen (after first dividing between the Union and Confederacy) helped the blockade efforts in the rivers and intercoastal waterways.

During the late 1800s, the Revenue Cutters were instrumental in the United States's expansion to the Alaskan territories. In fact, Captain Michael A. Healy is known for establishing a program that provided steady food (reindeer) to the area. The Cutters also helped starving whalers in the Overland Expedition and transported wiped out miners during the Snake River Gold Rush.

The Revenue-Marine Division was renamed the Revenue Cutter Service, on July 31, 1894.

The first training center for the Cutters, The School of Instruction of the Revenue Cutter Service, was established in 1876. The location moved from Massachusetts to Maryland then finally to Fort Trumbull, Connecticut in 1910. Officers and engineers were trained in two- to three-year programs in small classrooms or tutored aboard ships. The name changed to the Revenue Cutter Academy in 1914 and then was quickly changed to the United States Coast Guard Academy, as the Revenue Cutter Service, Life Saving Service, The Lighthouse Service, and The Bureau of Marine Inspection and Navigation merged to create the United States Coast Guard. The Academy again relocated to New London on the Thames River and used the USRC Dobbin for training exercises.

# The Revenue Cutter Service in World War 1

World War I was declared on April 6, 1917. Prior to this war, the USCG was swift to prepare for international conflict. Communications were strengthened along the shores between stations and lighthouses. The Coast Guard also began aviation training with the Navy. The Commandant of the Navy issued a Confidential Order stating, "Mobilization of the U.S. Coast Guard When Required to Operate as a part of the U.S. Navy."

After the formal declaration of war, operational control of the Coast Guard was given to the Department of the Navy, and all cutters and CG personnel reported to the Navy for orders. Coast Guard Cutters were looked upon by the Navy as ready assets and were used primarily in the war as fill-ins for Navy expansion. Coast Guard officers and petty officers were reduced to serve under less experienced Sailors for less pay while under the Navy's control. During this time, the Coast Guard consisted of almost 4,000 personnel. The USCG had about 300 rescue stations and around 45 cutters. While somewhat disorganized, the USCG still provided valuable maritime skills and dedication to all actions requested by the Navy.

## The Coast Guard enforces the law

During the 1920s, the United States Coast Guard played a large role enforcing the Prohibition of alcohol. The Eighteenth Amendment to the United States Constitution prohibited, ". . . manufacture, sale, or transportation of intoxicating liquors within, the importation thereof into, or the exportation thereof from the United States . . ." The Navy gave the Coast Guard four stack destroyers to help enforce prohibition and smuggling around the waterways. This continued until the ban was repealed in 1933.

The 1934 Coast Guard regulations show official meaning to the unofficial motto, "You have to go out, but you don't have to come back." It states:

> "In attempting a rescue, the keeper will select either the boat, breeches buoy, or life car, as in his judgment is best suited to effectively cope with the existing conditions. If the device first selected fails after such trial as satisfies him that no further attempt with it is feasible, he will resort to one of the others, and if that fails, then to the remaining one, and he will not desist from his efforts until by actual trial the impossibility of effecting a rescue is demonstrated. The statement of the keeper that he did not try to use the boat because the sea or surf was too heavy will not be accepted unless attempts to launch it were actually made and failed [underlining added], or unless the conformation of the coast — as bluffs, precipitous banks, etc. — is such as to unquestionably preclude the use of a boat."

An example of this exemplary Coast Guard service was shown during the devastating 1927 Mississippi River Flood. The USCG rescued over 43,000 persons from danger. It also saved an outstanding number of livestock and transported the injured to hospitals. Almost 700 Coast Guard personnel served in these rescue operations, using about 130 vessels.

In 1933, the Gold Lifesaving Medal was awarded to Lieutenant Commander Carl von Paulsen for his heroic actions during a Coast Guard rescue. A young boy ran adrift in a skiff off the coast of Cape Canaveral. During the open water rescue landing, Paulsen's aircraft sustained immobilizing damages, stranding all involved. However, the aircraft, *Arcturus,* washed ashore with all aboard, saving the boy from certain disaster.

# The Coast Guard in World War II

The USCG were helpful in operations across the globe during America's entry into World War II. A major duty was to oversee The Greenland Patrol's duties in protecting the International Ice Patrol and the cryolite mines the United States used for refining aluminum. Greenland was also a hot spot for the Coast Guard to accurately predict weather forecasts for Europe. The Coast Guard maintained its duties along the coasts of Greenland throughout the war.

The U.S. Coast Guard was involved in continuous rescue operations after the Germans started attacking and sinking American ships off the coast. Interestingly, it was the Coast Guard that took the first prisoners taken by combat during the war, when it sank German U-boat 352 off the coast of Charleston, South Carolina. The USCG retained 33 German prisoners. Throughout the war, the Coast Guard was helpful in anti-submarine operations. The Coast Guard also worked well with the Navy and the Marine Corps. Coast Guard personnel received amphibious training with Marine Corps cooperation for amphibious landings during the war, and the Navy allocated Coast Guard cutters to perform several deployments overseas in conjunction with the Navy. Throughout World War II, the Coast guard would continue to assist in the war with the Navy, rescue and protect allied vessels in danger at sea, and patrol the waters. Many Coast Guard personnel lost their lives during World War II battles.

Interestingly, women played a large role in assisting with Coast Guard duties. In November 1942, Congress passed legislation creating the Coast Guard Women's Reserve. Captain Dorothy C. Stratton, leader, renamed the group SPARS after the Coast Guard's motto, *Semper Paradus,* meaning "Always Ready." The main goal of the SPARS was to take over various stateside duties such as administration and supply, freeing up the men to deploy for war overseas. During the war, approximately 11,000 women served in the Coast Guard Women's Reserve.

Douglas Albert Munro (October 11, 1919 — September 27, 1942) is the only member of the United States Coast Guard to receive the Medal of Honor, the U.S. military's highest decoration. Munro received the award posthumously for his actions as officer-in-charge of a group of landing craft on September 27, 1942, during the September Matanikau action in the Guadalcanal campaign of World War II. His official Medal of Honor citation reads:

> *"For extraordinary heroism and conspicuous gallantry in action above and beyond the call of duty as Officer-in-Charge of a group of Higgins boats, engaged in the evacuation of a Battalion of Marines trapped by enemy Japanese forces at Point Cruz, Guadalcanal, on September 27, 1942. After making preliminary plans for the evacuation of nearly 500 beleaguered*

*Marines, Munro, under constant risk of his life, daringly led five of his small craft toward the shore. As he closed the beach, he signaled the others to land, and then in order to draw the enemy's fire and protect the heavily loaded boats, he valiantly placed his craft with its two small guns as a shield between the beachhead and the Japanese. When the perilous task of evacuation was nearly completed, Munro was killed by enemy fire, but his crew, two of whom were wounded, carried on until the last boat had loaded and cleared the beach. By his outstanding leadership, expert planning, and dauntless devotion to duty, he and his courageous comrades undoubtedly saved the lives of many who otherwise would have perished. He gallantly gave up his life in defense of his country."*

The official enlisted training center was established in Cape May, New Jersey, in 1948 and is still in operation today. Anyone enlisting in the Coast Guard will ultimately travel to this location for basic training.

# The Coast Guard in Korea

The Korean War began in 1950. The responsibility for the Coast Guard in this matter was to help evacuate the Korean Peninsula during the North's invasion. During this time, Congress passed the *Magneson Act,* which permanently directed the Coast Guard to ensure the safety and security of all ports and harbors within the United States. The Coast Guard also began to serve in the north Pacific Ocean, using weather ships and assisting with military and civilian distress calls.

On April 1, 1967, the Coast Guard was transferred from the Department of the Treasury to the newly formed Department of Transportation under the authority of PL 89-670, which was signed into law on October 15, 1966.

# The Coast Guard in Vietnam

The Coast Guard became activated under the control of the Navy for the Vietnam War on May 27, 1965. Many cutters were deployed to the area to assist in operations. The responsibility of the Coast Guard was mainly to interrupt resupply by sea of the North Vietnamese and Viet Cong. The Coast Guard was also responsible for assisting the Navy in coastal interdiction for enemy forces and gunfire support for shore-line operations in the South. Coast Guard forces also assisted in combat search and rescue, as the USCG teamed up with the U.S. Air Force 37th & 40th Aerospace Rescue and Recovery Squadrons. The Coast Guard also teamed up with the Army during Vietnam, providing Explosive Loading Detachments (ELD) that would assist the Army in dealing with explosive supply aboard merchant ships and maintaining port security operations. The Coast Guard was even tasked to assist the Vietnamese with Aids to Navigation, marking safe routes among the Vietnamese waterways. The activities of the Coast Guard in Vietnam ended when it turned over responsibilities to the newly trained South Vietnamese Navy in 1975. Seven Coast Guardsmen would lose their lives in the war during combat search-and-rescue operations.

## Changes made in the Coast Guard

Several changes were made in the Coast Guard during the '70s. The Coast Guard replaced its Navy-style uniforms with a distinctive uniform of its own (similar to the uniforms seen today). Coast Guard personnel would all wear the same uniform, but denote status only by their rank insignia and cap devices.

Women were allowed to enlist in the Coast Guard as early as 1973, when the SPARS Reserves were disbanded. Mixed gender crews were allowed by 1977, and the opening of all ratings to women was allowed by 1978. Today, the Coast Guard is the only military service in which women may hold any of its ratings.

The United States Coast Guard was officially transferred from the Department of Transportation to the newly created Department of Homeland Security on March 1, 2003. The Department of Homeland Security is a cabinet department created by the U.S. Government in response to the terrorist attacks which occurred on September 11, 2001 with the primary responsibilities of protecting the territory of the United States from terrorist attacks and responding to natural disasters.

This seems like a pretty good fit for the U.S. Coast Guard. To this day, the Coast Guard continues to protect and serve with over 40,000 active duty personnel, over 8,000 Reservists, and over 7,000 civilian employees. The Coast Guard also possesses 244 cutters, almost 2,000 boats, and over 200 aircraft. The Coast Guard remains, "Always Ready."

The following, written by VADM Harry G. Hamlet, USCG, exemplifies the uniform beliefs and values of all Coastguardsmen on duty today:

**Creed of the United States Coast Guardsman**

*I am proud to be a United States Coast Guardsman.*

*I revere that long line of expert seamen who by their devotion to duty and sacrifice of self have made it possible for me to be a member of a service honored and respected, in peace and in war, throughout the world.*

*I never, by word or deed, will bring reproach upon the fair name of my service, nor permit others to do so unchallenged.*

*I will cheerfully and willingly obey all lawful orders.*

*I will always be on time to relieve, and shall endeavor to do more, rather than less, than my share.*

*I will always be at my station, alert and attending to my duties.*

*I shall, so far as I am able, bring to my seniors solutions, not problems.*

*I shall live joyously, but always with due regard for the rights and privileges of others.*

*I shall endeavor to be a model citizen in the community in which I live.*

*I shall sell life dearly to an enemy of my country, but give it freely to rescue those in peril.*

*With God's help, I shall endeavor to be one of His noblest Works . . .*

*A UNITED STATES COAST GUARDSMAN.*

# Index

●●●●●●●●●●●●●●●●●●●●●●●●●●●●●●●●●●●●●●●●●●●●●●●●●●●●●●●●●●●●●●●●

## • S •